HOUGHTON MIFFLIN LITERARY READERS

BOOK 6

HOUGHTON MIFFLIN COMPANY   BOSTON

Atlanta   Dallas   Geneva, Illinois   Palo Alto   Princeton   Toronto

Program Authors

William K. Durr, John J. Pikulski, Rita M. Bean, J. David Cooper, Nicholas A. Glaser, M. Jean Greenlaw, Hugh Schoephoerster, Mary Lou Alsin, Kathryn Au, Rosalinda B. Barrera, Joseph E. Brzeinski, Ruth P. Bunyan, Jacqueline C. Comas, Frank X. Estrada, Robert L. Hillerich, Timothy G. Johnson, Pamela A. Mason, Joseph S. Renzulli

Senior Consultants

Jacqueline L. Chaparro, Alan N. Crawford, Alfredo Schifini, Sheila Valencia

Program Reviewers

Donna Bessant, Mara Bommarito, Yetive Bradley, Patricia M. Callan, Marjorie Delbut, Mary Goosby, Clara J. Hanline, Gloria Hooks, Sannie Humphrey, Barbara H. Jeffus, Beverly Jimenez, Sue Cramton Johnson, Michael P. Klentschy, Petra Montante, Nancy Rhodes, Julie Ryan, Lily Sarmiento, Ellis Vance, Kathleen Ware, Sandy Watson, Judy Williams, Leslie M. Woldt, Janet Gong Yin

Acknowledgments

For each of the selections listed below, grateful acknowledgement is made for permission to adapt and/or reprint original or copyrighted material, as follows:

"Ben and Me," from *Ben and Me* by Robert Lawson, copyright 1939 by Robert Lawson. Copyright renewed © 1967 by John W. Boyd. By permission of Little, Brown and Company.

"The Black Pearl," adapted from *The Black Pearl* by Scott O'Dell. Copyright © 1967 by Scott O'Dell. Reprinted by permission of Houghton Mifflin Company.

"The Boy Who Shaped Stone," adapted from *Tool-maker* by Jill Paton Walsh. Copyright © 1973 by Jill Paton Walsh. Reprinted by permission of William Heinemann, Ltd.

"Change," from *River Winding,* (poems) by Charlotte Zolotow: Text copyright © 1970 by Charlotte Zolotow. Reprinted by permission of Harper and Row, Publishers, Inc.

"Cobie's Courage," adapted from *Winter Wheat* by Jeanne Williams. Copyright © 1975 by Jeanne Williams. Reprinted by permission of Harold Ober Associates, Incorporated.

"Dear Mr. Henshaw," from *Dear Mr. Henshaw* by Beverly Cleary. Illustrated by Paul O. Zelinsky. Copyright © 1983 by Beverly Cleary. Reprinted by permission of William Morrow & Company.

Continued on page 487.

Printed in the U.S.A.

ISBN: 0-395-47703-4

CDEFGHIJ-D-96543210/89

Contents

1. Friendships

Houghton Mifflin Literature
Responsibilities

2. Building a Nation

Houghton Mifflin Literature
Night Journeys

3. Confronting Nature

Houghton Mifflin Literature
Heroes and Villains

4. Images and Illusions

6. Accepting Challenges

1

Friendships

The Dragon Doctor

From a book by Jo Manton

Long, long ago, in the days of the Yellow Emperor, lived a countryman called Huang. His home was in a remote place, where three or four farmhouses clustered round a horse pond. The men of the hamlet ploughed, the boys minded the geese and ducks, the women and girls tended the gardens. Each farm had its horse in the stable, sheep or cow in the paddock, hens in the roost, doves on the roof-ridge, pigs snug in the sty and cat stretched out in the sun. Far off you could see hazy smoke rise from the roofs. Nearer at hand you might hear a dog bark somewhere in the lanes, a cock crow at the top of the mulberry tree or the girls gossip as they milked the cows. Anyone who was not happy in that place would never be happy at all.

All these country neighbors honored Huang, for he was a wonderful doctor of sick animals. When the sheep coughed, or the cow would not calve or the piglets failed to thrive, they would run to fetch him. Then Huang would look at the sick beast intently, speak to it quietly and handle it gently with steady brown hands. He seemed to see through the illness to the nature of the creature itself, and the animals he treated with herbs or surgery were always healed. No wonder the farmers called him Dr. Horse, in Chinese Dr. Ma.

Ma was standing at the door one day, looking round his walled courtyard with its stables and barns, when a sudden shadow blotted out the sun. Slowly a flying dragon circled above the farm and glided down to land in front of him. Naturally Ma knew all about the dragons in theory, for the dragon was chief of the three-hundred and sixty scaly reptiles. He knew that four Dragon Kings rule the four seas, that the Celestial Dragon rules the sky, that the Earth Dragon marks out lakes and rivers, and that the Hidden Treasure Dragon guards the gold and silver deep in the earth. Dragons, he knew, were certainly magical. A foolish man once invented a recipe for cooking dragon-meat, but he never could catch one, so his skill was all wasted. The great Confucius himself said, "Birds fly, fishes swim and beasts run; you may snare those that run, hook those that swim and shoot those that fly. But when it comes to a dragon — he can ride on the wind and I can't imagine how to catch one." Like everyone else, Ma also knew that a friendly dragon brings good luck and that is why people so often have them painted on dishes or screens. Yet, strangely enough, he had never seen one.

Now the dragon shuffled towards him on golden claws. Red, green and azure rippled through its golden scales from head to snaky tail, wreathing and dissolving into changing patterns with every breath. Yet the gorgeous dragon's head and tail hung slack, its ears drooped and from its open jaws a trail of spittle fell to the stones. Its topaz eyes gazed at him piteously.

"Why," thought Ma in instant recognition, "this dragon is ill and wants me to cure it!" Seeing only a suffering beast, he lost all sense of the fabulous monster. He

examined it with a strong, delicate touch; searching the scaly temples, he felt the racing pulse of pain. The trouble was not hard to find — a red and angry abscess gathering on the jaw.

"Steady, old fellow," said Ma, as though to a horse; and the dragon, hearing the authority in that quiet voice, stood trustingly under his hands. Ma fetched his case of acupuncture needles. Deftly, still talking calmly to the patient, he slid the fine gold and silver needles into the skin. After five minutes he withdrew them, so delicately that the dragon seemed to feel nothing.

Ma knew all the three-hundred and sixty-five points of the body at which a surgeon may practice this craft. "Unhealthy fluids will drain away," he explained reassuringly, "the swelling will lessen, the healthy balance of the body will be restored and the pain will vanish." Topaz eyes gazed at him, as though the dragon understood.

The dragon rested that night in his barn. Ma, in his still room, pounded licorice root with pestle and mortar to make soothing medicine, which the dragon appeared to enjoy for it finished every drop and licked its chops. Next day Ma was satisfied to see the abscess draining, and the dragon resting comfortably, coiled in the straw. By the third morning it was cured, and flew away, rainbow scales glittering along the white fingers of the clouds, until it dwindled into the distance. Next day, it came back, with a pair of red jade slippers in its claws. Ma was deeply touched. "Bless you, I want no reward," he said. "Jade slippers are not for the likes of me; nor any of your magic tricks like floating through the air or passing through solid rock. If you feel well, that's all the thanks I need."

The dragon, like many human patients, was now deeply attached to its doctor. It went to live in the depths of the village pond, and every time it felt out of sorts appeared in Huang's courtyard like a persistent invalid at morning surgery. Ma knew what it wanted, and kept a jar always filled with the dragon's favorite dark, treacly licorice medicine.

Of course, this strange friendship could not long remain unknown. A dragon is only a dragon, you might think, but foolish people can make it a god. Soon news spread through the land that a Holy Dragon lived in the village horse pond. Happiness or grief, rain or drought, before long people were saying that it was all the dragon's doing. Crowds came on foot, nobles on horse-back and ladies in carrying chairs. They built a stone shrine beside the pool. They poured offerings of wine over the water-mint and burned sacrifices of young pig on the rocks; the foxes which came at night grew fat and drunk with finishing it all up. All day the crowds chanted prayers, waved silk umbrellas, threw paper money into the water or

banged gongs and drums. Sightseers from town trampled the barley fields, picked the flowers and frightened the hens until they stopped laying. No longer did the villagers stoop to see how their grain was growing, look up into their mulberry boughs or enjoy a friendly chat with the neighbors about the weather or crops. They were all too busy selling tea and rice cakes to the tourists. Ma escaped

to gather herbs in the calm shadows of the summer woods; yet even there loud picnic parties drove him away. "It's as bad as a barbarian invasion," he thought gloomily.

What did the dragon think of this incessant hubbub? Though worshippers implored it loudly, it refused to come out from its lair at the bottom of the pond, until one morning before sunrise Ma found it waiting at its old place in the yard. Bowing its head and spreading its great bat wings, the dragon invited him to mount. No sooner had Ma swung a leg over the scaly golden back than the dragon soared into the clouds. They winged through the sky, red mists of morning wrapping them round like a cloak under the high canopy of space. The doors of the Jade Emperor's heavenly palace swung open and Ma wandered freely through the halls of the stars. Servants washed him in showers of rainbow spray, dressed him in silk robes and girded him with a belt of jewels, while the dragon vanished to the stables of the sky. Then they led Ma to the banquet hall, to eat the Food of Long Life. Now his fame and glory would last for ever.

Like most men, Ma had expected one short life. "The world is an inn," he had said to himself, "and we are passing travelers." He was prepared to grow old, to find his hair and beard every day a little whiter, to lean each day a little more heavily on his thornwood stick, to drink a cup of wine in memory of friends gone before, and in his turn to meet the Common Change of death. "By then," he had said, "the world and I will have had our fill of one another."

Yet now that the dragon had carried him to the kingdom of the sky, Ma found everything quite unexpectedly usual. For there, every department of the Chinese Empire on earth has an everlasting counterpart. The Celestial Emperor has his court, his eighteen provinces with their governors, his judges, treasurers and mandarins, each with his host of attendant clerks, door-keepers and police. Naturally there is a celestial Ministry of Health, and the Minister soon sent for Ma.

"Welcome to our Ministry," he said, with a polished official smile. "I hereby appoint you to my staff, with the

title of Infallible Dr. Ma. Your duties will be to make a survey of all the medicinal plants on earth for the Office of Remedies. When you have completed it, kindly present your report to your senior officers, the Superintendent of the Celestial Pharmacy and the Eternal Apothecary." Before Ma had time to open his mouth, a black-robed clerk bowed him out of the door.

So, as Infallible Dr. Ma, he labored many centuries collecting healing plants on earth, and planting a physic garden in the sky. There he grew, in neatly labelled flower beds, eight-hundred and ninety-eight vegetable drugs: peppermint and rhubarb for the stomach, horehound for coughs, wintergreen for sprains, witch hazel for bruises, lime-blossom for headache, vervain to calm the thoughts, balsam for wounds, soya beans for strength and poppy for sleep. For centuries to come, everyone in China swore by

Dr. Ma's infallible remedies. When this garden was finished, Ma received another appointment — to be the patron and protector of all the veterinary surgeons on earth. What an important job for a country horse doctor!

Indeed, Ma might have felt overwhelmed but for one faithful friend. Every so often the golden dragon would appear outside the Celestial Pharmacy and wait patiently, with drooping ears and appealing gaze. Ma did his best not to show how pleased he was to see it.

"There is really nothing the matter with you at all," he said in as firm a voice as he could manage. Yet the dragon continued to look up in its peculiar manner, knowing that if it waited long enough, its favorite Dr. Ma would pour it a dose of Heavenly Licorice Medicine.

Author

British author Jo Manton has written several distinguished books for adults and children. She often collaborates with her husband, poet and biographer Robert Gittings. The short story you have just read is from her book *The Flying Horses: Tales from China*.

The Hundred Dresses

by Eleanor Estes

Wanda

Today, Monday, Wanda Petronski was not in her seat. But nobody, not even Peggy and Madeline, the girls who started all the fun, noticed her absence.

Usually Wanda sat in the next to the last seat in the last row in Room 13. She sat in the corner of the room where the rough boys who did not make good marks on their report cards sat; the corner of the room where there was most scuffling of feet, most roars of laughter when anything funny was said, and most mud and dirt on the floor.

Wanda did not sit there because she was rough and noisy. On the contrary she was very quiet and rarely said anything at all. And nobody had ever heard her laugh out loud. Sometimes she twisted her mouth into a crooked sort of smile, but that was all.

Nobody knew exactly why Wanda sat in that seat unless it was because she came all the way from Boggins Heights, and her feet were usually caked with dry mud that she picked up coming down the country roads. Maybe the teacher liked to keep all the children who were apt to come in with dirty shoes in one corner of the room. But no one really thought much about Wanda Petronski once she was in the classroom. The time they thought about her was outside of school hours, at noontime when they were coming back to school, or in the morning early before school began, when groups of two or three or even more would be talking and laughing on their way to the school yard.

Then sometimes they waited for Wanda — to have fun with her.

The next day, Tuesday, Wanda was not in school either. And nobody noticed her absence again, except the teacher and probably big Bill Byron, who sat in the seat behind Wanda's and who could now put his long legs around her empty desk, one on each side, and sit there like a frog, to the great entertainment of all in his corner of the room.

But on Wednesday, Peggy and Maddie, who sat in the front row along with other children who got good marks and didn't track in a whole lot of mud, did notice that Wanda wasn't there. Peggy was the most popular girl in school. She was pretty; she had many pretty clothes and her auburn hair was curly. Maddie was her closest friend.

The reason Peggy and Maddie noticed Wanda's absence was because Wanda had made them late to school. They had waited and waited for Wanda — to have some fun with her — and she just hadn't come. They kept thinking she'd come any minute. They saw Jack Beggles running to school, his necktie askew and his cap at a precarious tilt. They knew it must be late, for he always managed to slide into his chair exactly when the bell rang as though he were making a touchdown. Still they waited one minute more and one minute more, hoping she'd come. But finally they had to race off without seeing her.

The two girls reached their classroom after the doors had been closed. The children were reciting in unison the Gettysburg Address, for that was the way Miss Mason always began the session. Peggy and Maddie slipped into their seats just as the class was saying the last lines . . . "that these dead shall not have died in vain; that the nation shall, under God, have a new birth of freedom, and that government of the people, by the people, for the people, shall not perish from the earth."

The Dresses Game

After Peggy and Maddie stopped feeling like intruders in a class that had already begun, they looked across the room and noticed that Wanda was not in her seat. Furthermore her desk was dusty and looked as though she hadn't been there yesterday either. Come to think of it, they hadn't seen her yesterday. They had waited for her a little while but had forgotten about her when they reached school.

They often waited for Wanda Petronski — to have fun with her.

Wanda lived way up on Boggins Heights, and Boggins Heights was no place to live. It was a good place to go and pick wild flowers in the summer, but you always held your breath till you got safely past old man Svenson's yellow house. People in the town said old man Svenson was no good. He didn't work and, worse still, his house and yard were disgracefully dirty, with rusty tin cans strewn about and even an old straw hat. He lived alone with his dog and his cat. No wonder, said the people of the town. Who would live with him? And many stories circulated about him and the stories were the kind that made people scurry past his house even in broad daylight and hope not to meet him.

Beyond Svenson's there were a few small scattered frame houses, and in one of these Wanda Petronski lived with her father and her brother Jake.

Wanda Petronski. Most of the children in Room 13 didn't have names like that. They had names easy to say, like Thomas, Smith, or Allen. There was one boy named Bounce, Willie Bounce, and people thought that was funny but not funny in the same way that Petronski was.

Wanda didn't have any friends. She came to school alone and went home alone. She always wore a faded blue dress that didn't hang right. It was clean, but it looked as though it had never been ironed properly. She didn't have any friends, but a lot of girls talked to her. They waited for her under the maple trees on the corner of Oliver Street.

Or they surrounded her in the school yard as she stood watching some little girls play hopscotch on the worn hard ground.

"Wanda," Peggy would say in a most courteous manner, as though she were talking to Miss Mason or to the principal perhaps. "Wanda," she'd say, giving one of her friends a nudge, "tell us. How many dresses did you say you had hanging up in your closet?"

"A hundred," said Wanda.

"A hundred!" exclaimed all the girls incredulously, and the little girls would stop playing hopscotch and listen.

"Yeah, a hundred, all lined up," said Wanda. Then her thin lips drew together in silence.

"What are they like? All silk, I bet," said Peggy.

"Yeah, all silk, all colors."

"Velvet too?"

"Yeah, velvet too. A hundred dresses," repeated Wanda stolidly. "All lined up in my closet."

Then they'd let her go. And then before she'd gone very far, they couldn't help bursting into shrieks and peals of laughter.

A hundred dresses! Obviously the only dress Wanda had was the blue one she wore every day. So what did she say she had a hundred for? What a story! And the girls laughed derisively, while Wanda moved over to the sunny place by the ivy-covered brick wall of the school building where she usually stood and waited for the bell to ring.

But if the girls had met her at the corner of Oliver Street, they'd carry her along with them for a way, stopping every few feet for more incredulous questions. And it wasn't always dresses they talked about. Sometimes it was hats, or coats, or even shoes.

"How many shoes did you say you had?"

"Sixty."

"Sixty! Sixty pairs or sixty shoes?"

"Sixty pairs. All lined up in my closet."

"Yesterday you said fifty."

"Now I got sixty."

Cries of exaggerated politeness greeted this.

"All alike?" said the girls.

"Oh, no. Every pair is different. All colors. All lined up." And Wanda would shift her eyes quickly from Peggy to a distant spot, as though she were looking far ahead, looking but not seeing anything.

Then the outer fringe of the crowd of girls would break away gradually, laughing, and little by little, in pairs, the group would disperse. Peggy, who had thought up this game, and Maddie, her inseparable friend, were always the last to leave. And finally Wanda would move up the street, her eyes dull and her mouth closed tight, hitching her left shoulder every now and then in the funny way she had, finishing the walk to school alone.

Peggy was not really cruel. She protected small children from bullies. And she cried for hours if she saw an animal mistreated. If anybody had said to her, "Don't you think that is a cruel way to treat Wanda?" she would have been very surprised. Cruel? What did the girl want to go and say she had a hundred dresses for? Anybody could tell that was a lie. Why did she want to lie? And she wasn't just an ordinary person, else why would she have a name like that? Anyway, they never made her cry.

As for Maddie, this business of asking Wanda every day how many dresses and how many hats and how many this and that she had was bothering her. Maddie was poor herself. She usually wore somebody's hand-me-down clothes. Thank goodness, she didn't live up on Boggins Heights or have a funny name. And her forehead didn't shine the way

Wanda's round one did. What did she use on it? Sapolio? That's what all the girls wanted to know.

Sometimes when Peggy was asking Wanda those questions in that mock polite voice, Maddie felt embarrassed and studied the marbles in the palm of her hand, rolling them around and saying nothing herself. Not that she felt sorry for Wanda exactly. She would never have paid any attention to Wanda if Peggy hadn't invented the dresses game. But suppose Peggy and all the others started in on her next! She wasn't as poor as Wanda perhaps, but she was poor. Of course she would have more sense than to say a hundred dresses. Still she would not like them to begin on her. Not at all! Oh, dear! She did wish Peggy would stop teasing Wanda Petronski.

A Bright Blue Day

Somehow Maddie could not buckle down to work.

She sharpened her pencil, turning it around carefully in the little red sharpener, letting the shavings fall in a neat heap on a piece of scrap paper, and trying not to get any of the dust from the lead on her clean arithmetic paper.

A slight frown puckered her forehead. In the first place she didn't like being late to school. And in the second place she kept thinking about Wanda. Somehow Wanda's desk, though empty, seemed to be the only thing she saw when she looked over to that side of the room.

How had the hundred dresses game begun in the first place, she asked herself impatiently. It was hard to remember the time when they hadn't played that game with Wanda; hard to think all the way back from now, when the hundred dresses was like the daily dozen, to then, when everything seemed much nicer. Oh, yes. She remembered.

It had begun that day when Cecile first wore her new red dress. Suddenly the whole scene flashed swiftly and vividly before Maddie's eyes.

It was a bright blue day in September. No, it must have been October, because when she and Peggy were coming to school, arms around each other and singing, Peggy had said, "You know what? This must be the kind of day they mean when they say, 'October's bright blue weather.'"

Maddie remembered that because afterwards it didn't seem like bright blue weather any more, although the weather had not changed in the slightest.

As they turned from shady Oliver Street into Maple, they both blinked. For now the morning sun shone straight in their eyes. Besides that, bright flashes of color came from a group of a half-dozen or more girls across the street. Their sweaters and jackets and dresses, blues and golds and reds, and one crimson one in particular, caught the sun's rays like bright pieces of glass.

A crisp, fresh wind was blowing, swishing their skirts and blowing their hair in their eyes. The girls were all exclaiming and shouting and each one was trying to talk louder than the others. Maddie and Peggy joined the group, and the laughing, and the talking.

"Hi, Peg! Hi, Maddie!" they were greeted warmly. "Look at Cecile!"

What they were all exclaiming about was the dress that Cecile had on — a crimson dress with cap and socks to match. It was a bright new dress and very pretty. Everyone was admiring it and admiring Cecile. For long, slender Cecile was a toe-dancer and wore fancier clothes than most of them. And she had her black satin bag with her precious white satin ballet slippers slung over her shoulders. Today was the day for her dancing lesson.

Maddie sat down on the granite curbstone to tie her

29

shoelaces. She listened happily to what they were saying. They all seemed especially jolly today, probably because it was such a bright day. Everything sparkled. Way down at the end of the street the sun shimmered and turned to silver the blue water of the bay. Maddie picked up a piece of broken mirror and flashed a small circle of light edged with rainbow colors onto the houses, the trees, and the top of the telegraph pole.

And it was then that Wanda had come along with her brother Jake.

They didn't often come to school together. Jake had to get to school very early because he helped old Mr. Heany, the school janitor, with the furnace, or raking up the dry leaves, or other odd jobs before school opened. Today he must be late.

Even Wanda looked pretty in this sunshine, and her pale blue dress looked like a piece of the sky in summer; and that old gray toboggan cap she wore — it must be something Jake had found — looked almost jaunty. Maddie watched them absent-mindedly as she flashed her piece of broken mirror here and there. And only absent-mindedly she noticed Wanda stop short when they reached the crowd of laughing and shouting girls.

"Come on," Maddie heard Jake say. "I gotta hurry. I gotta get the doors open and ring the bell."

"You go the rest of the way," said Wanda. "I want to stay here."

Jake shrugged and went on up Maple Street. Wanda slowly approached the group of girls. With each step forward, before she put her foot down she seemed to hesitate for a long, long time. She approached the group as a timid animal might, ready to run if anything alarmed it.

Even so, Wanda's mouth was twisted into the vaguest

suggestion of a smile. She must feel happy too because everybody must feel happy on such a day.

As Wanda joined the outside fringe of girls, Maddie stood up too and went over close to Peggy to get a good look at Cecile's new dress herself. She forgot about Wanda, and more girls kept coming up, enlarging the group and all exclaiming about Cecile's new dress.

"Isn't it lovely!" said one.

"Yeah, I have a new blue dress, but it's not as pretty as that," said another.

"My mother just bought me a plaid, one of the Stuart plaids."

"I got a new dress for dancing school."

"I'm gonna make my mother get me one just like Cecile's."

Everyone was talking to everybody else. Nobody said anything to Wanda, but there she was, a part of the crowd. The girls closed in a tighter circle around Cecile, still talking all at once and admiring her, and Wanda was somehow enveloped in the group. Nobody talked to Wanda, but nobody even thought about her being there.

Maybe, thought Maddie, remembering what had happened next, maybe she figured all she'd have to do was say something and she'd really be one of the girls. And this would be an easy thing to do because all they were doing was talking about dresses.

Maddie was standing next to Peggy. Wanda was standing next to Peggy on the other side. All of a sudden, Wanda impulsively touched Peggy's arm and said something. Her light blue eyes were shining and she looked excited like the rest of the girls.

"What?" asked Peggy. For Wanda had spoken very softly.

Wanda hesitated a moment and then she repeated her words firmly.

"I got a hundred dresses home."

"That's what I thought you said. A hundred dresses. A hundred!" Peggy's voice raised itself higher and higher.

"Hey, kids!" she yelled. "This girl's got a hundred dresses."

Silence greeted this, and the crowd which had centered around Cecile and her new finery now centered curiously around Wanda and Peggy. The girls eyed Wanda, first incredulously, then suspiciously.

"A hundred dresses?" they said. "Nobody could have a hundred dresses."

"I have though."

"Wanda has a hundred dresses."

"Where are they then?"

"In my closet."

"Oh, you don't wear them to school."

"No. For parties."

"Oh, you mean you don't have any everyday dresses."

"Yes, I have all kinds of dresses."

"Why don't you wear them to school?"

For a moment Wanda was silent to this. Her lips drew together. Then she repeated stolidly as though it were a lesson learned in school, "A hundred of them. All lined up in my closet."

"Oh, I see," said Peggy, talking like a grown-up person. "The child has a hundred dresses, but she wouldn't wear them to school. Perhaps she's worried of getting ink or chalk on them."

With this everybody fell to laughing and talking at once. Wanda looked stolidly at them, pursing her lips together, wrinkling her forehead up so that the gray toboggan slipped way down on her brow. Suddenly from down the street the school gong rang its first warning.

"Oh, come on, hurry," said Maddie, relieved. "We'll be late."

"Good-by, Wanda," said Peggy. "Your hundred dresses sound bee-you-tiful."

More shouts of laughter greeted this, and off the girls ran, laughing and talking and forgetting Wanda and her hundred dresses. Forgetting until tomorrow and the next day and the next, when Peggy, seeing her coming to school, would remember and ask her about the hundred dresses. For now Peggy seemed to think a day was lost if she had not had some fun with Wanda, winning the approving laughter of the girls.

Yes, that was the way it had all begun, the game of the hundred dresses. It all happened so suddenly and unexpectedly, with everybody falling right in, that even if you felt uncomfortable as Maddie had there wasn't anything you could do about it. Maddie wagged her head up and down. Yes, she repeated to herself, that was the way it began, that day, that bright blue day.

And she wrapped up her shavings and went to the front of the room to empty them in the teacher's basket.

The Contest

Now today, even though she and Peggy had been late to school, Maddie was glad she had not had to make fun of Wanda. She worked her arithmetic problems absent-mindedly. Eight times eight . . . let's see . . . nothing she could do about making fun of Wanda. She wished she had the nerve to write Peggy a note, because she knew she'd never have the courage to speak right out to Peggy, to say, "Hey, Peg, let's stop asking Wanda how many dresses she has."

When she finished her arithmetic, she did start a note to Peggy. Suddenly she paused and shuddered. She pictured herself in the school yard, a new target for Peggy and the girls. Peggy might ask her where she got the dress she had on, and Maddie would have to say that it was one of Peggy's old ones that Maddie's mother had tried to disguise with new trimmings so that no one in Room 13 would recognize it.

If only Peggy would decide of her own accord to stop having fun with Wanda. Oh, well! Maddie ran her hand through her short blonde hair as though to push the uncomfortable thoughts away. What difference did it make? Slowly Maddie tore the note she had started into bits. She was Peggy's best friend, and Peggy was the best-liked girl in the whole room. Peggy could not possibly do anything that was really wrong, she thought.

As for Wanda, she was just some girl who lived up on Boggins Heights and stood alone in the school yard. Nobody in the room thought about Wanda at all except when it was her turn to stand up for oral reading. Then they all hoped she would hurry up and finish and sit down, because it took her forever to read a paragraph. Sometimes she stood up and just looked at her book and couldn't, or wouldn't, read at all. The teacher tried to help her, but she'd just stand there until the teacher told her to sit down. Was she dumb or what? Maybe she was just timid. The only time she talked was in the school yard about her hundred dresses. Maddie remembered her telling about one of her dresses, a pale blue one with cerise-colored trimmings. And she remembered another that was brilliant jungle green with a red sash. "You'd look like a Christmas tree in that," the girls had said in pretended admiration.

Thinking about Wanda and her hundred dresses all lined up in the closet, Maddie began to wonder who was going to win the drawing and color contest. For girls this contest consisted of designing dresses, and for boys, of designing motor boats. Probably Peggy would win the girls' medal. Peggy drew better than anyone else in the room. At least that's what everybody thought. You should see the way she could copy a picture in a magazine or some film star's head. You could almost tell who it was. Oh, Maddie did hope Peggy would win. Hope so? She was sure Peggy would win. Well, tomorrow the teacher was going to announce the winners. Then they'd know.

Thoughts of Wanda sank further and further from Maddie's mind, and by the time the history lesson began she had forgotten all about her.

The Hundred Dresses

The next day it was drizzling. Maddie and Peggy hurried to school under Peggy's umbrella. Naturally on a day like this they didn't wait for Wanda Petronski on the corner of Oliver Street, the street that far, far away, under the railroad tracks and up the hill, led to Boggins Heights. Anyway they weren't taking chances on being late today, because today was important.

"Do you think Miss Mason will surely announce the winners today?" asked Peggy.

"Oh, I hope so, the minute we get in," said Maddie, and added, "Of course you'll win, Peg."

"Hope so," said Peggy eagerly.

The minute they entered the classroom they stopped short and gasped. There were drawings all over the room, on every ledge and window sill, tacked to the tops of the blackboards, spread over the bird charts, dazzling colors and brilliant lavish designs, all drawn on great sheets of wrapping paper.

There must have been a hundred of them all lined up!

These must be the drawings for the contest. They were! Everybody stopped and whistled or murmured admiringly.

As soon as the class had assembled Miss Mason announced the winners. Jack Beggles had won for the boys, she said, and his design of an outboard motor boat was on exhibition in Room 12, along with the sketches by all the other boys.

"As for the girls," she said, "although just one or two sketches were submitted by most, one girl — and Room 13 should be very proud of her — this one girl actually drew one hundred designs — all different and all beautiful. In the opinion of the judges, any one of her drawings is worthy of winning the prize. I am happy to say that Wanda Petronski is the winner of the girls' medal. Unfortunately Wanda has been absent from school for some days and is not here to receive the applause that is due her. Let us hope she will be back tomorrow. Now, class, you may file around the room quietly and look at her exquisite drawings."

The children burst into applause, and even the boys were glad to have a chance to stamp on the floor, put their fingers in their mouths and whistle, though they were not interested in dresses. Maddie and Peggy were among the first to reach the blackboard to look at the drawings.

"Look, Peg," whispered Maddie, "there's that blue one she told us about. Isn't it beautiful?"

"Yeah," said Peggy, "and here's that green one. Boy, and I thought I could draw!"

While the class was circling the room, the monitor from the principal's office brought Miss Mason a note. Miss Mason read it several times and studied it thoughtfully for a while. Then she clapped her hands and said, "Attention, class. Everyone back to his seat."

When the shuffling of feet had stopped and the room was still and quiet, Miss Mason said, "I have a letter from Wanda's father that I want to read to you."

Miss Mason stood there a moment and the silence in the room grew tense and expectant. The teacher adjusted her glasses slowly and deliberately. Her manner indicated that what was coming — this letter from Wanda's father — was a matter of great importance. Everybody listened closely as Miss Mason read the brief note:

"Dear teacher: My Wanda will not come to your school any more. Jake also. Now we move away to big city. No more holler Polack. No more ask why funny name. Plenty of funny names in the big city. Yours truly,

Jan Petronski."

A deep silence met the reading of this letter. Miss Mason took her glasses off, blew on them and wiped them on her soft white handkerchief. Then she put them on again and looked at the class. When she spoke her voice was very low.

"I am sure none of my boys and girls in Room 13 would purposely and deliberately hurt anyone's feelings because his name happened to be a long unfamiliar one. I prefer to think that what was said was said in thoughtlessness. I know that all of you feel the way I do, that this is a very unfortunate thing to have happen. Unfortunate and sad, both. And I want you all to think about it."

The first period was a study period. Maddie tried to prepare her lessons, but she could not put her mind on her work. She had a very sick feeling in the bottom of her stomach. True, she had not enjoyed listening to Peggy ask Wanda how many dresses she had in her closet, but she had said nothing. She had stood by silently, and that was just as bad as what Peggy had done. Worse. She was a coward. At least Peggy hadn't considered they were being mean, but she, Maddie, had thought they were doing wrong. She had thought, supposing she was the one being made fun of. She could put herself in Wanda's shoes. But she had done just as much as Peggy to make life miserable for Wanda by simply standing by and saying nothing. She had helped to make someone so unhappy that she had had to move away from town.

Goodness! Wasn't there anything she could do? If only she could tell Wanda she hadn't meant to hurt her feelings. She turned around and stole a glance at Peggy, but Peggy did not look up. She seemed to be studying hard.

Well, whether Peggy felt badly or not, she, Maddie, had to do something. She had to find Wanda Petronski. Maybe she had not yet moved away. Maybe Peggy would climb the Heights with her and they would tell Wanda she had won the contest. And that they thought she was smart and the hundred dresses were beautiful.

When school was dismissed in the afternoon, Peggy said with pretended casualness, "Hey, let's go and see if that kid has left town or not."

So Peggy had had the same idea as Maddie had had! Maddie glowed. Peggy was really all right, just as she always thought. Peg was really all right. She was o.k.

Up on Boggins Heights

The two girls hurried out of the building, up the street toward Boggins Heights, the part of town that wore such a forbidding air on this kind of a November afternoon, drizzly, damp, and dismal.

"Well, at least," said Peggy gruffly, "I never did call her a foreigner or make fun of her name. I never thought she had the sense to know we were making fun of her anyway. I thought she was too dumb. And gee, look how she can draw! And I thought I could draw."

Maddie could say nothing. All she hoped was that they would find Wanda. Just so she'd be able to tell her they were sorry they had all picked on her. And just to say how wonderful the whole school thought she was, and please not to move away and everybody would be nice. She and Peggy would fight anybody who was not nice.

Maddie fell to imagining a story in which she and Peggy assailed any bully who might be going to pick on Wanda. "Petronski — Onski!" somebody would yell, and she and Peggy would pounce on the guilty one. For a time Maddie consoled herself with these thoughts, but they soon vanished and again she felt unhappy and wished everything could be nice the way it was before any of them had made fun of Wanda.

Br-r-r! How drab and cold and cheerless it was up here on the Heights! In the summer time the woods, the sumac, and the ferns that grew along the brook on the side of the road were lush and made this a beautiful walk on Sunday afternoons. But now it did not seem beautiful. The brook had shrunk to the merest trickle, and today's drizzle sharpened the outlines of the rusty tin cans, old shoes, and forlorn remnants of a big black umbrella in the bed of the brook.

The two girls hurried on. They hoped to get to the top of the hill before dark. Otherwise they were not certain they could find Wanda's house. At last, puffing and panting, they rounded the top of the hill. The first house, that old rickety one, belonged to old man Svenson. Peggy and Maddie hurried past it almost on tiptoe. Somebody said once that old man Svenson had shot a man. Others said "Nonsense! He's an old good-for-nothing. Wouldn't hurt a flea."

But, false or true, the girls breathed more freely as they rounded the corner. It was too cold and drizzly for old man Svenson to be in his customary chair tilted against the house. Even his dog was nowhere in sight and had not barked at the girls from wherever he might be.

"I think that's where the Petronskis live," said Maddie, pointing to a little white house with lots of chicken coops at the side of it. Wisps of old grass stuck up here and there along the pathway like thin wet kittens. The house and its sparse little yard looked shabby but clean. It reminded Maddie of Wanda's one dress, her faded blue cotton dress, shabby but clean.

There was not a sign of life about the house except for a yellow cat, half grown, crouching on the one small step close to the front door. It leapt timidly with a small cry half way up a tree when the girls came into the yard. Peggy knocked firmly on the door, but there was no answer. She and Maddie went around to the back yard and knocked there. Still there was no answer.

"Wanda!" called Peggy. They listened sharply, but only a deep silence pressed against their eardrums. There was no doubt about it. The Petronskis were gone.

"Maybe they just went away for a little while and haven't really left with their furniture yet," suggested Maddie hopefully. Maddie was beginning to wonder how

she could bear the hard fact that Wanda had actually gone and that she might never be able to make amends.

"Well," said Peggy, "let's see if the door is open."

They cautiously turned the knob of the front door. It opened easily, for it was a light thing and looked as though it furnished but frail protection against the cold winds that blew up here in the winter time. The little square room that the door opened into was empty. There was absolutely nothing left in it, and in the corner a closet with its door wide open was empty too. Maddie wondered what it had held before the Petronskis moved out. And she thought of Wanda saying, "Sure, a hundred dresses . . . all lined up in the closet."

Well, anyway, real and imaginary dresses alike were gone. The Petronskis were gone. And now how could she and Peggy tell Wanda anything? Maybe the teacher knew where she had moved to. Maybe old man Svenson knew. They might knock on his door and ask on the way down. Or the post office might know. If they wrote a letter, Wanda might get it because the post office might forward it. Feeling very downcast and discouraged, the girls closed the door and started for home. Coming down the road, way, way off in the distance, through the drizzle they could see the water of the bay, gray and cold.

"Do you suppose that was their cat and they forgot her?" asked Peggy. But the cat wasn't anywhere around now, and as the girls turned the bend they saw her crouching under the dilapidated wooden chair in front of old man Svenson's house. So perhaps the cat belonged to him. They lost their courage about knocking on his door and asking when the Petronskis had left and anyway, goodness! here was old man Svenson himself coming up the road. Everything about Svenson was yellow; his house, his cat, his trousers, his drooping mustache and tangled hair, his hound loping behind him. The two girls drew over to the side of the path as they hurried by. When they were a good way past, they stopped.

"Hey, Mr. Svenson!" yelled Peggy. "When did the Petronskis move?"

Old man Svenson turned around, but said nothing. Finally he did answer, but his words were unintelligible, and the two girls turned and ran down the hill as fast as they could. Old man Svenson looked after them for a moment and then went on up the hill, muttering to himself and scratching his head.

When they were back down on Oliver Street again, the girls stopped running. They still felt disconsolate, and Maddie wondered if she were going to be unhappy about Wanda and the hundred dresses forever. Nothing would ever seem good to her again, because just when she was about to enjoy something — like going for a hike with Peggy to look for bayberries or sliding down Barley Hill — she'd bump right smack into the thought that she had made Wanda Petronski move away.

"Well, anyway," said Peggy, "she's gone now, so what can we do? Besides, when I was asking her about all of her dresses she probably was getting good ideas for her drawings. She might not even have won the contest otherwise."

Maddie carefully turned this idea over in her head, for if there were anything in it she would not have to feel so bad. But that night she could not get to sleep. She thought about Wanda and her faded blue dress and the little house she had lived in; and old man Svenson living a few steps away. And she thought of the glowing picture those hundred dresses made — all lined up in the classroom.

At last Maddie sat up in bed and pressed her forehead

tight in her hands and really thought. This was the hardest thinking she had ever done. After a long, long time she reached an important conclusion.

She was never going to stand by and say nothing again.

If she ever heard anybody picking on someone because they were funny looking or because they had strange names, she'd speak up. Even if it meant losing Peggy's friendship. She had no way of making things right with Wanda, but from now on she would never make anybody else so unhappy again. Finally, all tired out, Maddie fell asleep.

The Letter to Room 13

On Saturday Maddie spent the afternoon with Peggy. They were writing a letter to Wanda Petronski.

It was just a friendly letter telling about the contest and telling Wanda she had won. They told her how pretty her drawings were, and that now they were studying about Winfield Scott in school. And they asked her if she liked where she was living now and if she liked her new teacher. They had meant to say they were sorry, but it ended up with their just writing a friendly letter, the kind they would have written to any good friend, and they signed it with lots of X's for love.

They mailed the letter to Boggins Heights, writing "Please Forward" on the envelope. The teacher had not known where Wanda had moved to, so their only hope was that the post office knew. The minute they dropped the letter in the mail box they both felt happier and more care-free.

Days passed and there was no answer, but the letter did not come back so maybe Wanda had received it. Perhaps she was so hurt and angry she was not going to answer. You could not blame her. And Maddie remembered the way she hitched her left shoulder up as she walked off to school alone, and how the girls always said, "Why does her dress always hang funny like that, and why does she wear those queer, high, laced shoes?"

They knew she didn't have any mother, but they hadn't thought about it. They hadn't thought she had to do her own washing and ironing. She only had one dress and she must have had to wash and iron it overnight. Maybe sometimes it wasn't dry when it was time to put it on in the morning. But it was always clean.

Several weeks went by and still Wanda did not answer. Peggy had begun to forget the whole business, and Maddie put herself to sleep at night making speeches about Wanda, defending her from great crowds of girls who were trying to tease her with, "How many dresses have you got?" Before Wanda could press her lips together in a tight line the way she did before answering, Maddie would cry out, "Stop! This girl is just a girl just like you are. . . ." And then everybody would feel ashamed the way she used to feel. Sometimes she rescued Wanda from a sinking ship or the hoofs of a runaway horse. "Oh, that's all right," she'd say when Wanda thanked her with dull pained eyes.

Now it was Christmas time and there was snow on the ground. Christmas bells and a small tree decorated the classroom. And on one narrow blackboard Jack Beggles had drawn a jolly fat Santa Claus in red and white chalk. On the last day of school before the holidays, the children in Peggy's and Maddie's class had a Christmas party. The teacher's desk was rolled back and a piano rolled in. First the children had acted the story of Tiny Tim. Then they had sung songs and Cecile had done some dances in different costumes. The dance called the "Passing of Autumn" in which she whirled and spun like a red and golden autumn leaf was the favorite.

After the party the teacher said she had a surprise, and she showed the class a letter she had received that morning.

"Guess who this is from," she said. "You remember Wanda Petronski? The bright little artist who won the drawing contest? Well, she has written me and I am glad to know where she lives because now I can send her medal. And I hope it gets there for Christmas. I want to read her letter to you."

The class sat up with a sudden interest, and listened intently to Miss Mason as she read the letter.

> Dear Miss Mason,
>
> How are you and Room 13? Please tell the girls they can keep those hundred dresses because in my new house I have a hundred new ones all lined up in my closet. I'd like that girl Peggy to have the drawing of the green dress with the red trimming and her friend Maddie to have the blue one.
> For Christmas. I miss that school and my new teacher does not equalize with you.
> Merry Christmas to you and everybody.
>
> Yours truly,
>
> Wanda Petronski

The teacher passed the letter around the room for everybody to see. It was pretty, decorated with a picture of a Christmas tree lighted up in the night in a park surrounded by high buildings.

On the way home from school Maddie and Peggy held their drawings very carefully. They had stayed late to help straighten up after the play and it was getting dark. The houses looked warm and inviting with wreaths and holly and lighted trees in their windows. Outside the grocery store hundreds of Christmas trees were stacked, and in the window candy peppermint canes and cornucopias of shiny bright transparent paper were strung. The air smelled like Christmas and bright lights everywhere reflected different colors on the snow.

"The colors are like the colors in Wanda's hundred dresses," said Maddie.

"Yes," said Peggy, holding her drawing out to look at it under the street lamp. "And boy! This shows she really liked us. It shows she got our letter and this is her way of saying that everything's all right. And that's that," she said with finality.

Peggy felt happy and relieved. It was Christmas and everything was fine.

"I hope so," said Maddie sadly. She felt sad because she knew she would never see the little tight-lipped Polish girl again and couldn't ever really make things right between them.

She went home and she pinned her drawing over a torn place in the pink-flowered wall-paper in the bedroom. The shabby room came alive from the brilliancy of the colors. Maddie sat down on the edge of her bed and looked at the drawing. She had stood by and said nothing, but Wanda had been nice to her anyway.

Tears blurred her eyes and she gazed for a long time at the picture. Then hastily she rubbed her eyes and studied it intently. The colors in the dress were so vivid she had scarcely noticed the face and head of the drawing. But it looked like her, Maddie! It really did. The same short blonde hair, blue eyes, and wide straight mouth. Why, it really looked like her own self! Wanda had really drawn this for her. Wanda had drawn her! In excitement she ran over to Peggy's.

"Peg!" she said. "Let me see your picture."

"What's the matter?" asked Peggy as they clattered up the stairs to her room, where Wanda's drawing was lying face down on the bed. Maddie carefully lifted it up.

"Look! She drew you. That's you!" she exclaimed. And the head and face of this picture did look like the auburn-haired Peggy.

"What did I say!" said Peggy. "She must have really liked us anyway."

"Yes, she must have," agreed Maddie, and she blinked away the tears that came every time she thought of Wanda standing alone in that sunny spot in the school yard close to the wall, looking stolidly over at the group of laughing girls after she had walked off, after she had said, "Sure, a hundred of them — all lined up . . ."

Author

Born and raised in West Haven, Connecticut, Eleanor Estes says it was the perfect town to grow up in. She has used it as the setting for many of her books. She says, "I like to feel I am holding up a mirror of childhood. I feel that the impressions I have gathered through the years must be woven into a structure of the imagination — a book written purely for the enjoyment and the entertainment of children." Among the many books she has written for children are the more humorous books *The Moffats* and *The Witch Family*. She has received two awards, including the Newbery Medal for distinguished contribution to children's literature in 1952, for her book *Ginger Pye*.

An excerpt from

Thank You, Jackie Robinson

by Barbara Cohen

This story takes place in the late 1940's. Sam loves baseball, especially the Brooklyn Dodgers. Sam's special friend is Davy, a sixty-year-old man who shares Sam's love for baseball and takes him to his first major-league game. When Davy goes into the hospital, Sam buys a baseball and sets off for the ball park to get it autographed as a get-well present for Davy.

All the baseball players named in the story were real people. Jackie Robinson was the first black player in major-league baseball and played for the Brooklyn Dodgers from 1947 until he retired in 1956. In 1962, Robinson became the first black player to be named to the Baseball Hall of Fame.

I had gone into the kitchen real early in the morning, before anyone else was up, and made myself a couple of egg-salad sandwiches. I had them and my money and the baseball in its little cardboard box. I walked the mile and a half to the bus station because there'd be no place to leave my bike if I rode there. I took the bus into New York City and I took a subway to Ebbets Field. I didn't have to ask anyone anything except the bus driver for a ticket to New York City and the man in the subway booth for change of a quarter. There was one thing I'd learned and that was that if you know how to read you can do anything. Right in the middle of the subway was this big map of the subway system and Ebbets Field was marked right on it in large black letters.

You could see flags flying above the ball park when you climbed up out of the subway station. You had to walk three blocks and there you were. Inside it was as it always had been, as bright and green as ever, remote from the sooty streets that surrounded it, remote from all the world. In the excitement of being there, I almost forgot about Davy for a moment. I almost forgot why I had come. Then, when the Cubs' pitcher, Warren Hacker, began to warm up, I turned to Davy to ask him if he thought the Dodger's manager Shotton was going to give Jackie Robinson's sore heel a rest that day, but Davy wasn't there, and I remembered.

I thought maybe I'd better start trying right away. My chances were probably better during batting practice than they would be later. I took my ball out of its box and stashed the box underneath my bleacher seat. Then I walked around to the first-base side and climbed all the way down to the box seats right behind the dugout. I leaned over the rail. Billy Cox was trotting back to the dugout from home plate, where Carl Erskine had been throwing to him.

I swallowed my heart, which seemed to be beating in my throat, and called out, "Billy, hey Billy," waving my ball as hard and high as I could. But I was scared, and my voice wasn't very loud. I don't think Billy Cox heard me. He disappeared into the dugout.

Marv Rackley came out of the dugout and then Carl Furillo. I called to them too, but they didn't seem to hear me either.

This method was getting me nowhere. I had to try something else before the game began and I'd really lost my chance. I looked around to see if there were any ushers nearby, but none was in sight. It was kind of early and the place hadn't really started to fill up yet. I guess the ushers were loafing around the refreshment stand.

I climbed up on the railing and then hoisted myself onto the roof of the dugout. That was something you could not do at many places besides Ebbets Field. That was one of the few advantages of such a small ball park. Of course, you know, you couldn't go see Ebbets Field now if you wanted to. They tore it down and put an apartment building there.

I could have stood up and walked across the dugout roof to the edge, but I figured if I did that an usher surely would see me. I sneaked across the roof on my belly until I came to the edge and then I leaned over.

It was really very nice in the dugout. I had always kind of pictured it as being literally dug out of the dirt, like a trench in a war, but it had regular walls and a floor and benches and a water cooler. The only trouble was, there were just a couple of guys in there — Eddie Miksis, and Billy Cox, whom I'd seen out on the field a few minutes before. I was disappointed. I had certainly hoped for

Campy's signature, and Gil Hodges', and Pee Wee Reese's, and of course Jackie Robinson's, but I figured Davy would be thrilled with Miksis and Billy Cox, since their names on a ball would be more than he'd ever expected. Anyway I figured a few more guys might come meandering in before I was through.

But no matter how hard I swallowed, my heart was still stuck in my throat. "Eddie," I called. "Eddie, Billy." Hardly any sound came out of my mouth at all.

And then all of a sudden I heard a voice calling real loud. Whoever it was didn't have any trouble getting the sound out of *his* mouth. "Hey you, kid, get down off that roof," the voice said. "What do you think you're doing?" I sat up and turned around. An angry usher was standing at the foot of the aisle, right by the railing, screaming at me. "Get yourself off that roof," he shouted. "Right now, or I'll throw you out of the ball park."

I scrambled down fast as I could. Boy, was I a mess. My chino pants and my striped jersey were absolutely covered with dust and grime from that roof. I guess my face and arms weren't any too clean either. I looked like a bum.

"I'm going to throw you out anyway," the usher said, "because you don't have a ticket."

I got real mad when I heard him say that. People had been throwing me out of places all week long and I was plenty sick of it. Especially since I certainly did have a ticket.

"You can't throw me out," I shouted back at him. "I've got as much right to be here as you have." I had suddenly found my voice. I was scared of the ball players, but this usher didn't frighten me one bit. I pulled my ticket stub out of my pocket. "See?" I said, thrusting it into his face, "I certainly do have a ticket."

He made as if to take it out of my hand. I guess he wanted to look at it close, to make sure it was a stub from that day and not an old one I carried around in my pocket for emergencies. But I pulled my hand back.

"Oh, no, you don't," I said. "You can't take this ticket away from me. You won't give it back to me and then you'll throw me out because I don't have a ticket!"

"You crazy, kid?" he asked, shaking his head. "This is what I get for working in Ebbets Field. A bunch of crazy people. Next year I'm applying for a job at the Polo Grounds."

"Go, ahead," I said, "you traitor. Who needs you?" I turned away from him and leaned over the rail.

"I better not see you on that roof again," the usher said. "I'll have my eye out for you — and so will all the other ushers."

"Don't worry," I said.

Then I felt his hand on my shoulder. "As a matter of fact, kid," he said, "I think I'll escort you to your seat where you belong. Up in the bleachers where you can't make any trouble!"

Well, right then and there the whole enterprise would have gone up in smoke if old Jackie Robinson himself had not come trotting out onto the field from the dugout that very second. "Hey, Jackie," I called, "Hey, Jackie," in a voice as loud as a thunderbolt. I mean there were two airplanes flying overhead right that minute and Jackie Robinson heard me anyway.

He glanced over in the direction he could tell my voice was coming from, and I began to wave frantically, still calling "Jackie, hey, Jackie."

He lifted up his hand, gave one wide wave, and smiled. "Hey, kid," he called, and continued on his way to the

batting cage. In another instant he'd have been too busy with batting practice to pay any attention to me.

"Sign my ball," I screamed. "Sign my ball."

He seemed to hesitate briefly. I took this as a good omen. "You gotta," I went on frantically. "Please, please, you gotta."

"He don't gotta do nothing," the usher said. "That's Jackie Robinson and everyone knows that he don't gotta do nothing."

I went right on screaming.

"Come on, kid," the usher said, "we're getting out of here." He was a big hulking usher who must have weighed about eight hundred pounds, and he began pulling on me. Even though I gripped the cement with my sneakers and held onto the rail with my hand, he managed to pull me loose. But he couldn't shut me up.

"Please, Jackie, please," I went right on screaming.

It worked. Or something worked. If not my screaming, then maybe the sight of that monster usher trying to pull me up the aisle and scrungy old me pulling against him for dear life.

"Let the kid go," Jackie Robinson said when he got to the railing. "All he wants is an autograph."

"He's a fresh kid," the usher said, but he let me go.

"Kids are supposed to be fresh," Jackie Robinson said.

I thrust my ball into Jackie Robinson's face. "Gee, thanks, Mr. Robinson," I said. "Sign it, please."

"You got a pen?" he asked.

"A pen?" I could have kicked myself. "A pen?" I'd forgotten a pen! I turned to the usher. "You got a pen?"

"If I had," the usher said triumphantly, "I certainly wouldn't lend it to you!"

"Oh, come on," Jackie Robinson said, "don't be so vindictive. What harm did the kid do, after all?"

"Well, as it happens, I don't have one," the usher replied smugly.

"Wait here," I said. "Wait right here, Mr. Robinson. I'll go find one."

Jackie Robinson laughed. "Sorry, kid, but I've got work to do. Another time, maybe."

"Please, Mr. Robinson," I said. "It's for my friend. My friend, Davy."

"Well, let Davy come and get his own autographs," he said. "Why should you do his dirty work for him?"

"He can't come," I said. The words came rushing out of me, tumbling one on top of the other. I had to tell Jackie Robinson all about it, before he went away. "Davy can't come because he's sick. He had a heart attack."

"A heart attack?" Jackie Robinson asked. "A kid had a heart attack?"

"He's not a kid," I explained. "He's sixty years old. He's my best friend. He's black like you. He's always loved the Dodgers, but lately he's loved them more than ever."

Now that I think about it, what I said could have annoyed Jackie Robinson very much. But at the time, it didn't. I guess he could tell how serious I was about what I was saying. "How did this Davy get to be your best friend?" he asked.

So I told him. I told him everything, or as near to everything as I could tell in five minutes. I told him how Davy worked for my mother, and how I had no father, so it was Davy who took me to my first ball game. I told him how they wouldn't let me into the hospital to see Davy and how we had always talked about catching a ball that was hit into the stands and getting it autographed.

Jackie listened silently, nodding every once in a while. When I was done at last, he said, "Well, now, kid, I'll tell you what. You keep this ball you brought with you. Keep it to play with. And borrow a pen from someone. Come back to the dugout the minute, the very second, the game is over, and I'll get you a real ball, one we played with, and I'll get all the guys to autograph it for you."

"Make sure it's one you hit," I said.

What nerve. I should have fainted dead away just because Jackie Robinson had deigned to speak to me. But here he was, making me an offer beyond my wildest dreams, and for me it wasn't enough. I had to have more. However, he didn't seem to care.

"O.K.," he said, "*if* I hit one." He had been in a little slump lately.

"You will," I said, "you will."

And he did. He broke the ball game wide open in the sixth inning when he hit a double to left field, scoring Rackley and Duke Snider. He scored himself when the Cubs pitcher, Warren Hacker, tried to pick him off second base. But Hacker overthrew, and Jackie, with that incredible speed he had, ran all the way home. Besides, he worked two double plays with Preacher Roe and Gil Hodges. On consecutive pitches, Carl Furillo and Billy Cox both hit home runs, shattering the 1930 Brooklyn home-run record of 122 for a season. The Dodgers scored six runs, and they scored them all in the sixth inning. They beat the Cubs, 6–1. They were hot, really hot, that day and that year.

But I really didn't watch the game as closely as I had all the others I'd been to see. I couldn't. My mind was on too many other things — on Jackie Robinson, on what was going to happen after the game was over, on that monster usher who I feared would yet find some way of spoiling things for me, but above all on Davy and the fact that he was missing all of the excitement.

And then I had to worry about getting hold of a pen. You could buy little pencils at the ball park for keeping

box scores, but no pens. It was the first — and last — time in my life I walked into a ball park without something to write with. And I didn't see how I could borrow one from someone, since in all that mess of humanity I'd never find the person after the game to return it to him. Unless I took the guy's name and address and mailed it back to him later.

It didn't look to me like the guys in the bleachers where I was sitting had pens with them anyway. Most of them had on tee shirts, and tee shirts don't have pockets in them for pens. I decided to walk over to the seats along the first-base line to see if any of those fans looked more like pen owners. I had to go in that direction anyway to make sure I was at the dugout the second the ball game ended. I took with me my ball in its box.

On my way over I ran into this guy hawking cold drinks and I decided to buy one in order to wash down the two egg-salad sandwiches I had eaten during the third inning.

This guy had a pen in his pocket. As a matter of fact he had two of them. "Look," I said to him, as I paid him for my soda, "could I borrow one of those pens?"

"Sure," he said, handing it to me after he had put my money into his change machine. He stood there, waiting, like he expected me to hand it back to him after I was done with it.

"Look," I said again, "maybe I could sort of buy it from you."

"Buy it from me? You mean the pen?"

"Yeah."

"What do you want my pen for?"

"I need it because Jackie Robinson promised me that after the game he and all the other guys would autograph a ball for me." Getting involved in all these explanations was really a pain in the neck.

"You don't say," the hawker remarked. I could tell he didn't believe me.

"It's true," I said. "Anyway, are you going to sell me your pen?"

"Sure. For a dollar."

I didn't have a dollar. Not any more. I'd have to try something else. I started to walk away.

"Oh, don't be silly, kid," he called to me. "Here, take the darn pen. Keep it." It was a nice pen. It was shaped like a bat, and on it, it said, "Ebbets Field, Home of the Brooklyn Dodgers."

"Hey, mister, thanks," I said. "That's real nice of you."
It seemed to me I ought to do something for him, so I
added, "I think I'd like another soda." He sold me another
soda, and between sipping first from one and then from
the other and trying to watch the game, I made very slow
progress down to the dugout. I got there just before the
game ended in the top of the ninth. The Dodgers didn't
have to come up to bat at all in that final inning, and I was
only afraid that they'd all have disappeared into the club-
house by the time I got there. I should have come down at

the end of the eighth. But Jackie Robinson had said the end of the game. Although my nerve had grown by about seven thousand per cent that day, I still didn't have enough to interrupt Jackie Robinson during a game.

I stood at the railing near the dugout, waiting, and sure enough, Jackie Robinson appeared around the corner of the building only a minute or two after Preacher Roe pitched that final out. All around me people were getting up to leave the ball park, but a lot of them stopped when they saw Jackie Robinson come to the rail to talk to me.

Roy Campanella, Pee Wee Reese, and Gil Hodges were with him.

"Hi, kid," Jackie Robinson said. He was carrying a ball. It was covered with signatures. "Pee Wee here had a pen."

"And a good thing, too," Pee Wee said, "because most of the other guys left the field already."

"But these guys wanted to meet Davy's friend," Jackie Robinson said.

By that time, Preacher Roe had joined us at the railing. Jackie handed him the ball. "Hey, Preacher," he said, "got enough strength left in that arm to sign this ball for Davy's friend here?"

"Got a pen?" Preacher Roe asked.

I handed him the pen the hawker had given me. I was glad I hadn't gone through all the trouble of getting it for nothing.

"Not much room left on this ball," Roe said. He squirmed his signature into a little empty space beneath Duke Snider's and then he handed me both the pen and the ball. Everybody was waving programs and pens in the faces of the ball players who stood by the railing. But before they signed any of them, they all shook my hand. So did Jackie Robinson. I stood there, clutching Davy's ball and watching while those guys signed the programs of the other fans. Finally, though, they'd had enough. They smiled and waved their hands and walked away, five big men in white uniforms, etched sharply against the bright green grass. Jackie Robinson was the last one into the dugout and before he disappeared around the corner, he turned and waved to me.

I waved back. "Thank you, Jackie Robinson," I called. "Thanks for everything." He nodded and smiled. I guess he heard me. I'm glad I remembered my manners before it was too late.

When everyone was gone, I looked down at the ball in my hands. Right between the rows of red seaming, Jackie Robinson had written, above his own signature, "For Davy. Get well soon." Then all the others had put their names around that.

I took the ball I had bought out of the box and put it in my pocket. I put the ball Jackie Robinson had given me in the box. Then I went home.

Author

Barbara Cohen always wanted to be a writer and began writing in the fifth grade. She writes from her own experience. *Thank You, Jackie Robinson* and another of her books, *Gooseberries to Oranges,* were named American Library Association Notable Books.

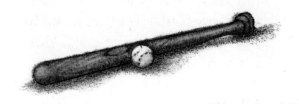

A Time to Talk

by Robert Frost

When a friend calls to me from the road
And slows his horse to a meaning walk,
I don't stand still and look around
On all the hills I haven't hoed,
And shout from where I am, "What is it?"
No, not as there is a time to talk.
I thrust my hoe in the mellow ground,
Blade-end up and five feet tall,
And plod: I go up to the stone wall
For a friendly visit.

An excerpt from

Dear Mr. Henshaw

by Beverly Cleary

Leigh has been Boyd Henshaw's Number One fan ever since his second-grade teacher read aloud Ways to Amuse a Dog. *Now in the sixth grade, Leigh lives with his mother and is "the new kid" in school. Troubled by the absence of his father, a cross-country trucker, and angry because a mysterious lunch-bag thief steals all the "good stuff" from his lunch, Leigh feels his only friend is Mr. Fridley, the school custodian. Then Leigh's teacher assigns a project that requires writing letters asking questions of authors. Naturally Leigh chooses to write to Mr. Henshaw, whose surprising answer changes Leigh's life.*

May 12

Dear Mr. Henshaw,

My teacher read your book about the dog to our class. It was funny. We licked it.

Your freind,
Leigh Botts (boy)

December 3

Dear Mr. Henshaw,

I am the boy who wrote to you last year when I was in the second grade. Maybe you didn't get my letter. This year I read the book I wrote to you about called *Ways to Amuse a Dog*. It is the first thick book with chapters that I have read.

The boy's father said city dogs were bored so Joe could not keep the dog unless he could think up seven ways to amuse it. I have a black dog. His name is Bandit. He is a nice dog.

If you answer I get to put your letter on the bulletin board.

My teacher taught me a trick about friend. The *i* goes before *e* so that at the end it will spell *end*.

Keep in tutch.

Your fri*end*,
Leigh (Lēē) Botts

November 13

Dear Mr. Henshaw,

I am in the fourth grade now. I made a diorama of *Ways to Amuse a Dog,* the book I wrote to you about two times before. Now our teacher is making us write to authors for Book Week. I got your answer to my letter last year, but it was only printed. Please would you write to me in your own handwriting? I am a great enjoyer of your books.

My favorite character in the book was Joe's Dad because he didn't get mad when Joe amused his dog by playing a tape of a lady singing, and his dog sat and howled like he was singing, too. Bandit does the same thing when he hears singing.

Your best reader,
Leigh Botts

Dear Mr. Henshaw,

I got to thinking about *Ways to Amuse a Dog*. When Joe took his dog to the park and taught him to slide down the slide, wouldn't some grownup come along and say he couldn't let his dog use the slide? Around here grownups, who are mostly real old with cats, get mad if dogs aren't on leashes every minute. I hate living in a mobile home park.

I saw your picture on the back of the book. When I grow up I want to be a famous book writer with a beard like you.

I am sending you my picture. It is last year's picture. My hair is longer now. With all the millions of kids in the U.S., how would you know who I am if I don't send you my picture?

Your favorite reader,
Leigh Botts

Enclosure: Picture of me.
(We are studying
business letters.)

October 2

Dear Mr. Henshaw,

I am in the fifth grade now. You might like to know that I gave a book report on *Ways to Amuse a Dog*. The class liked it. I got an A−. The minus was because the teacher said I didn't stand on both feet.

Sincerely,
Leigh Botts

November 7

Dear Mr. Henshaw,

I got your letter and did what you said. I read a different book by you. I read *Moose on Toast*. I liked it almost as much as *Ways to Amuse a Dog*. It was really funny the way the boy's mother tried to think up ways to cook the moose meat they had in their freezer. 1000 pounds is a lot of moose. Mooseburgers, moose stew and moose meat loaf don't sound too bad. Maybe moose mincemeat pie would be OK because with all the raisins and junk you wouldn't know you were eating moose. Creamed chipped moose on toast, yuck.

I don't think the boy's father should have shot the moose, but I guess there are plenty of moose up there in Alaska, and maybe they needed it for food.

If my Dad shot a moose I would feed the tough parts to my dog Bandit.

Your number 1 fan,
Leigh Botts

Dear Mr. Henshaw,

This year I am in the sixth grade in a new school in a different town. Our teacher is making us do author reports to improve our writing skills, so of course I thought of you. Please answer the following questions.

1. How many books have you written?
2. Is Boyd Henshaw your real name or is it fake?
3. Why do you write books for children?
4. Where do you get your ideas?
5. Do you have any kids?
6. What is your favorite book that you wrote?
7. Do you like to write books?
8. What is the title of your next book?
9. What is your favorite animal?
10. Please give me some tips on how to write a book. This is important to me. I really want to know so I can get to be a famous author and write books exactly like yours.

Please send me a list of your books that you wrote, an autographed picture and a bookmark. I need your answer by next Friday. This is urgent!

Sincerely,
Leigh Botts

De Liver
De Letter
De Sooner
De Better
De Later
De Letter
De Madder
I Getter

Dear Mr. Henshaw,

At first I was pretty upset when I didn't get an answer to my letter in time for my report, but I worked it out OK. I read what it said about you on the back of *Ways to Amuse a Dog* and wrote real big on every other line so I filled up the paper. On the book it said you lived in Seattle, so I didn't know you had moved to Alaska although I should have guessed from *Moose on Toast*.

When your letter finally came I didn't want to read it to the class, because I didn't think Miss Martinez would like silly answers, like your real name is Messing A. Round, and you don't have kids because you don't raise goats. She said I had to read it. The class laughed and Miss Martinez smiled, but she didn't smile when I came to the part about your favorite animal was a purple monster who ate children who sent authors long lists of questions for reports instead of learning to use the library.

Your writing tips were OK. I could tell you meant what you said. Don't worry. When I write something, I won't send it to you. I understand how busy you are with your own books.

I hid the second page of your letter from Miss Martinez. That list of questions you sent for me to answer really made me mad. Nobody else's author put in a list of questions to be answered, and I don't think it's fair to make me do more work when I already wrote a report.

Anyway, thank you for answering my questions. Some kids didn't get any answers at all, which made them mad, and one girl almost cried, she was so afraid she would get a bad grade. One boy got a letter from an author who sounded real excited about getting a letter and wrote such a long answer the boy had to write a long report. He guessed nobody ever wrote to that author before, and he sure wouldn't again. About ten kids wrote to the same author, who wrote one answer to all of them. There was a big argument about who got to keep it until Miss Martinez took the letter to the office and duplicated it.

About those questions you sent me. I'm not going to answer them, and you can't make me. You're not my teacher.

Yours truly,
Leigh Botts

P.S. When I asked you what the title of your next book was going to be, you said, Who knows? Did you mean that was the title or you don't know what the title will be? And do you really write books because you have read every book in the library and because writing beats mowing the lawn or shoveling snow?

November 16

Dear Mr. Henshaw,

Mom found your letter and your list of questions which I was dumb enough to leave lying around. We had a big argument. She says I have to answer your questions because authors are working people like anyone else, and if you took time to answer my questions, I should answer yours. She says I can't go through life expecting everyone to do everything for me. She used to say the same thing to Dad when he left his socks on the floor.

Well, I got to go now. It's bedtime. Maybe I'll get around to answering your ten questions, and maybe I won't. There isn't any law that says I have to. Maybe I won't even read any more of your books.

Disgusted reader,
Leigh Botts

P.S. If my Dad was here, he would tell you to go climb a tree.

Dear Mr. Henshaw,

Mom is nagging me about your dumb old questions. She says if I really want to be an author, I should follow the tips in your letter. I should read, look, listen, think and <u>write.</u> She says the best way she knows for me to get started is to apply the seat of my pants to a chair and answer your questions and answer them fully. So here goes.

1. Who are you?

Like I've been telling you, I am Leigh Botts. Leigh Marcus Botts. I don't like Leigh for a name because some people don't know how to say it or think it's a girl's name. Mom says with a last name like Botts I need something fancy but not too fancy. My Dad's name is Bill and Mom's name is Bonnie. She says Bill and Bonnie Botts sounds like something out of a comic strip.

I am just a plain boy. This school doesn't say I am Gifted and Talented, and I don't like soccer very much the way everybody at this school is supposed to. I am not stupid either.

2. What do you look like?

I already sent you my picture, but maybe you lost it. I am sort of medium. I don't have red hair or anything like that. I'm not real big like my Dad. Mom says I take after her family, thank goodness. That's the way she always says it. In first and second grades kids used to call me Leigh the Flea, but I have grown. Now when the class lines up according to height, I am in the middle. I guess you could call me the mediumest boy in the class.

This is hard work. To be continued, maybe.

Leigh Botts

Dear Mr. Henshaw,

I wasn't going to answer any more of your questions, but Mom won't get the TV repaired because she says it was rotting my brain. This is Thanksgiving vacation and I am so bored I decided to answer a couple of your rotten questions with my rotten brain. (Joke.)

3. What is your family like?

Since Dad and Bandit went away, my family is just Mom and me. We all used to live in a mobile home outside of Bakersfield which is in California's Great Central Valley we studied about in school. When Mom and Dad got divorced, they sold the mobile home, and Dad moved into a trailer.

Dad drives a big truck, a cab-over job. That means the cab is over the engine. Some people don't know that. The truck is why my parents got divorced. Dad used to drive for someone else, hauling stuff like cotton, sugar beets and other produce around Central California and Nevada, but he couldn't get owning his own rig for cross-country hauling out of his head. He worked practically night and day and saved a down payment. Mom said we'd never get out of that mobile home when he had to make such big payments on that rig, and she'd never know where he was when he hauled cross-country. His big rig sure is a beauty, with a bunk in the cab and everything. His rig, which truckers call a tractor but everyone else calls a truck, has ten wheels, two in front and eight in back so he can hitch up to anything — flatbeds, refrigerated vans, a couple of gondolas.

In school they teach you that a gondola is some kind of boat in Italy, but in the U.S. it is a container for hauling loose stuff like carrots.

My hand is all worn out from all this writing, but I try to treat Mom and Dad the same so I'll get to Mom next time.

Your pooped reader,
Leigh Botts

November 23

Mr. Henshaw:

Why should I call you "dear," when you are the reason I'm stuck with all this work? It wouldn't be fair to leave Mom out so here is Question 3 continued.

Mom works part time for Catering by Katy which is run by a real nice lady Mom knew when she was growing up in Taft, California. Katy says all women who grew up in Taft had to be good cooks because they went to so many potluck suppers. Mom and Katy and some other ladies make fancy food for weddings and parties. They also bake cheesecake and apple strudel for restaurants. Mom is a good cook. I just wish she would do it more at home, like the mother in *Moose on Toast*. Almost every day Katy gives Mom something good to put in my school lunch.

Mom also takes a couple of courses at the community college. She wants to be an LVN which means Licensed Vocational Nurse. They help real nurses except they don't stick needles in people. She is almost always home when I get home from school.

Your ex-friend,
Leigh Botts

Mr. Henshaw:

Here we go again.

4. *Where do you live?*

After the divorce Mom and I moved from Bakersfield to Pacific Grove which is on California's Central Coast about twenty miles from the sugar refinery at Spreckels where Dad used to haul sugar beets before he went cross-country. Mom said all the time she was growing up in California's Great Central Valley she longed for a few ocean breezes, and now we've got them. We've got a lot of fog, especially in the morning. There aren't any crops around here, just golf courses for rich people.

We live in a little house, a *really* little house, that used to be somebody's summer cottage a long time ago before somebody built a two-story duplex in front of it. Now it is what they call a garden cottage. It is sort of falling apart, but it is all we can afford. Mom says at least it keeps the

rain off, and it can't be hauled away on a flatbed truck. I have a room of my own, but Mom sleeps on a couch in the living room. She fixed the place up real nice with things from the thrift shop down the street.

Next door is a gas station that goes ping-ping, ping-ping every time a car drives in. They turn off the pinger at 10:00 P.M., but most of the time I am asleep by then. Mom doesn't want me to hang around the gas station. On our street, besides the thrift shop, there is a pet shop, a sewing machine shop, an electric shop, a couple of junk stores they call antique shops, plus a Taco King and a Softee Freeze. I am not supposed to hang around those places either. Mom is against hanging around anyplace.

Sometimes when the gas station isn't pinging, I can hear the ocean and the sea lions barking. They sound like dogs, and I think of Bandit.

To be continued unless we get the TV fixed.

Still disgusted,
Leigh Botts

Mr. Henshaw:

If our TV was fixed I would be looking at "Highway Patrol," but it isn't so here are some more answers from my rotten brain. (Ha-ha.)

5. Do you have any pets?

I do not have any pets. (My teacher says always answer questions in complete sentences.) When Mom and Dad got divorced and Mom got me, Dad took Bandit because Mom said she couldn't work and look after a dog, and Dad said he likes to take Bandit in his truck because it is easier to stay awake on long hauls if he has him to talk to. I really miss Bandit, but I guess he's happier riding around with Dad. Like the father said in *Ways to Amuse a Dog,* dogs get pretty bored just lying around the house all day. That is what Bandit would have to do with Mom and me gone so much.

Bandit likes to ride. That's how we got him. He just jumped into Dad's cab at a truck stop in Nevada and sat there. He had a red bandanna around his neck instead of a collar, so we called him Bandit.

Sometimes I lie awake at night listening to the gas station ping-pinging and thinking about Dad and Bandit hauling tomatoes or cotton bales on Interstate 5, and I am glad Bandit is there to keep Dad awake. Have you ever seen Interstate 5? It is straight and boring with nothing much but cotton fields and a big feedlot that you can smell a long way before you come to it. It is so boring that the cattle on the feedlot don't even bother to moo. They just stand there. They don't tell you that part in school when they talk about California's Great Central Valley.

I'm getting writer's cramp from all this writing. I'll get to No. 6 next time. Mom says not to worry about the postage, so I can't use that as an excuse for not answering.

Pooped writer,

Leigh Botts

Mr. Henshaw:

Here we go again. I'll never write another list of questions for an author to answer, no matter what the teacher says.

6. *Do you like school?*

School is OK, I guess. That's where the kids are. The best thing about sixth grade in my new school is that if I hang in, I'll get out.

7. *Who are your friends?*

I don't have a whole lot of friends in my new school. Mom says maybe I'm a loner, but I don't know. A new boy in school has to be pretty cautious until he gets to know who's who. Maybe I'm just a boy nobody pays much attention to. The only time anybody paid much attention to me was in my last school when I gave the book report on *Ways to Amuse a Dog*. After my report some people went to the library to get the book. The kids here pay more attention to my lunch than they do to me. They really watch to see what I have in my lunch because Katy gives me such good things.

I wish somebody would ask me over sometime. After school I stay around kicking a soccer ball with some of the other kids so they won't think I am stuck up or anything, but nobody asks me over.

8. *Who is your favorite teacher?*

I don't have a favorite teacher, but I really like Mr. Fridley. He's the custodian. He's always fair about who gets to pass out milk at lunchtime, and once when he had to clean up after someone who threw up in the hall, he didn't even look cross. He just said, "Looks like somebody's been whooping it up," and started sprinkling sawdust around. Mom used to get mad at Dad for whooping it up, but she didn't mean throwing up. She meant he stayed too long at the truck stop outside of town.

Two more questions to go. Maybe I won't answer them. So there. Ha-ha.

Leigh Botts

December 1

Mr. Henshaw:

OK, you win, because Mom is still nagging me, and I don't have anything else to do. I'll answer your last two questions if it takes all night.

9. *What bothers you?*

What bothers me about what? I don't know what you mean. I guess I'm bothered by a lot of things. I am bothered when someone steals something out of my lunchbag. I don't know enough about the people in the school to know who to suspect. I am bothered about little kids with runny noses. I don't mean I am fussy or anything like that. I don't know why. I am just bothered.

I am bothered about walking to school *slow*. The rule is nobody is supposed to be on the school grounds until ten minutes before the first bell rings. Mom has an early class. The house is so lonely in the morning when she is gone that I can't stand it and leave when she does. I don't mind being alone after school, but I do in the morning before the fog lifts and our cottage seems dark and damp.

Mom tells me to go to school but to walk slow which is hard work. Once I tried walking around every square in the sidewalk, but that got boring. So did walking heel-toe, heel-toe. Sometimes I walk backwards except when I cross the street, but I still get there so early I have to sort of hide behind the shrubbery so Mr. Fridley won't see me.

I am bothered when my Dad telephones me and finishes by saying, "Well, keep your nose clean, kid." Why can't he say he misses me, and why can't he call me Leigh? I am bothered when he doesn't phone at all which is most of the time. I have a book of road maps and try to follow his trips when I hear from him. When the TV worked I watched the weather on the news so I would know if he was driving through blizzards, tornadoes, hail like golf balls or any of that fancy weather they have other places in the U.S.

10. What do you wish?

I wish somebody would stop stealing the good stuff out of my lunchbag. I guess I wish a lot of other things, too. I wish someday Dad and Bandit would pull up in front in the rig. Maybe Dad would be hauling a forty-foot reefer (that means refrigerated trailer) which would make his outfit add up to eighteen wheels altogether. Dad would yell out of the cab, "Come on, Leigh. Hop in and I'll give you a lift to school." Then I'd climb in and Bandit would wag his tail and lick my face. We'd take off with all the men in the gas station staring after us. Instead of going straight to school, we'd go barreling along the freeway looking down on the tops of ordinary cars, then down the offramp and back to school just before the bell rang. I guess I wouldn't seem so medium then, sitting up there in the cab in front of a forty-foot reefer. I'd jump out, and Dad would say, "So long, Leigh. Be seeing you," and Bandit would give a little bark like good-bye. I'd say, "Drive carefully, Dad," like I always do. Dad would take a minute to write in the truck's logbook, "Drove my son to school." Then the truck would pull away from the curb with all the kids staring and wishing their Dads drove big trucks, too.

There, Mr. Henshaw. That's the end of your crummy questions. I hope you are satisfied for making me do all this extra work.

Fooey on you,
Leigh Botts

Dear Mr. Henshaw,

I am sorry I was rude in my last letter when I finished answering your questions. Maybe I was mad about other things, like Dad forgetting to send this month's support payment. Mom tried to phone him at the trailer park where, as Mom says, he hangs his hat. He has his own phone in his trailer so the broker who lines up jobs for him can reach him. I wish he still hauled sugar beets over to the refinery in Spreckels so he might come to see me. The judge in the divorce said he has a right to see me.

When you answered my questions, you said the way to get to be an author was to <u>write.</u> You underlined it twice. Well, I sure did a lot of writing, and you know what? Now that I think about it, it wasn't so bad when it wasn't for a book report or a report on some country in South America or anything where I had to look things up in the library. I even sort of miss writing now that I've finished your questions. I get lonesome. Mom is working overtime at Catering by Katy because people give a lot of parties this time of year.

When I write a book maybe I'll call it *The Great Lunchbag Mystery*, because I have a lot of trouble with my lunchbag. Mom isn't so great on cooking roasts and steaks now that Dad is gone, but she makes me good lunches with sandwiches on whole wheat bread from the health food store with good filling spread all the way to the corners. Katy sends me little cheesecakes baked just for me or stuffed mushrooms and little things she calls canapés (kà-nà-pāýs). Sometimes I get a slice of quiche (kēēsh).

Today I was supposed to have a deviled egg. Katy buys the smallest eggs for parties so half an egg can be eaten in one bite and won't spill on people's carpets. She puts a little curry powder in with the mashed-up yolk which she squirts out of a tube so it looks like a rose. At lunchtime when I opened my lunchbag, my egg was gone. We leave our lunchbags and boxes (mostly bags because no sixth grader wants to carry a lunchbox) lined up along the wall under our coathooks at the back of the classroom behind a sort of partition.

Are you writing another book? Please answer my letter so we can be pen pals.

Still your No. 1 fan,
Leigh Botts

Dear Mr. Henshaw,

I was surprised to get your postcard from Wyoming, because I thought you lived in Alaska.

Don't worry. I get the message. You don't have a lot of time for answering letters. That's OK with me, because I'm glad you are busy writing a book and chopping wood to keep warm.

Something nice happened today. When I was hanging around behind the bushes at school waiting for the ten minutes to come before the first bell rings, I was watching Mr. Fridley raise the flags. Maybe I better explain that the state flag of California is white with a brown bear in the middle. First Mr. Fridley fastened the U.S. flag on the halyard (that's a new word in my vocabulary) and then fastened the California flag below it. When he pulled the flags to the top of the flagpole, the bear was upside down with his feet in the air. I said, "Hey, Mr. Fridley, the bear is upside down."

This is a new paragraph because Miss Martinez says there should be a new paragraph when a different person speaks. Mr. Fridley said, "Well, so it is. How would you like to turn him right side up?"

So I got to pull the flags down, turn the bear flag the right way and raise both flags again. Mr. Fridley said maybe I should come to school a few minutes early every morning to help him with the flags, but please stop walking backwards because it made him nervous. So now I don't have to walk quite so slow. It was nice to have somebody notice me. Nobody stole anything from my lunch today because I ate it on the way to school.

I've been thinking about what you said on your postcard about keeping a diary. Maybe I'll try it.

Sincerely,
Leigh Botts

December 13

Dear Mr. Henshaw,

I bought a composition book like you said. It is yellow with a spiral binding. On the front I printed

DIARY OF LEIGH MARCUS BOTTS
PRIVATE—KEEP OUT
THIS MEANS YOU!!!!!

When I started to write in it, I didn't know how to begin. I felt as if I should write, "Dear Composition Book," but that sounds dumb. So does "Dear Piece of Paper." The first page still looks the way I feel. Blank. I don't think I can keep a diary. I don't want to be a nuisance to you, but I wish you could tell me how. I am stuck.

Puzzled reader,
Leigh Botts

December 21

Dear Mr. Henshaw,

I got your postcard with the picture of the bears. Maybe I'll do what you said and pretend my diary is a letter to somebody. I suppose I could pretend to write to Dad, but I used to write to him and he never answered. Maybe I'll pretend I am writing to you because when I answered all your questions, I got the habit of beginning, "Dear Mr. Henshaw." Don't worry. I won't send it to you.

Thanks for the tip. I know you're busy.

Your grateful friend,
Leigh Botts

Author

Beverly Cleary is one of America's most popular authors of children's fiction. She has won many awards for her work, such as the American Library Association's Laura Ingalls Wilder Award. Two of her books, *Ramona and her Father* and *Ramona Quimby, Age 8,* were named Newbery Honor Books. Not only have her books won these well-known awards, but she has won twenty-five statewide awards based on votes from her young readers. Her characters such as Henry Huggins, Ellen Tebbits, and Ramona Quimby are known and loved by many.

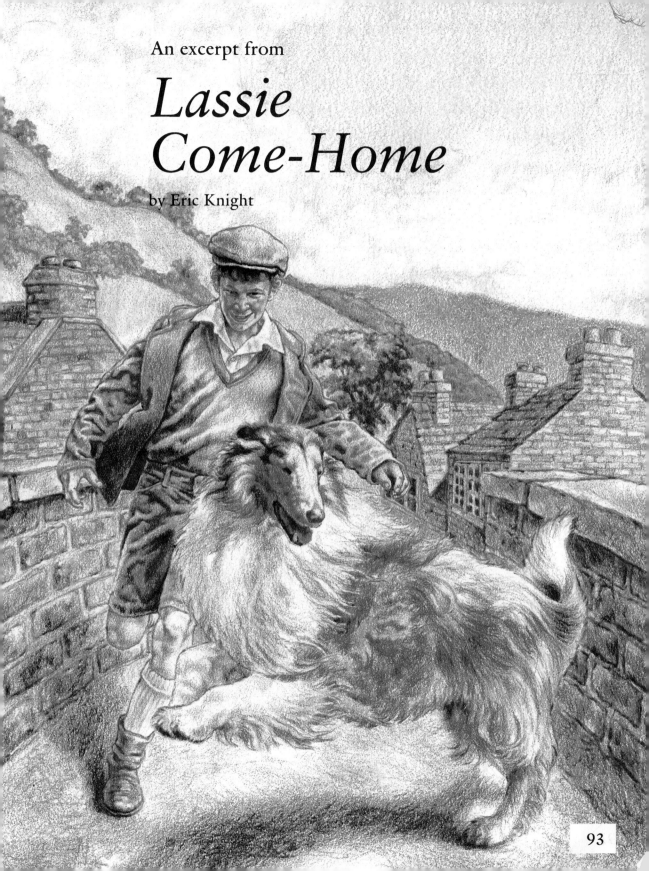

An excerpt from

Lassie Come-Home

by Eric Knight

The Carraclough family loved their collie dog Lassie, but they had little money, and finally they had to sell her. They sold her to the Duke of Rudling, but she kept running away and coming back to the Carracloughs. Finally the duke took her away from the village that had been her home in York-shire, England, to his estate in the north of Scotland. Even there, Lassie escaped and headed south—longing to get home and meet young Joe Carraclough after school once again. Lassie's story is told in Eric Knight's book, Lassie Come-Home, from which this excerpt is taken.

Journey's End

Now Lassie was crossing a great, high moor, where the wind swept without halt. The snowstorm drove from behind her, blowing the hair in sodden wisps forward from her thin flanks.

She found it hard to keep going. The snow was getting deeper, and it took more and more strength from her tired muscles to lift her feet clear of the snow at each step. At last she staggered and fell. Coiling up, she began biting the matted ice from the hair between her claws. Again she tried, but the snow was too deep. She began plunging at it like a horse, rearing and leaping forward, but before very long she found herself utterly exhausted.

She stood, her head down, the panted breath coming like white steam. She lifted her head and whined; but the snow was still there. She jumped and bucketed again, trying to leap through the drifts. Again she stopped, without power to go farther.

Then, lifting her head, she gave a long cry—the cry of a dog lost, cold, and helpless. It was a long, high call that went out over the wide moor, through the driving snow where the darkness was descending.

The snow blanketed all sounds. There was no one for miles on that flat, wild land. Even if there had been someone within a few hundred yards, it is doubtful whether or not he could have heard that snow-muffled cry.

At last Lassie sank to the ground. The white expanse of snow softly covered her. Below that white blanket she lay, exhausted but warm.

Sam Carraclough had spoken the truth early that year when he told his son Joe that it was a long way from Greenall Bridge in Yorkshire to the Duke of Rudling's place in Scotland. And it is just as many miles coming the other way, a matter of four hundred miles.

But that would be for a man, traveling straight by road or by train. For an animal how far would it be — an animal that must circle and quest at obstacles, wander and err, back-track and sidetrack till it found a way?

A thousand miles it would be — a thousand miles through strange terrain it had never crossed before, with nothing but instinct to tell direction.

Yes, a thousand miles of mountain and dale, of highland and moor, plowland and path, ravine and river and beck and burn; a thousand miles of tor and brae, of snow and rain and fog and sun; of wire and thistle and thorn and flint and rock to tear the feet — who could expect a dog to win through that?

Yet, if it were almost a miracle, in his heart Joe Carraclough tried to believe in that miracle — that somehow, wonderfully, inexplicably, his dog would be there some day; there, waiting by the school gate. Each day as he came out of school, his eyes would turn to the spot where Lassie had always waited. And each day there was nothing there, and Joe Carraclough would walk home slowly, silently, stolidly as did the people of his country.

Always, when school ended, Joe tried to prepare himself — told himself not to be disappointed, because there could be no dog there. Thus, through the long weeks, Joe began to teach himself not to believe in the impossible. He had hoped against hope so long that hope began to die.

But if hope can die in a human, it does not in an animal. As long as it lives, the hope is there and the faith is there. And so, coming across the schoolyard that day, Joe Carraclough would not believe his eyes. He shook his head and blinked, and rubbed his fists in his eyes, for he thought what he was seeing was a dream. There, walking the last few yards to the school gate was — his dog!

He stood, for the coming of the dog was terrible — her

walk was a thing that tore at her breath. Her head and her tail were down almost to the pavement. Each footstep forward seemed a separate effort. It was a crawl rather than a walk. But the steps were made, one by one, and at last the animal dropped in her place by the gate and lay still.

Then Joe roused himself. Even if it were a dream, he must do something. In dreams one must try.

He raced across the yard and fell to his knees, and then, when his hands were touching and feeling fur, he knew it was reality. His dog had come to meet him!

But what a dog was this — no prize collie with fine tricolor coat glowing, with ears lifted gladly over the proud, slim head with its perfect black mask. It was not a dog whose bright eyes were alert, and who jumped up to bark a glad welcome. This was a dog that lay, weakly trying to lift a head that would no longer lift; trying to move a tail that was torn and matted with thorns and burrs, and managing to do nothing very much except to whine in a weak, happy, crying way. For she knew that at last the terrible driving instinct was at peace. She was at the place. She had kept her lifelong rendezvous, and hands were touching her that had not touched her for so long a time.

By the Labor Exchange, Ian Cawper stood with the other out-of-work miners, waiting until it was tea time so that they could all go back to their cottages.

You could have picked out Ian, for he was much the biggest man even among the many big men that Yorkshire grows. In fact, he was reputed to be the biggest and strongest man in all that Riding of Yorkshire. A big man, but gentle and often very slow of thinking and speech.

And so Ian was a few seconds behind the others in realizing that something of urgency was happening in the village. Then he too saw it — a boy struggling, half running,

along the main street, his voice lifted in excitement, a great bundle of something in his arms.

The men stirred and moved forward. Then, when the boy was nearer, they heard his cry:

"She's come back! She's come back!"

The men looked at each other and blew out their breath and then stared at the bundle the boy was carrying. It was true. Sam Carraclough's collie had walked back home from Scotland.

"I must get her home, quick!" the boy was saying. He staggered on.

Ian Cawper stepped forward.

"Here," he said. "Run on ahead, tell 'em to get ready."

His great arms cradled the dog — arms that could have carried ten times the weight of this poor, thin animal.

"Oh, hurry, Ian!" the boy cried, dancing in excitement.

"I'm hurrying, lad. Go on ahead."

So Joe Carraclough raced along the street, turned up the side street, ran down the garden path, and burst into the cottage:

"Mother! Feyther!"

"What is it, lad?"

Joe paused. He could hardly get the words out — the excitement was choking up in his throat, hot and stifling. And then the words were said:

"Lassie! She's come home! Lassie's come home!"

He opened the door, and Ian Cawper, bowing his head to pass under the lintel, carried the dog to the hearth and laid her there.

There were many things that Joe Carraclough was to remember from that evening. He was never to forget the look that passed over his father's face as he first knelt beside the dog that had been his for so many years, and let

his hands travel over the emaciated frame. He was to remember how his mother moved about the kitchen, not grumbling or scolding now, but silently and with a sort of terrific intensity, poking the fire quickly, stirring the condensed milk into warm water, kneeling to hold the dog's head and lift open the jowl.

Not a word did his parents speak to him. They seemed to have forgotten him altogether. Instead, they both worked over the dog with a concentration that seemed to put them in a separate world.

Joe watched how his father spooned in the warm liquid, he saw how it drooled out again from the unswallowing dog's jowls and dribbled down onto the rug. He saw his mother warm up a blanket and wrap it round the dog. He saw them try again and again to feed her. He saw his father rise at last.

"It's no use, lass," he said to his mother.

Between his mother and father many questions and answers passed unspoken except through their eyes.

"Pneumonia," his father said at last. "She's not strong enough now . . ."

For a while his parents stood, and then it was his mother who seemed to be somehow wonderfully alive and strong.

"I won't be beat!" she said. "I just *won't* be beat."

She pursed her lips, and as if this grimace had settled something, she went to the mantlepiece and took down a vase. She turned it over and shook it. The copper pennies came into her hand. She held them out to her husband, not explaining nor needing to explain what was needed. But he stared at the money.

"Go on, lad," she said. "I were saving it for insurance, like."

"But how'll we . . ."

"Hush," the woman said.

Then her eyes flickered over her son, and Joe knew that they were aware of him again for the first time in an hour. His father looked at him, at the money in the woman's hand, and at last at the dog. Suddenly he took the money. He put on his cap and hurried out into the night. When he came back he was carrying bundles — eggs and a small bottle of brandy — precious and costly things in that home.

Joe watched as they were beaten together, and again and again his father tried to spoon some into the dog's mouth. Then his mother blew in exasperation. Angrily she snatched the spoon. She cradled the dog's head on her lap, she lifted the jowls, and poured and stroked the throat — stroked it and stroked it, until at last the dog swallowed.

"Aaaah!"

It was his father, breathing a long, triumphant exclamation. And the firelight shone gold on his mother's hair as she crouched there, holding the dog's head — stroking its throat soothing it with soft, loving sounds.

Joe did not clearly remember about it afterwards, only a faint sensation that he was being carried to bed at some strange hour of darkness.

And in the morning when he rose, his father sat in his chair, but his mother was still on the rug, and the fire was still burning warm. The dog, swathed in blankets, lay quiet.

"Is she — dead?" Joe asked.

His mother smiled weakly.

"Shhh," she said. "She's just sleeping. And I suppose I ought to get breakfast — but I'm that played out—if I nobbut[1] had a nice strong cup o' tea . . ."

And that morning, strangely enough, it was his father who got the breakfast, boiling the water, brewing the tea, cutting the bread. It was his mother who sat in the rocking chair, waiting until it was ready.

That evening when Joe came home from school, Lassie still lay where he had left her when he went off to school. He wanted to sit and cradle her, but he knew that ill dogs are best left alone. All evening he sat, watching her, stretched out, with the faint breathing the only sign of life. He didn't want to go to bed.

"Now she'll be all right," his mother cried. "Go to bed — she'll be all right."

---

[1]local expression for *nothing but a*

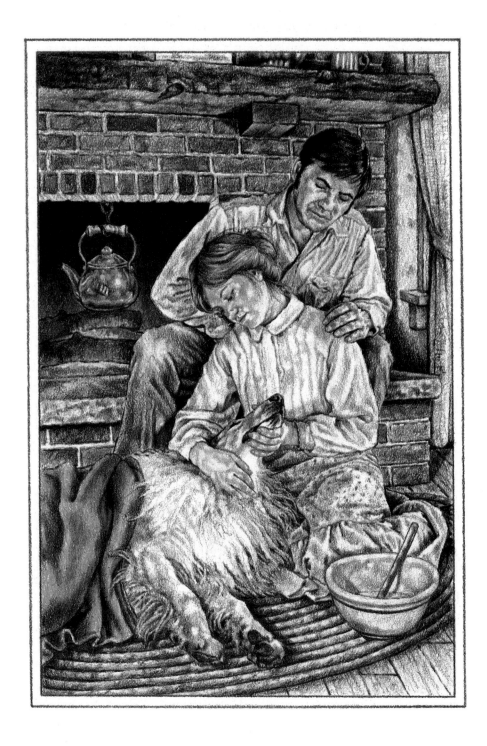

"Are you sure she'll get better, Mother?"

"Ye can see for yourself, can't you? She doesn't look any worse, does she?"

"But are you sure she's going to be better?"

The woman sighed.

"Of course — I'm sure — now go to bed and sleep."

And Joe went to bed, confident in his parents.

That was one day. There were others to remember. There was the day when Joe returned and, as he walked to the hearth, there came from the dog lying there a movement that was meant to be a wag of the tail.

There was another day when Joe's mother sighed with pleasure, for as she prepared the bowl of milk, the dog stirred, lifted herself unsteadily, and waited. And when the bowl was set down, she put down her head and lapped, while her pinched flanks quivered.

And finally there was that day when Joe first realized that — even now — his dog was not to be his own again. So again the cottage rang with cries and protests, and again a woman's voice was lifted, tired and shrilling:

"Is there never to be any more peace and quiet in my home?"

And long after Joe had gone to bed, he heard the voices continuing — his mother's clear and rising and falling; his father's in a steady, reiterative monotone, never changing, always coming to one sentence:

"But even if he would sell her back, where'd Ah get the brass to buy her — where's the money coming fro'? Ye know we can't get it."

To Joe Carraclough's father, life was laid out in straight rules. When a man could get work, he worked his best and got the best wage he could. If he raised a dog, he raised the best one he could. If he had a wife and children, he took care of them the best he could.

In this out-of-work collier's mind, there were no devious exceptions and evasions concerning life and its codes. Like most simple men, he saw all these things clearly. Lying, cheating, stealing — they were wrong, and you couldn't make them right by twisting them round in your mind.

So it was that, when he was faced with any problem, he so often brought it smack up against elemental truths.

"Honest is honest, and there's no two ways about it," he would say.

He had a habit of putting it like that. "Truth is truth." Or, "Cheating is cheating."

And the matter of Lassie came up against this simple, direct code of morals. He had sold the dog and taken the money and spent it. Therefore the dog did not belong to him any more, and no matter how you argued you could not change that.

But a man has to live with his family, too. When a woman starts to argue with a man . . . well . . .

That next morning when Joe came down to breakfast, while his mother served the oatmeal with pursed lips, his father coughed and spoke as if he had rehearsed a set speech over in his mind many times that night:

"Joe, lad. We've decided upon it — that is, thy mother and me — that Lassie can stay here till she's all better.

"That's all reight, because I believe true in ma heart that nobody could nurse her better and wi' more care nor we're doing. So that's honest. But when she's better, well . . .

"Now ye have her for a little while yet, so be content. And don't plague us, lad. There's enough things to worry us now wi'out more. So don't plague us no more — and try to be a man about it — and be content."

With the young, "for a little while" has two shapes. Seen from one end, it is a great, yawning stretch of time extending into the unlimitable future. From the other, it is a ghastly span of days that has been cruelly whisked away before the realization comes.

Joe Carraclough knew that it was the latter that morning when he went to school and heard a mighty, booming voice. As he turned to look, he saw in an automobile a fearsome old man and a girl with her flaxen hair cascading from under a beret. And the old man, with his ferocious white moustaches looking like an animal's misshapen fangs, was waving an ugly blackthorn stick to the danger of the car, the chauffeur, and the world in general, and shouting at him:

"Hi! Hi, there! Yes, I mean you, m' lad! Jenkins, will you make this smelly contraption stand still a moment? Whoa, there, Jenkins! Whoa! Why we ever stopped using horses is more than any sane man can understand. Country's going to pot, that's what! Here, m'lad! Come here!"

For a moment Joe thought of running — doing anything to get all these things he feared out of his sight, so that they might, miraculously, be out of his mind, too. But a machine can go faster than a boy, and then, too, Joe had in him the blood of men who might think slowly and stick to old ideas and bear trouble patiently — but who do not run away. So he stood sturdily on the pavement and remembered his manners as his mother had taught him, and said:

"Yes, sir?"

"You're Whosis — What's-his-name's lad, aren't you?"

Joe's eyes had turned to the girl. She was the one he had seen long ago when he was putting Lassie in the Duke's kennels. Her face was not hearty-red like his own.

It was blue-white. On the hand that clutched the edge of the car the veins stood out clear-blue. That hand looked thin. He was thinking that, as his mother would say, she could do with some plumduff.

She was looking at him, too. Something made him draw himself up proudly.

"My father is Sam Carraclough," he said firmly.

"I know, I know," the old man shouted impatiently. "I never forget a name. Never! Used to know every last soul in this village. Too many of you growing up now — younger generation. And, by gad, they're all of them not worth one of the old bunch — not the whole kit and caboodle. The modern generation, why . . ."

He halted, for the girl beside him was tugging his sleeve.

"What is it? Eh? Oh, yes. I was just coming to it. Where's your father, m'lad? Is he home?"

"No, sir."

"Where is he?"

"He's off over Allerby, sir."

"Allerby, what's he doing there?"

"A mate spoke for him at the pit, I think, and he's gone to see if there's a chance of getting taken on."

"Oh, yes — yes, of course. When'll he be back?"

"I don't know, sir. I think about tea."

"Don't mumble! Not till tea. Very inconvenient — very! Well, I'll drop round about five-ish. You tell him to stay home and I want to see him — it's important. Tell him to wait."

Then the car was gone, and Joe hurried to school. There was never such a long morning as that one. The minutes in the classroom crawled past as the lessons droned on.

Joe had only one desire — to have it become noon. And

when at last the leaden moments that were years were
gone, he raced home and burst through the door. It was
the same cry — for his mother.

"Mother, Mother!"

"Goodness, don't knock the door down. And close it —
anyone would think you were brought up in a barn.
What's the matter?"

"Mother, he's coming to take Lassie away!"

"Who is?"

"The Duke . . . he's coming . . ."

"The Duke? How in the world does he know that
she's . . ."

"I don't know. But he stopped me this morning. He's
coming at tea time . . ."

"Coming here? Are ye sure?"

"Yes, he said he'd come at tea. Oh, Mother,
please . . ."

"Now, Joe. Don't start! Now I warn ye!"

"Mother, you've got to listen. Please, please!"

"You hear me? I said . . ."

"No, Mother. Please help me. Please!"

The woman looked at her son and heaved a sigh of
weariness and exasperation. Then she threw up her hands
in despair.

"Eigh, dearie me! Is there never to be any more peace in
this house? Never?"

She sank into her chair and looked at the floor. The boy
went to her and touched her arm.

"Mother—do something," the boy pleaded. "Can't we
hide her? He'll be here at five. He told me to tell Father
he'd be here at five. Oh, Mother . . ."

"Nay, Joe. Thy father won't . . ."

"Won't you beg him? Please, please! Beg Father
to . . ."

"Joe!" his mother cried angrily. Then her voice became patient again. "Now, Joe, it's no use. So stop thy plaguing. It's just that thy father won't lie. That much I'll give him. Come good, come bad, he'll not lie."

"But just this once, Mother."

The woman shook her head sadly and sat by the fire, staring into it as if she would find peace there. Her son went to her and touched her bare forearm.

"Please, Mother. Beg him. Just this once. Just one lie wouldn't hurt him. I'll make it up to him, I will. I will, truly!"

The words began to race from his mouth quickly.

"I'll make it up to both of you. When I'm growed up, I'll get a job. I'll earn money. I'll buy him things — I'll buy you things, too. I'll buy you both anything you ever want, if you'll only please, please . . ."

And then, for the first time in all his trouble, Joe Carraclough became a child, his sturdiness gone, and the tears choked his voice. His mother could hear his sobs, and she patted his hand, but she would not look at him. From the magic of the fire she seemed to read deep wisdom, and she spoke slowly.

"Tha mustn't, Joe," she said, her words soft. "Tha mustn't want like that. Tha must learn never to want anything i' life so hard as tha wants Lassie. It doesn't do."

It was then that she felt her son's hand trembling with impatience, and his voice rising clear.

"Ye don't understand, Mother. Ye don't understand. It ain't me that wants her. It's her that wants us — so terrible bad. That's what made her come home all that way. She wants us, so terrible bad."

It was then that Mrs. Carraclough looked at her son at last. She could see his face, contorted, and the tears rolling openly down his cheeks. And yet, in that moment of childishness, it was as if he were suddenly all the more grown up. Mrs. Carraclough felt as if time had jumped, and she were seeing this boy, this son of her own, for the first time in many years.

She stared at him and then she clasped her hands together. Her lips pressed together in a straight line and she got up.

"Joe, come and eat, then. And go back to school and be content. I'll talk to thy father."

She lifted her head, and her voice sounded firm.

"Yes — I'll talk to him, all right. I'll talk to Mr. Samuel Carraclough. I will indeed!"

At five that afternoon, the Duke of Rudling, fuming and muttering in his bad-tempered way, got out of a car that had stopped by a cottage gate. And behind the gate was a boy, who stood sturdily, his feet apart, as if to bar the way.

"Well, well, m' lad! Did ye tell him?"

"Go away," the boy said fiercely. "Go away! Thy tyke's not here."

For once in his life the Duke of Rudling stepped backward. He stared at the boy in amazement.

"Well, drat my buttons, Priscilla," he breathed. "Th' lad's touched. He is — he's touched!"

"Thy tyke's net here. Away wi' thee," the boy said stoutly. And it seemed as if in his determination he spoke in the broadest dialect he could command.

"What's he saying?" Priscilla asked.

"He's saying my dog isn't here. Drat my buttons, are you going deaf, Priscilla? I'm supposed to be deaf, and I can hear him all right. Now, ma lad, what tyke o' mine's net here?"

The Duke, when he answered, also turned to the broadest tones of Yorkshire dialect, as he always did to the people of the cottages—a habit which many of the members of the Duke's family deplored deeply.

"Coom, coom, ma lad. Speak up! What tyke's net here?"

As he spoke he waved his cane ferociously and advanced. Joe Carraclough stepped back from the fearful old man, but he still barred the path.

"No tyke o' thine," he cried stoutly.

But the Duke continued to advance. The words raced from Joe's mouth with a torrent of despair.

"Us hasn't got her. She's not here. She couldn't be here. No tyke could ha' done it. No tyke could come all them miles. It's not Lassie — it's — it's just another one that looks like her. It isn't Lassie."

"Well, bless my heart and soul," puffed the Duke. "Bless my heart and soul. Where's thy father, lad?"

Joe shook his head grimly. But behind him the cottage door opened and his mother's voice spoke.

"If it's Sam Carraclough ye're looking for — he's out in the shed, and been shut up there half the afternoon."

"What's this lad talking about — a dog o' mine being here?"

"Nay, ye're mistaken," the woman said stoutly.

"I'm mistaken?" roared the Duke.

"Yes. He didn't say a tyke o' thine was here. He said it wasn't here."

"Drat my buttons," the Duke sputtered angrily. "Don't twist my words up."

Then his eyes narrowed, and he stepped a pace forward.

"Well, if he said a dog of mine *isn't,* perhaps you'll be good enough to tell me just *which* dog of mine it is that isn't here. Now," he finished triumphantly. "Come, come! Answer me!"

Joe, watching his mother, saw her swallow and then look about her as if for help. She pressed her lips together.

The Duke stood waiting for his answer, peering out angrily from beneath his jutting eyebrows. Then Mrs. Carraclough drew a breath to speak.

But her answer, truth or lie, was never spoken. For they all heard the rattle of a chain being drawn from a door, and then the voice of Sam Carraclough said clearly:

"This, I give ye my word, is th' only tyke us has here. So tell me, does it look like any dog that belongs to thee?"

Joe's mouth was opening for a last cry of protest, but as his eyes fell on the dog by his father, the exclamation died. And he stared in amazement.

There he saw his father, Sam Carraclough, the collie fancier, standing with a dog at his heels the like of which few men had ever seen before, or would wish to see. It was a dog that sat patiently at his left heel, as any well-trained dog should do — just as Lassie used to do. But this dog — it was ridiculous to think of it at the same moment as Lassie.

For where Lassie's skull was aristocratic and slim, this dog's head was clumsy and rough. Where Lassie's ears stood in the grace of twin-lapped symmetry, this dog had one screw ear and the other standing up Alsatian fashion, in a way that would give any collie breeder the cold shivers.

More than that. Where Lassie's coat faded to delicate sable, this curious dog had ugly splashes of black; and where Lassie's apron was a billowing expanse of white, this dog had muddy puddles of off-color, blue-merle mixture. Lassie had four white paws, and this one had only one white, two dirty-brown, and one almost black. Lassie's tail flowed gracefully behind her, and this dog's tail looked like something added as an afterthought.

And yet, as Joe Carraclough looked at the dog beside his father, he understood. He knew that if a dog coper could treat a dog with cunning so that its bad points came to look like good ones, he could also reverse the process and make all its good ones look like bad ones — especially if that man were his father, one of the most knowing of dog fanciers in all that Riding of Yorkshire.

In that moment, he understood his father's words, too. For in dog-dealing, as in horse-dealing, the spoken word is a binding contract, and once it is given, no real dog-man will attempt to go back on it.

And that was how his father, in his patient, slow way, had tried to escape with honor. He had not lied. He had not denied anything. He had merely asked a question:

"Tell me, does this dog look like any dog that belongs to thee?"

And the Duke had only to say:

"Why, that's not my dog," and forever after, it would not be his.

So the boy, his mother and his father, gazed steadily at the old man, and waited with held breath as he continued to stare at the dog.

But the Duke of Rudling knew many things too — many, many things. And he was not answering. Instead he was walking forward slowly, the great cane now tapping as he leaned on it. His eyes never left the dog for a second. Slowly, as if he were in a dream, he knelt down, and his hand made one gentle movement. It picked up a forepaw and turned it slightly. So he knelt by the collie, looking with eyes that were as knowing about dogs as any man in Yorkshire. And those eyes did not waste themselves upon twisted ears or blotched markings or rough head. Instead, they stared steadily at the underside of the paw, seeing only the five black pads, crossed and recrossed with half-healed scars where thorns had torn and stones had lacerated.

Then the Duke lifted his head, but for a long time he knelt, gazing into space, while they waited. When he did get up, he spoke, not using Yorkshire dialect any more, but speaking as one gentleman might address another.

"Sam Carraclough," he said. "This is no dog of mine. 'Pon my soul and honor, she never belonged to me. No! Not for a single second did she ever belong to me!"

Then he turned and walked down the path, thumping his cane and muttering: "Bless my soul! I wouldn't ha' believed it! Bless my soul! Four hundred miles! I wouldn't ha' believed it."

It was at the gate that his granddaughter tugged his sleeve.

"What you came for," she whispered. "Remember?"

The Duke seemed to come from his dream, and then he suddenly turned into his old self again.

"Don't whisper! What's that? Oh, yes, of course. You don't need to tell me — I hadn't forgotten!"

He turned and made his voice terrible.

"Carraclough! Carraclough! Drat my buttons, where are ye? What're ye hiding for?"

"I'm still here, sir."

"Oh, yes. Yes. Of course. There you are. You working?"

"Eigh, now — working," Joe's father said. That was the best he could manage.

"Yes, working — working! A job! A job! Do you have one?" the Duke fumed.

"Well, now — it's this road . . ." began Carraclough.

As he fumbled his words, Mrs. Carraclough came to his rescue, as good housewives will in Yorkshire—and in most other parts of the world.

"My Sam's not exactly working, but he's got three or four things that he's been considering. Sort of investigating, as ye might say. But — he hasn't quite said yes or no to any of them yet."

"Then he'd better say no, and quickly," snapped the Duke. "I need somebody up at my kennels. And I think, Carraclough . . ." His eyes turned to the dog still sitting at the man's heel. ". . . I think you must know — a lot — about dogs. So there. That's settled."

"Nay, hold on," Carraclough said. "Ye see, I wouldn't like to think I got a chap into trouble and then took his job. Ye see, Mr. Hynes couldn't help . . ."

"Hynes!" snorted the Duke. "Hynes? Utter nincompoop. Had to sack him. Didn't know a dog from a ring-tailed filly. Should ha' known no Londoner could ever run a kennel for a Yorkshireman's taste. Now, I want you for the job."

"Nay, there's still summat," Mrs. Carraclough protested.

"What now?"

"Well, how much would this position be paying?"

The Duke puffed his lips.

"How much do you want, Carraclough?"

"Seven pounds a week, and worth every penny," Mrs. Carraclough cut in, before her husband could even get round to drawing a preparatory breath.

But the Duke was a Yorkshireman, too, and that meant he would scorn himself if he missed a chance to be "practical," as they say, where money is concerned.

"Five," he roared. "And not a penny more."

"Six pounds, ten," bargained Mrs. Carraclough.

"Six even," offered the Duke cannily.

"Done," said Mrs. Carraclough, as quick as a hawk's swoop.

They both glowed, self-righteously pleased with themselves. Mrs. Carraclough would have been willing to settle for three pounds a week in the first place — and as for the Duke, he felt he was getting a man for his kennels who was beyond price.

"Then it's settled," the Duke said.

"Well, almost," the woman said. "I presume, of course . . ." She liked the taste of what she considered a very fine word, so she repeated it. ". . . I presume that means we get the cottage on the estate, too."

"Ye drive a fierce bargain, ma'am," said the Duke, scowling. "But ye get it — on one condition." He lifted his voice and roared. "On condition that as long as ye live on my land, you never allow that thick-skulled, screw-lugged, gay-tailed eyesore of an excuse for a collie on my property. Now, what do ye say?"

He waited, rumbling and chuckling happily to himself as Sam Carraclough stooped, perplexed. But it was the boy who answered gladly: "Oh, no, sir. She'll be down at school waiting for me most o' the time. And, anyway, in a day or so we'll have her fixed up so's ye'd never recognize her."

"I don't doubt that," puffed the Duke, as he stumped toward his car. "I don't doubt ye could do exactly that. Hmm . . . Well, I never . . ."

It was afterwards in the car that the girl edged close to the old man.

"Now don't wriggle," he protested. "I can't stand anyone wriggling."

"Grandfather," she said. "You are kind — I mean about their dog."

The old man coughed and cleared his throat.

"Nonsense," he growled. "Nonsense. When you grow up, you'll understand that I'm what people call a hardhearted Yorkshire realist. For five years I've sworn I'd have that dog. And now I've got her."

Then he shook his head slowly.

"But I had to buy the man to get her. Ah, well. Perhaps that's not the worst part of the bargain."

Author

Eric Knight was born in the Yorkshire countryside of *Lassie Come-Home*. He later moved to the United States, where he had a distinguished career as a writer. His works included newspaper columns, cartoons, film scripts, books, magazine articles, and short stories.

One story was based on his collie, Toots, who made a long journey home after being lost. Mr. Knight expanded the story into his only full-length children's book, *Lassie Come-Home*. The book was the basis of a feature film with many sequels and a popular television series.

RESPONSIBILITIES

MY
FRIEND
FLICKA
Mary O'Hara

THE
APPRENTICE
Dorothy Canfield

OLD BEN
Jesse Stuart

~ *Houghton Mifflin Literature* ~

In the selections you have just read from *Friendships,* two aspects of friendship were explored: having a friend, and being one. A special type of "friendship" is that which exists between a human being and an animal.

The friendship between humans and animals is further explored in the selections you are about to read. The responsibilities and the benefits of caring for a pet are presented through the stories of a horse, a dog, and even a snake. These selections show the many forms "care" can take.

2

Building
a Nation

Five Under Cover

by Myrtle Nord

Characters

Anna Strong   **Caleb Brewster**
Ben Tallmadge   **Abe Woodhull**
Robert Townsend   **Two British Soldiers**

Scene 1

Time: *Summer, 1778, during the British occupation of New York.*

Setting: *Anna Strong's home in Setauket, Long Island. A table and two chairs are center. There are a few other chairs placed around stage. At right rear is a sideboard with display dishes as well as a cup and saucer placed close to edge of counter top. A bolted door at left leads outside; a door at right leads to cellar; a door at center rear leads to rest of house. Window beside left door, through which clothesline can be seen, may be painted on backdrop.*

At Rise: Anna Strong, *who has graying hair, sits at sideboard sipping from cup. The stage is lighted only by a candle beside her. A gentle rap is heard at the front door. Startled and afraid, Anna rises as the rapping becomes louder.*

Ben (*In hoarse whisper; offstage*): Anna. (*Louder*) Anna! (*Anna, candle in hand, moves slowly to front stage, holding light ahead of her. Ben raps again.*) It's Ben. Ben Tallmadge. Open the door!

Anna: Oh! Ben! (*Relieved, she sets candle on table and hurries to unbolt and open door. Stage lights rise.*) Come in. I'm so glad to see you!

Ben (*Furtively*): Are you alone?

Anna: Yes.

Ben: Good. *(Turns, bolting the door.)*

Anna: I've been plundered twice, Ben, and when you knocked, I was afraid it was the British again.

Ben *(Grimly)*: Those rascals! Now, Anna, are you sure no one could have seen me come in here?

Anna: Yes. *(Sadly)* I've been especially careful since they took Selah prisoner. He's been on the prison ship, *Jersey*, since last January. It's terrible!

Ben *(Gently leading* Anna *to chair)*: Anna, I'm sorry about Mr. Strong. Come, sit down. I want to talk to you.

Anna: It's about the occupation, isn't it, Ben? The Redcoats are everywhere in Setauket, and so many of our neighbors are Loyalists now. We patriots don't have a chance. What about you? I thought you were a lieutenant with Colonel Chester's minutemen. *(She lowers her voice.)* You haven't gone to the other side, have you?

Ben *(Impatiently)*: Of course not! But, listen. General Washington is in White Plains, while New York and all of Long Island are held by the English. He needs to know the British plans so he can block them. He needs secret information, Anna, and I'm looking for your help.

Anna *(Shocked)*: Ben! You're talking about spying!

Ben *(Calmly)*: Yes, Anna — spying. Our side must have information about what the enemy is going to do, to help fight for independence. You can be sure the British have spies, too. *(Step is heard offstage, then rap at door.* Anna *and* Ben *stand, fearful.)*

Anna: Good heavens! They mustn't find you here, Ben. Quick! Go to the cellar. *(Loud rapping is heard again.* Anna *calls out.)* I'm coming! I'm coming! *(Then, softly to* Ben, *as she pushes him out door at right)* If there's danger you can escape down the outside stairs. I'll drop my cup against the floor. You'll hear it, surely, and that will be

your signal to run for your life. *(Loud rapping is heard.)* Coming! *(She closes cellar door, grabs candle, goes left and opens door to* Robert, *dressed in Quaker garb, including hat, which he keeps on all the time.)*

Robert *(Entering)*: Good evening, Mrs. Strong. I hope I didn't frighten thee.

Anna *(With sigh of relief)*: Oh, it's you, Robert. Come in. I've been so afraid, and so alone . . .

Robert: That is why I came. To visit thee awhile.

Anna *(Returning candle to table)*: Well, come sit down, then.

Robert *(Pulling small newspaper from pocket)*: I brought the *Gazette.* I'm writing for Mr. Rivington as a regular reporter now. *(Holds out paper)* See, here are my news items.

Anna *(Taking paper and reading)*: All about the parties in New York! Admiral Lord Howe entertains some disguished guests, including Mrs. Loring. *(Scans paper)* And Robert Murray serves cake to the great General Clinton. *(Looking up)* Well, I must say, Robert, you write well.

Robert: I thank thee, ma'am.

Anna *(Again reading paper)*: What's this? Benjamin Franklin thrown out of the French palace? Breaking his leg? And Washington ready to give up?

Robert *(Laughing)*: Those are all lies. Mr. Rivington makes up those stories, and you know he's a Tory. He has a great imagination, and it helps him sell his papers.

Anna *(Aghast)*: And you are working for him?

Robert: Yes, but *I* don't tell lies! *(Indignantly)* I couldn't. Even though I had to swear the oath of allegiance to England's king, I am still a Quaker! Thou knowest that, Anna Strong!

Anna: Of course I do, Robert.

Robert: Working for the *Gazette* allows me to gather news about the British. British soldiers will talk with me as a *Gazette* reporter.

Anna: You do a fine job, Robert.

Robert: Well, Mrs. Strong, I must be going.

Anna: Come again, Robert. *(Accompanies him to door)*

Robert: Yes, whenever I get back from New York. Good night to thee. *(She closes and bolts door.)*

Anna *(Going to cellar door; calling)*: Ben, you can come up. (Ben *enters through door.)* That was Robert Townsend. Now, you were saying you need help for General Washington.

Ben: Yes, Anna. I want to talk to Abe Woodhull and Caleb Brewster tonight. They're both patriots.

Anna: Yes, I know them.

Ben: Caleb is in Fairfield, Connecticut, serving under Colonel Smith, and still working on his whaling boats.

Anna: Making successful raids, too, I hear. But Abe's resigned from the Army. He's just running his father's farm, and after that terrible beating the Tories gave him, he's sick most of the time.

Ben: Yes, I've heard that. That's why I thought that Abe would be willing to go to New York occasionally, make observations, and report them back to me.

Anna *(Musing)*: His sister, Mary, lives there. He could visit her, as an excuse.

Ben: Exactly. But we all need to talk about it. Would you let us meet here later tonight?

Anna *(Hesitating briefly, then firmly)*: Of course.

Ben: Good. *(He turns to go, hand on door bolt.)* I'll go find them.

Anna *(Stopping him, her hand on his arm)*: Ben, wait a minute. Robert Townsend is writing social news for Jammy Rivington's *Gazette,* and I've been thinking . . . He might be persuaded to help in your cause.

Ben: A Quaker? *(Shakes his head)* I don't think so.

Anna: You might ask him. You know his father, old Samuel? Well, the Loyalists picked him up and before they freed him, they made him swear the oath of allegiance to the King. They even made Robert swear it. It went against all their beliefs.

Ben *(Angrily)*: The devils!

Anna: If you remember, it was Robert who hid Nathan Hale on Captain Klaas' boat as a crew member, and got him across the British lines. Robert has connections in New York, and he's in touch with the British all the time.

Ben: I don't think he'd be of any help, but we'll see. *(Opens door)* We'll be back this evening, Anna.

Anna: Yes, Ben. I'll be waiting. *(Ben exits. Anna closes door, bolts it, takes candle and exits through rear door. Curtain)*

Scene 2

Time: *That evening.*
Setting: *The same.*
At Rise: Anna, Robert, Ben, Caleb Brewster *and* Abe Wood-hull *are sitting on stage.*

Ben: Robert, you'll not be telling tales of what you learn here tonight, all over town and in New York, will you?

Robert *(Seriously):* On my word, Ben. I'll never breathe a word of it to anyone.

Ben: We all have to know what needs to be done, so I'll tell you right out. It's spying . . . that's what General Washington wants, here in Setauket, and in New York.

Caleb *(Chuckling):* Spying, eh? Nothing I'd rather do than spy on old King George's scallawags. *(Rubs hands in satisfaction)*

Ben: Your job, Caleb, will be running messages across the Sound, from here to Fairfield. Then you'll have to deliver them to me so I can send them on to General Washington.

Caleb: Is that all?

Ben: It's no small matter, Caleb. The trick will be to cross that Sound and not get caught with secret messages.

Caleb: I'm ready to start.

Ben: Abe, we'll need you to go to New York once in a while, learn of the embattlement positions, listen around for troop movements, and then write down what you learn from memory.

Abe *(Nervously):* I'm . . . I'm not so sure. A farmer in Manhattan? It doesn't make sense. They'd be suspicious.

Ben: But your sister Mary runs the boardinghouse there, so there would be no questions asked if you were visiting her.

Abe *(Uncomfortably)*: I don't know. The lobsterbacks watch us. They know our every move. They'd be sure to make something of it.

Ben: Look, we even have John Jay's invisible ink for you to use.

Robert: Invisible ink?

Ben: Yes. No one can read it without the secret formula that brings it to light. So you see, Abe, it wouldn't put you in a spot. To the British, it would only be a blank piece of paper.

Abe: I'd like to help, but why can't Robert write the messages? He's already in New York, and it sounds as if he knows what's going on.

Ben: Abe, we all know the difficult time you had with the Tories. But we need you.

Abe: *(Uncertainly)*: I guess I could pick up the messages at Mary's. And I could probably get them to Caleb. *(Turns to* Robert*)* But Robert, you can write the messages in that invisible ink. You know how to write.

Robert *(Adamantly)*: No. I will tell you what I see, and hear, about the British plans, but I cannot write the messages. Writing messages would not allow me to stay neutral.

Ben: Well, Abe?

Abe: I just don't think I can do it. The danger of being discovered is too great.

Ben *(Sighing)*: I'll tell you what. We'll give you a false name. How about . . . *(Pauses)* Samuel Culper. Robert will give you the news from New York. You write it down under the name of Samuel Culper and pass it along to Caleb.

Caleb *(Laughing)*: And Robert can be Samuel Culper, Junior!

Abe *(Doubtfully)*: I still don't know. Wouldn't the British be suspicious about why I travel to New York all the time?

Anna: You and Robert could take turns. You go to New York once in a while to get information and Robert could bring it here sometimes. *(To Robert)* You come home to see your father quite often, don't you?

Robert: Yes. Yes, I do. *(To Ben)* This plan is agreeable to me.

Ben: Wonderful! You could meet at Mary's in New York, and in Setauket, you can meet here at Anna's house.

Anna: Will you do it, Abe?

Abe *(Frantically)*: But how will Caleb pick up the messages? How will he know where to meet me? I can't deliver them to the same place every time.

Ben: Let's figure that out right now.

Anna: I have an idea. I can hang some things on my clothesline, as a signal. How about a black petticoat? That would mean a message is ready.

Ben: Then something white . . .

Anna: Yes! Handkerchiefs! To tell the meeting place on the Sound.

Ben *(Excitedly)*: Great idea! One would mean Strong's Neck Point, by the oak where the lightning struck . . .

Anna: Two would mean Setauket Harbor.

Ben: And three would mean Crane's Neck Bend!

Caleb: Four would mean Drowned Meadow, and five could be Old Man's Bay!

Ben: Anna, will you do that?

Anna: Of course I will!

Ben: We have a debt to our country. None of us can forget Nathan Hale.

Robert *(Thoughtfully)*: I will never forget Nathan Hale. He was my friend.

Caleb: He was a friend and neighbor to all of us. He died for his country. *(After a pause)* Well, Abe. Will you do it?

Abe *(After a long pause; weakly)*: I'll . . . I'll try.

Ben *(Standing; to Abe, pleased)*: You're a good man, Abe. *(To others)* We'll call ourselves the Samuel Culper Ring, but no one must ever know! *(Lights dim. Quick curtain)*

Scene 3

Time: *Several weeks later.*

Setting: *The same.*

At Rise: Anna *enters and hurries to front door. She unbolts lock, opens door to* Robert.

Anna *(Furtively)*: Come in, Robert. Abe is already here.

Robert: Good. *(Soberly)* The news is bad, Mrs. Strong. *(Bolts door)* We must hurry.

Anna: I'll call Abe up from the cellar. *(Goes to cellar door)* Did you have any trouble getting through today?

Robert: No. I was stopped and searched, but I had no problems. I've used the same method for the last several weeks.

Anna *(Opening cellar door, calling)*: Abe! Robert's here. *(Then, to* Robert*)* Bringing supplies for your father's store is a good method.

Robert: Yes, ma'am. The Redcoats go through my wagon, but there's nothing there. Cabbages, flour, buttons, hatchets . . . there's always something different. And my father needs the supplies, in these times.

Abe *(Entering, carrying ink bottle of clear liquid, pen, and white paper; nervously)*: Are you sure no one saw you come, Robert?

Robert: I'm sure, Abe. I was very careful. (*Abe puts writing supplies on table, then pulls up a chair and sits.*)

Anna: I'll hang the black petticoat on the line. (*Exits at rear*)

Abe: Let's not delay. What's the message?

Robert: The news is all bad. The 54th Regiment and Lord Rawdon's Corps are southward bound, and the Greyhound Frigate, with Cornwallis, arrived last week with two thousand men, sailing for Carolina. (*Abe writes quickly.*) More troops have been stationed in Jamaica and Brooklyn and the Hessians are guarding the ferries now.

Abe (*Looking up*): Is there any word that General Clinton will leave Manhattan open, giving Washington a chance to regain it?

Robert: No. They're tightening up everywhere. Fortifying Governor's Island and the Narrows, and repairing the works at Paulus Hook. (*Abe continues to write.*)

Anna (*Entering*): How many handkerchiefs should I hang on the line, Abe? I need to signal Caleb while it's still daylight.

Abe: The cattle are grazing down on the Bay. It will be natural for me to go there. Hang out three, Anna. That means Crane's Neck Bend. (*Anna exits rear.*) Let's continue, Robert.

Robert: Two British regiments of Colonel Fanning's Corps, and a troop of Loyalists, are now at White Stone. They came yesterday from Rhode Island, and they plan to invade Connecticut . . . to plunder and scourge the entire colony.

Abe (*Jumping up*): Not Connecticut! Ben will need to know that right away! I'll tell Caleb about it when I see him. I'd better hurry. (*Grabs ink, paper, and quill, and hurries out through cellar door*)

Robert: But, Abe, I haven't finished! *(Anna re-enters.)*

Anna: Has Abe gone?

Robert: Yes. He left before we had finished. There's a British regiment headed for Connecticut, and Abe rushed off when he heard that. He wanted to be sure that Ben found out as soon as possible.

Anna: Connecticut? *(Sinks into chair)* Abe is right — Ben will want to know right away. So many patriots have gone to Connecticut for safety. *(Loud pounding on door is heard.)* Oh, dear, who can that be? *(Nervously)* Robert, go to the cellar. Wait there and listen. *(Gestures at cup on sideboard)* If there's danger, I'll drop the cup. *(Robert exits through cellar door. Anna goes to front door, unbolts it, and in burst Two British Soldiers. They push her aside.)*

1st Soldier *(Loudly):* Search the house to see who's here.

(2nd Soldier *looks through rear door.* Anna *hurries to sideboard, picks up cup.*)

Anna *(Loudly):* No need to search my house. Nobody's here but me. You've taken my husband. I'm all alone.

2nd Soldier: There's nobody else here. *(Opens cellar door, looks through doorway quickly, then closes door)* No one down there.

1st Soldier: Now, then, missus. We just want to know a few things. (Anna *returns cup to sideboard.*)

Anna *(Feigning deafness):* Eh? I can't hear you.

1st Soldier: I say, we want to ask you some questions.

Anna *(Shouting):* Questions?

1st Soldier: Yes.

Anna *(Shouting):* You'll have to speak louder. I'm going deaf.

1st Soldier *(Shouting):* We need to know what's going on here.

Anna *(Drawing back, afraid):* I don't know anything.

2nd Soldier: We think you do. We think you're a spy.

Anna: Eh?

1st Soldier: Just tell us about those clothes on your clothesline.

Anna: Clothes? What clothes?

1st Soldier: The handkerchiefs. What does three handkerchiefs on your clothesline mean?

Anna: Say that again? I can't hear you.

2nd Soldier *(Loudly):* Are those three handkerchiefs on your clothesline a signal? *(Pause)*

Anna *(Moving toward sideboard; shouting):* Signal? *(Frowning)* Handkerchiefs? *(Suddenly)* Oh! Yes, they're a signal. I need some potatoes and eggs. *(Louder)* And some milk!

1st Soldier: Potatoes? Eggs and milk? What do you mean?

2nd Soldier: Yes, you'd better tell us!

Anna *(Loudly):* Now, look here! I'm an old woman, and I can't get to the store — Sam Townsend's store. So when I see Robert Townsend coming with supplies for his Pa, I hang out some handkerchiefs.

2nd Soldier *(Suspiciously):* Then what?

Anna *(Counting off on her fingers):* Well, one handkerchief means potatoes. Two means eggs. And three means a can of milk. *(She shouts.)* When the black petticoat is hanging there, it means I need all three. *(She moves away from the sideboard.)*

1st Soldier: Who brings it?

Anna: Robert Townsend brings me what I need. He's a good man.

2nd Soldier: Do you think he's seen your signal today?

Anna: I don't know.

1st Soldier *(Pacing closer to sideboard):* You'd better be telling us the truth, or we'll . . . *(He swings around to point his finger at* Anna, *and as he does so, he hits cup and saucer, which crash to the floor.)*

Anna: What was that?

1st Soldier: It was a cup and saucer. That was all. *(Grimly)* But that's not all that will be broken if your Mr. Townsend doesn't show up pretty soon. Do you hear?

Anna *(Nervously):* Yes. Yes, I hear you.

1st Soldier: Then we'll just wait here, if you don't mind. *(Soldiers* sit, fold their arms, attentive. Anna *peers at broken cup on the floor, and in terror she picks up the pieces and carries them to table.)*

Anna *(In distress):* My pretty cup, all broken now. My husband will tell me I should have been more careful. I'll tell him the King's soldiers broke it by accident. *(Turns to* Soldiers, *shouting)* Then he won't be angry at me. *(Softly)* I wonder if I can put it back together again. Oh, dear, I wonder when Robert will come . . .

2nd Soldier (*Unpleasantly*): Madam, please stop your mumbling.

1st Soldier (*To* 2nd Soldier): Leave her alone. Once Townsend arrives, it's all over for them anyway.

2nd Soldier: *If* he comes. I'm ready to leave now. I'd like to get back to New York.

1st Soldier: So would I. But if our friend here is a spy, don't forget that we'll be commended for having found her out.

2nd Soldier: True, true. I'd like to get back to the fighting, all the same.

Anna (*Sighing*): My good cup and saucer. Maybe I can fix it. (*She shows pieces to* 1st Soldier, *shouting*) See, these two pieces fit together. I'll bet I can fix it.

1st Soldier (*Laughing*): I'll bet you can!

2nd Soldier (*Impatiently*): Oh, let's get out of here. The woman is crazy — and she's driving *me* crazy! (*Leaps to his feet. Loud rapping on front door is heard.*)

Robert (*Shouting from offstage*): Anna! Anna Strong! Come and open the door. I am loaded with your foodstuffs.

Anna (*Hand to her ear, listening*): Eh?

Robert: Anna! It's Robert!

Anna (*Softly*): Oh, it's Robert. (*She shuffles across to door, opens it.*)

Robert (*Entering, carrying gunny sack of potatoes, a bucket of eggs, and one of milk; shouting*): Here are the foods for thee, Anna Strong. Your potatoes, eggs, and milk.

Anna: Oh, thank you, Robert.

1st Soldier (*Softly; confronting* Robert): What does four handkerchiefs mean, Robert Townsend?

Robert: (*In natural voice*): Four handkerchiefs?

1st Soldier: Yes. On the clothesline.

Robert: Oh, four means Mrs. Strong wants me to bring a cabbage, or carrots — some vegetable, that's all.

2nd Soldier: And what about five on the line?

Robert: Five means flour. She uses a lot of flour.

1st Soldier: You're pretty clever, young Quaker. Now we'll test you!

2nd Soldier: If you're wrong, you'll both be locked in prison. Or we'll hang you, as we did Nathan Hale! *(He laughs.)*

1st Soldier *(Turning to Anna; shouting):* All right, now, old woman, you've got your potatoes, eggs, and milk. What does four handkerchiefs mean?

Anna: Eh?

1st Soldier *(Yelling):* Four handkerchiefs! What does that mean out there on your clothesline?

Anna: Oh, that means I want some cabbage or some turnips, or carrots, or whatever Mr. Townsend has on hand.

2nd Soldier: And what does five mean?

Anna: Five? That means I need some flour. I bake lots of bread. Do you want to taste my bread?

1st Soldier: No, thank you. We'll be going now.

Anna *(As Soldiers exit; after them):* You come back sometime and taste my bread. (Soldiers *exit, close front door.* Anna *and* Robert *sigh in relief.* Anna *shouts again.)* You're a good boy, Robert!

Robert *(Shouting):* Shall I take the handkerchiefs down for thee?

Anna *(Shouting):* Yes. Take the handkerchiefs down. (Robert *exits rear.* Anna *sinks into chair. He returns with three handkerchiefs, puts them on table. In natural voices, they continue.)*

Robert: Anna, what a narrow escape! It was so dark in the cellar I could hardly find the potatoes, or the eggs and milk. Then I feared the outside door would squeak.

Anna: I keep it well oiled. Robert, thank you for telling the lie about the handkerchiefs. You did it for me.

Robert: I did not lie for thee, Anna Strong. I only repeated what I heard from you. I did not lie.

Anna: But you made up the story about the cabbages and the flour.

Robert: I made it up, but I did not lie. The imagination is a gift to use for a good purpose. Some of us have imaginations, and others, like Caleb Brewster, have physical strength.

Anna *(Smiling):* Well, I just hope Caleb saw the signal and Abe found him at the Bend.

Robert: So do I. But I didn't give Abe all the information I have. I hope he returns for it.

Anna: He will.

Robert: What will we do now about our signals? We'll need to change them after today.

Anna: We'll change them, Robert, but we'll still get our information through. And we'll never give up our fight for independence. *(Brushes bits of china on table)* I'm glad the cup is broken. It was from England. We must do the same thing with the ties they hold on America.

Robert: Dost thou think that we can break those ties?

Anna: Yes, Robert. We must break them. *(She stands, smiles confidently.)* And somehow, Robert, we will! *(Curtain)*

The End

Author

Myrtle Nord has written a number of plays for adults and young people. Her plays have been performed in many parts of the country, and two have won awards.

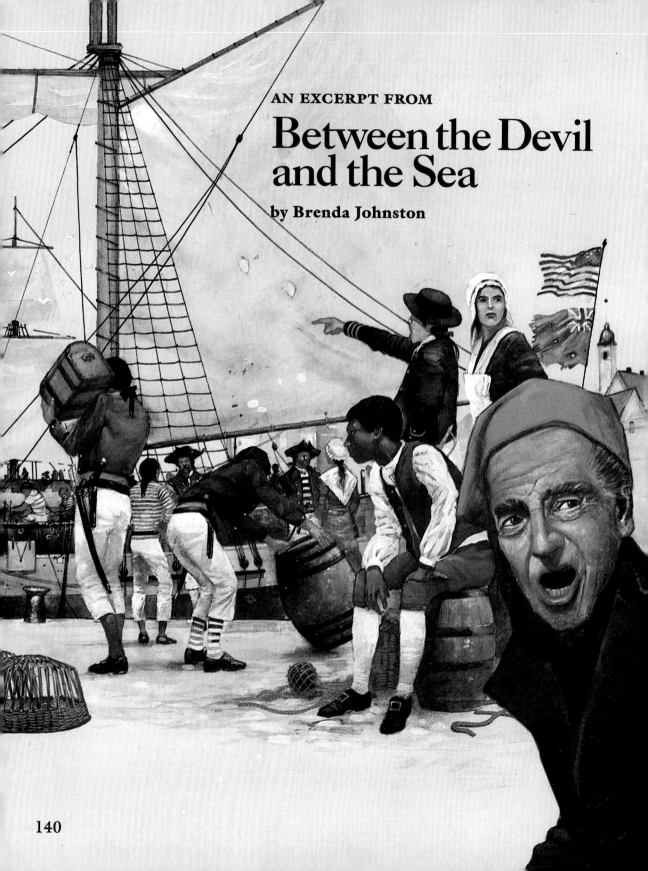

AN EXCERPT FROM

Between the Devil and the Sea

by Brenda Johnston

In 1781, the city of Philadelphia was a center of activity for the American Revolution. Coming and going from the harbor were many ships whose mission was to capture British ships. James Forten was one of many young Americans who wanted to seek adventure at sea.

James was a fifteen-year-old who lived with his mother and sister in a community of free blacks. James's father, a sailmaker, had drowned when James was ten. Educated in a school for blacks, James helped to support his family by doing jobs for the sailmaker who had once employed Mr. Forten.

James Forten Goes to Sea

There was excitement along the harbor, and James joined the crowds watching the *Royal Lewis,* Philadelphia's own privateer, bringing its captured British vessel into port. Since Philadelphia was the capital of the new nation, James witnessed many auctions of captured British cargo at the wharves and marveled at the proceeds that the captain and the crew shared as a reward. The privateers were not part of the navy, but American pirate ships whose mission was to stop the British merchant ships. Their reward was patriotic glory, the wealthy cargo from the captured ships, and a small monthly allotment as well.

James wanted to join the privateer crew more than anything else in the world, but he had already learned that it was useless to plead with his mother. As he walked home from the docks, he passed the London Coffee House, where he met his friends Larry and Fred standing outside.

"Guess what?" They greeted him in excitement.

"What?" asked James coolly, careful not to betray his curiosity.

"Guess who got signed up for the *Royal Lewis*'s next trip?"

James was interested. "Not you, I know," he said, hoping with all his heart that they were not going before he could.

"Daniel Brewton," they answered him. Daniel was one of their white friends.

"I'm going to sign up, too," said James decisively.

"You're too young," said Fred.

"Daniel and I are the same age almost," said James.

"Your mother'll kill you," declared Larry. "Besides, we already tried."

James left them standing there while he approached a man sitting at a table taking down names. He stood before the man and cleared his throat.

The man looked at him inquiringly for a moment, then asked sharply, "How old are you?"

"Sixteen," said James, thinking fast. He was already nearly six feet tall and walked with a slow, self-confident gait. Black bushy eyebrows framed a lean creamed-coffee face and gave him the appearance of a scowl until one of his slow smiles broke through, lit his eyes, and showed two rows of perfect white teeth. His smiles were rare though, and most of the time his face was expressionless. He had acquired the habit of gazing unfalteringly into a person's eyes while talking, but taking care that none of his own feelings were ever reflected in his dark eyes. He now fixed his gaze on the man and waited.

The man finally shrugged his shoulders and said, "Oh, well. You're on. What's your name?"

"James Forten," he answered quickly, already wondering what he was going to tell his mother.

The man's voice broke through his thoughts. "We sail in three days, James. See you then."

He walked back to his friends and with disdain in every

word said, "Well, boys, the *Royal Lewis* and *I* sail in three days."

They were astonished. "How?" they asked. "What did you say?"

James laughed at their dismay and patted their heads.

"I think," he said, "that you two are just a little too short." He started for home.

In spite of his apprehension about telling his mother the bad news, James was humming with joy when he reached home. His spirits were so high that even Abigail[1] and his mother caught his mood. James put off telling his mother until he had read to her from the Bible that evening. But as he closed the book, he looked at her and started.

---

[1]James's younger sister

"Mother, can I join the crew of the *Royal Lewis?*"

She didn't answer but just returned his direct look. For a panicky moment, he wondered if someone had already told her what he had done. She acted as if she knew.

"They are taking twenty black sailors with them, Mother," he finally said.

She still would not answer. James wildly thought that either she was a mind reader or she had talked to Larry's mother.

"I'm one of the twenty," he said at last, shamefacedly.

His mother folded her arms and shook her head but did not say anything. It was the only time James had ever defied her. Now he felt sorry.

"Is it all right?" he asked, his voice pleading.

"You did what you wanted to do already, didn't you?" She sounded tired.

"Oh, I'll never get a job in the sail loft so long as the war lasts," said James. "Business keeps getting slower and slower. This way I'll get a chance to do lots of things. Travel. Defend my country." His eyes sparkled in excitement, and he suddenly laughed aloud.

"Oh, Mother," he exclaimed, "I've always wanted to ride in a ship and see the sails from the other side."

"But, James," she said, her voice almost breaking, "it's so dangerous."

"Not for our ship," said James, "the *Royal Lewis,* commanded by Captain Decatur — King of the Sea."

"Promise me," his mother said, finally relenting, "that you will read your Bible every night. You'll never know how much your father wanted you to be able to read."

"I promise," said James. "Only, Mother, no one can forget how to read. It's like forgetting how to walk."

Three days later James went down to the docks, taking only the clothes he wore on his back, his mother's Bible, and a bag of marbles. On the way he stopped by the sail loft to say good-bye. He was surprised that Mr. Bridges[2] was more emotional about his leaving than his mother had been. They walked to the ship together, and Mr. Bridges stood on shore while James boarded the *Royal Lewis* and stood there waving as the ship weighed anchor and moved out to the open sea. His mother had stayed home and had waved good-bye to James from the door as if he were leaving, as always, only for the day.

Powder boy on the *Royal Lewis* was the lowest and dirtiest of jobs, and James soon realized that it consisted of more than just preparing for battle. He was often called to serve meals, act as cabin boy, and do whatever else no one in particular was assigned to do. James hid his resentment behind an expressionless face and slow smile and tried especially to make himself useful to Captain Decatur. He stood by ready to serve the captain's meals, to clear the table, or to clean the captain's quarters and was soon recognized as being reserved for the service of the captain. As a result, he escaped some of the dirtier jobs.

He was eager for his first battle, and it seemed forever until the day that the cry came from the ship's lookout that the British ship *Activist* had been spotted. The quiet *Royal Lewis* became a whirl of activity as the regular privateers, in a disciplined manner, began running to their respective posts and shouting out orders. James's head was spinning. He had forgotten all he had learned. He didn't know where to start.

"James Forten," a voice called out impatiently, sounding as if it had called him many times before. "Over here!"

---

[2] the man who had employed his father in his sail loft, where sails for boats are made

James ran over to the gun crew and stood in position near the powder and balls and waited, hoping that no one would notice his trembling. The *Royal Lewis* came remarkably close to the other ship, it seemed, before the voice of the British captain broke the silence.

"This is His Majesty's frigate *Activist*," he called. "What ship is that?"

Captain Decatur's answer was to signal his men to attack. Almost immediately there was a deafening roar followed by a flash of fire from the cannon, and the deck shook under James's feet. The smell of smoke filled the air and blinded him, making him cough and sneeze. He was so frightened that he froze until a sharp nudge on his shoulder reminded him of his job. By blind instinct, he began passing the powder and cannonballs to the loader, who forced them down the muzzle with a ramrod.

Now that the battle was really on, James could see the extreme danger of his job as powder boy. When the ammunition was low, James had to run below deck to the magazine for more powder and cannonballs. He would then have to run back to his post, shielding the explosive powder from the flying sparks, which could ignite an explosion fatal to him. All around him the sparks flew, forcing him to keep moving, although he had to step over the bodies of wounded, groaning men who cried out to him for help. The battle seemed to last an eternity, and both ships appeared to be utterly destroyed. The two ships were so close now that the crew from the *Royal Lewis* began jumping over to the deck of the *Activist* to continue the battle in man-to-man combat. James, however, stayed at his post, passing powder and balls until his arms felt like rubber. The battle finally took an upward swing when the *Activist* began burning in several places and the captain was seriously wounded. Soon the British flag was lowered in surrender, and the long battle had ended at last.

The *Activist* did not have the rich cargo that James and all the crew of the *Royal Lewis* had hoped for. As James looked around at the mangled ships and the wounded and dead men on both vessels, he wondered if it had been worth it. However, it was just the first of several battles for James, and some of the later ones brought important prisoners or goods that could be exchanged for large amounts of money. But too soon their luck changed.

One day, about three months after that first battle, as the *Royal Lewis* approached a British warship called the *Amphyon*, the lookout suddenly spotted two more British vessels in the distance. Realizing the impossibility of fighting three ships at one time, the *Royal Lewis* decided to make a run for it, but the British took up the chase. Before long, they were close enough to begin firing. At the first shot, Captain Decatur immediately gave orders to strike colors. The American flag fluttered down in surrender.

It was then that James went into a complete panic. He wanted to run and scream. He knew that black sailors were never kept for prisoner exchanges but were sold into slavery in the West Indies as part of the cargo. Running below to his bunk, he had just enough time to snatch up his blanket, Bible, and marbles before he was ordered on deck by one of the British officers. The crew of the *Royal Lewis* was divided into three groups and sent to the three British ships. James was with the group taken by the *Amphyon*. As the prisoners filed past the captain, James was stopped and the captain asked sharply, "What's in that bag, boy?"

"What bag?" said James in confusion, looking down. His marbles in a small cloth sack dangled from his wrist.

"How old are you?" demanded the captain.

"Fifteen," answered James quickly, forgetting his former lie.

"I said, 'What's in that bag?' " the captain demanded again.

"Marbles," James answered, feeling very embarrassed and childish. He didn't know now what had made him bring them.

"What's your name?" asked the captain.

James figured this was the end for him. The captain probably already had a prospective buyer in mind. He stood tall and answered without faltering, "My name is James Forten."

The captain smiled and waved him on. A few hours later, while James sat with the other prisoners, a British youth with rosy cheeks, straight brown hair, and a pouting mouth approached him.

"Are you James Forten, the powder boy from the *Royal Lewis?*" he asked.

James nodded.

"I am Willie Beasley, the son of Sir John, the captain of the *Amphyon,*" he said with a heavy British accent. "My father tells me that you brought a bag of marbles on board. I'm a champion. Would you like to play a game?"

James took out his marbles with great pride now and followed Willie on deck. They placed the marbles in a group on the floor between them. At first they played seriously and silently, but soon, in boyish glee, they were laughing and teasing. James was trying to decide whether or not to let Willie Beasley win, for he was sure he couldn't be beaten. His perfect aim and strong fingers had won him the neighborhood championship for years. He decided to win first and then to let Willie win. He was surprised to find out, however, that letting Willie win was no problem because he really was very good, and James had to play carefully to beat him. It was the first of many games, and in spite of

themselves, the boys became fast friends, so James was in no way treated as a prisoner. At first he thought the other prisoners would be angry, but they didn't seem to notice. Sir John was glad that Willie had met someone his own age to entertain him since the trip had turned out to be a long and boring one for the boy. During one of their long days together, Willie asked James to go back to England with him. James instantly flared.

"I'll never be a traitor!" he snapped.

"What difference does it make since you're nothing but a slave in your own country anyway?" asked Willie.

"I am not a slave!" said James angrily. "I was born free."

"Well, you're just a black prisoner now," retorted Willie. "And you have only two choices. You will either be sold as a slave, or you can come to England with me as a friend." He suddenly dropped his belligerent attitude. "Oh, come on, James," he begged. "England abolished slavery. You'll get an education and live in a beautiful home. Father likes you. He thinks you have a fine mind."

James didn't answer. He was tempted, but somehow it didn't seem right. When Sir John sent for him the next day, James stood before him and refused his offer to go to England.

"You must be a fool!" exclaimed Sir John in perplexed anger.

"I am an American prisoner," said James. "I cannot be a traitor to my country."

Willie broke in. "America is not your country, James. All you are there is a slave."

"I am not a slave," answered James, quietly this time.

"Well, all you are there, then, is a servant," said Willie. "I could understand your loyalty if you were white."

This time James didn't answer.

Sir John sighed. He had spoiled Willie by trying to give him everything he wanted. Now he hated to see him disappointed. In an effort to change James's mind, he said, "You know you'll have to be sold."

James didn't know what to say. He opened his mouth to speak, but changed his mind and said nothing.

"Well?" asked Willie.

"I cannot be a traitor," James answered. Lifting his dark pain-filled eyes and looking directly at Willie, he almost whispered, "I never want to be a slave." He turned and quickly left.

The next day before the prisoner exchange, Willie Beasley approached James.

"You will be transferred to the *Jersey* with the other prisoners," he said. As soon as he started talking, his eyes filled with tears. "It is nothing but a floating death trap. No one gets off alive." He handed James a white envelope. "This is from Father to the captain of the *Jersey*. It will help you. Good-bye, James." He turned and hurried away. Looking down at the white envelope, James realized that Willie was one of the best friends he would ever have. Somehow he knew that they would never meet again.

When James boarded the *Jersey,* he handed the white envelope to the officer in charge, who barely glanced at it and waved him on without comment. He was sent below to the main prisoner quarters, where his nostrils were immediately assailed by the loathsome odor of human filth, and all around the dark hole he could hear the ravings and groanings of the sick and dying. James knew that he was probably the only black on board. His mind went back to Mr. Benezet and his school lessons on how the slaves were captured and brought to America in the pits of ships. He now knew just how they must have felt. He knew why they were so submissive and broken when they were finally sold. They said that no man sentenced to the *Jersey* survived unless he was removed in a short time, but then, James thought, most prisoners were white. He thought of his great-grandfather who had survived the slave ship and of his grandfather who had bought his freedom. From the number of African slaves in America, James realized that quite a few of them must have survived, and in a sudden surge of pride, he realized that he was of the same race. He would make it, too.

When the prisoners were brought on deck the next day, James recognized Daniel Brewton,[3] who looked gravely ill. They were glad to see each other, and because of their past association, they quickly became friends. This relationship was hard on James because Daniel was so sickly that James ended up doing chores and hustling food for both of them. Nevertheless, James was still able to volunteer for extra jobs, and in his usual manner he picked the ones that kept him on deck and out of the stinking hole as much as possible. He loaded supplies, scrubbed the deck, and even volunteered to bring up the corpses of dead prisoners. After the first few times, this task no longer bothered him. Not only did James survive, but he also grew tough.

He never knew if it was the letter Sir John had written that prompted another prisoner to seek him out one morning while he was doing his chores. The man, who was an officer, told James he was being exchanged for a British prisoner and that he was taking a trunk with him that would hold one person. Joy flooded James's heart to think that he might finally escape, but instinct warned him not to tell Daniel. Somehow he felt like a traitor leaving him behind to die. He rudely avoided Daniel the remainder of the day.

---

[3]a white neighbor from Philadelphia

That night when Daniel sought him out in the dark pit where they usually huddled together and talked about Philadelphia, their mothers and sisters, and old times, James pretended he was sleepy.

"Leave me alone, Daniel!" he snapped.

"What's wrong?" asked Daniel.

"Nothing," James snapped again. "I'm just sick and tired of waiting to get off this boat."

"I don't think I'm ever going to get off," said Daniel. "I don't think I'm ever going to see Philadelphia or my home again." His voice cracked, and James knew that he was crying.

Long after Daniel had fallen asleep, James still lay awake, hating himself for what he knew he had to do. The next morning Daniel did not even want to go up on deck for fresh air, and James had to practically carry him up. His face was gray and his eyelids were red and swollen. His body was covered with sores. His eyes seemed to be constantly pleading with James. That evening James slipped Daniel into the trunk, and the next morning he and the officer carried the trunk down to the waiting boats, which took it and the officer to freedom. As the boat disappeared toward shore, James swallowed hard and fought back the tears, knowing that it was too late to change his mind now and that a golden opportunity had slipped through his fingers.

"I can make it," he whispered to himself. "I know I can make it." He put his hands in his pocket and felt the round hardness of his bag of marbles that he had childishly clung to since leaving home. In sudden anger, he tossed them into the sea. He would never need them again. He felt like a tired old man as he turned back to the *Jersey* and wondered how he could make it through another day.

He did make it through, though. That day and the next day and the next for three more months. Near the end of the war, he was freed in a general prisoner exchange. After the American ship, loaded with returning prisoners, docked in Philadelphia, James walked down the tiny streets of his boyhood home, wondering how the houses and streets could ever have looked so huge. A few people glanced at him curiously, some with recognition, but he barely noticed anyone. He was thinking of his mother and wondering if she knew he was on his way. He knew that even if she did know, she wouldn't be waiting at the door but would be in the kitchen cooking and would try to pretend that his walking through the door after all this time was nothing very exciting. But the smell of biscuits and gravy would soon fill the house, and her singing voice would float from the kitchen. Long before nightfall the whole neighborhood would know that Sarah Forten's boy was home.

James pushed the door open, and the aroma of cooking food filled his nostrils. She knew. When he walked into the kitchen, she didn't even look up until he whirled her around in a bear hug. In spite of herself, she could not help crying when she saw how much James looked like his father. He was now six feet two inches and thin as a rail.

"You're so skinny," she said, shaking her head.

"They don't cook like you do on the *Jersey*," replied James, laughing. "Where is Abigail?"

"Oh, she lives down the street now," said his mother. "There was no way to tell you. She's married."

"Married!" exclaimed James. To him Abigail was just a child. He couldn't imagine her married.

"Daniel Brewton was here and told us how you slipped him off the boat," his mother said. "I'm proud of you." After a moment, when James didn't answer, she went on. "Now that the war is over, you can go and see Mr. Bridges about a job in the sail loft."

"I won't be staying," said James in sudden decision. He

hadn't thought about it until now. "I'm going to England."

"England?" said his mother. "Whatever for?"

"There are no slaves in England," he said.

"But you don't have to worry about slavery, James."

"If slavery was abolished in England," he answered bitterly, "maybe it's the best country for blacks to live in. After what I've been through, I can't live in a country where my brothers are slaves."

They were interrupted by Abigail bursting through the door and throwing herself on James. She hadn't grown an inch.

"I hear you're a married woman now." He held her back from him.

"Yes," said Abigail almost shyly. "This is your brother now." Holding her hand out toward the young man who stood by the door, she said, "This is Charles Dunbar." Giggling, she added, "Everybody calls him Dunbar, though."

The two young men shook hands, and James decided that he would probably like this sandy-haired young man with gray eyes and yellowish-brown skin who laughed a lot and constantly teased Abigail.

"Dunbar is a sailor," said Abigail, "and he's been practically everywhere in the world. You should see the things he brings home. Things are much better now." She looked at her mother, busy preparing James a plate.

"Have you ever been to England?" asked James with interest.

"We'll talk about that later," broke in Sarah Forten nervously. "Right now James has to eat. See how skinny he is?"

She piled his plate high with rice and gravy and biscuits and pork chops and okra, just the way James had dreamed of her doing over and over again while he lay in the dark misery of the *Jersey,* counting off the passing days. It had taken 210 days for the dream to come true.

James went to live in England for a few years. When he returned home he did go to work in the sail loft, as he had planned. In a short time, he was promoted to foreman. Later he became the owner of the business and invented a device that made it easier to handle the vast, heavy sails used at that time.

James Forten used his wealth and position in the community in support of the rights of women and blacks. He was active in opposing slavery, and he taught black children in his home when they were excluded from public schools. He never stopped fighting for the justice that he knew all people deserved.

Author

Brenda Johnston has written books for adults as well as children. *Between the Devil and the Sea,* from which this story was taken, was chosen Book of the Year by the Child Study Association and received honorable mention from the Council on Interracial Books.

An excerpt from

BEN and ME

A New and Astonishing *LIFE* of
BENJAMIN FRANKLIN
As written by his Good Mouse
AMOS
Lately Discovered, Edited
& Illustrated by
**ROBERT
LAWSON**

Since the recent death of my lamented friend and patron Ben Franklin, many so-called historians have attempted to write accounts of his life and his achievements. Most of these are wrong in so many respects that I feel the time has now come for me to take pen in paw and set things right.

All of these ill-informed scribblers seem astonished at Ben's great fund of information, at his brilliant decisions, at his seeming knowledge of all that went on about him.

Had they asked me, I could have told them. It was ME.

For many years I was his closest friend and adviser and, if I do say it, was in great part responsible for his success and fame.

Not that I wish to claim too much: I simply hope to see justice done, credit given where credit is due, and that's to me — mostly.

Ben was undoubtedly a splendid fellow, a great man, a patriot and all that; but he *was* undeniably stupid at times, and had it not been for me — well, here's the true story, and you can judge for yourself.

I was the oldest of twenty-six children. My parents, in naming us, went right through the alphabet. I, being first, was **A**mos, the others went along through **B**athsheba, **C**laude, **D**aniel — and so forth down to the babies: **X**enophon, **Y**sobel, and **Z**enas.

We lived in the vestry of Old Christ Church on Second Street, in Philadelphia — behind the paneling. With that number of mouths to feed we were, naturally, not a very prosperous family. In fact we were really quite poor — as poor as church-mice.

But it was not until the Hard Winter of 1745 that things really became desperate. That was a winter long to be remembered for its severity, and night after night my poor father would come in tired and wet with his little sack practically empty.

We were driven to eating prayer-books, and when those gave out we took to the Minister's sermons. That was, for me, the final straw. The prayer-books were tough, but those sermons!

Being the oldest, it seemed fitting that I should go out into the world and make my own way. Perhaps I could in some way help the others. At least, it left one less to be provided for.

So, saying farewell to all of them — my mother and father and all the children from Bathsheba to Zenas — I set forth on the coldest, windiest night of a cold and windy winter.

Little did I dream, at that moment, of all the strange people and experiences I should encounter before ever I returned to that little vestry home! All I thought of were my cold paws, my empty stomach — and those sermons.

I have never known how far I traveled that night, for, what with the cold and hunger, I must have become slightly delirious. The first thing I remember clearly was being in a kitchen and smelling CHEESE! It didn't take long to find it; it was only a bit of rind and fairly dry, but how I ate!

Refreshed by this, my first real meal in many a day, I began to explore the house. It was painfully bare; clean, but bare. Very little furniture; and that all hard and shiny; no soft things, or dusty corners where a chap could curl up and have a good warm nap. It was cold too, almost as cold as outdoors.

Upstairs were two rooms. One was dark, and from it came the sound of snoring; the other had a light, and the sound of sneezing. I chose the sneezy one.

In a large chair close to the fireplace sat a short, thick, round-faced man, trying to write by the light of a candle. Every few moments he would sneeze, and his square-rimmed glasses would fly off. Reaching for these he would drop his pen; by the time he found that and got settled to write, the candle would flicker from the draught; when that calmed down, the sneezing would start again, and so it went. He was not accomplishing much in the way of writing.

Of course I recognized him. Everyone in Philadelphia knew the great Doctor Benjamin Franklin, scientist, inventor, printer, editor, author, soldier, statesman and philosopher.

He didn't look great or famous that night, though, he just looked cold — and a bit silly.

He was wrapped in a sort of dressing-gown, with a dirty fur collar; and on his head was perched an odd-looking fur cap.

The cap interested me, for I was still chilled to the bone — and this room was just as bleak as the rest of the house. It was a rather disreputable-looking affair, that cap; but in one side of it I had spied a hole — just about my size.

Up the back of the chair I went, and under cover of the next fit of sneezes, in I slid. What a cozy place *that* was! Plenty of room to move about a bit; just enough air; such soft fur, and such warmth!

"Here," said I to myself, "is my home. No more cold streets, or cellars, or vestries. HERE I stay."

At the moment, of course, I never realized how true this was to prove. All I realized was that I was warm, well fed and — oh, so sleepy!

And so to bed.

I slept late the next morning. When I woke my fur-cap home was hanging on the bedpost, and I in it.

Dr. Franklin was again crouched over the fire attempting to write, between fits of sneezing and glasses-hunting. The fire, what there was of it, was smoking, and the room was as cold as ever.

"Not wishing to be critical —" I said. "But, perhaps, a bit of wood on that smoky ember that you seem to consider a fire might —"

"WASTE NOT, WANT NOT," said he, severe, and went on writing.

"Well, just suppose," I said, "just suppose you spend two or three weeks in bed with pewmonia — would that be a waste or —"

"It would be," said he, putting on a log; "whatever your name might be."

"Amos," said I. . . . "And then there'd be doctors' bills —"

"BILLS!" said he, shuddering, and put on two more logs, quick. The fire blazed up then, and the room became a little better, but not much.

"Dr. Franklin," I said, "that fireplace is all wrong."

"You might call me Ben — just plain Ben," said he. . . . "What's wrong with it?"

"Well, for one thing, most of the heat goes up the chimney. And for another, you can't get *around* it. Now, outside our church there used to be a Hot-chestnut Man. Sometimes, when business was rushing, he'd drop a chestnut. Pop was always on the look-out, and almost before it touched the ground he'd have it in his sack — and down to the vestry with it. There he'd put it in the middle of the floor — and we'd all gather round for the warmth.

"Twenty-eight of us it would heat, and the room as well. It was all because it was OUT IN THE OPEN, not stuck in a hole in the wall like that fireplace."

"Amos," he interrupts, excited, "there's an idea there! But we couldn't move the fire out into the middle of the room."

"We could if there were something to put it in, iron or something."

"But the smoke?" he objected.

"PIPE," said I, and curled up for another nap.

I didn't get it, though.

Ben rushed off downstairs, came back with a great armful of junk, dumped it on the floor and was off for more. No one could have slept, not even a dormouse. After a few trips he had a big pile of things there. There were scraps of iron, tin and wire. There were a couple of old warming-pans, an iron oven, three flatirons, six pot-lids, a wire birdcage and an anvil. There were saws, hammers, pincers, files, drills, nails, screws, bolts, bricks, sand, and an old broken sword.

He drew out a sort of plan and went to work. With the clatter he made there was no chance of a nap, so I helped all I could, picking up the nuts and screws and tools that he dropped — and his glasses.

Ben was a fair terror for work, once he was interested. It was almost noon before he stopped for a bit of rest. We looked over what had been done and it didn't look so bad — considering.

It was shaped much like a small fireplace set up on legs, with two iron doors on the front and a smoke pipe running from the back to the fireplace. He had taken the andirons out of the fireplace and boarded that up so we wouldn't lose any heat up the chimney.

Ben walked around looking at it, proud as could be, but worried.

"The floor," he says. "It's the floor that troubles me, Amos. With those short legs and that thin iron bottom, the heat —"

"Down on the docks," said I, "we used to hear the ship-rats telling how the sailors build their cooking fires on board ship. A layer of sand right on the deck, bricks on top of that, and —"

"Amos," he shouts, "you've got it!" and rushed for the bricks and sand. He put a layer of sand in the bottom of the affair, the bricks on top of that, and then set the andirons in.

It looked pretty promising.

"Eureka!" he exclaims, stepping back to admire it — and tripping over the saw. "Straighten things up a bit, Amos, while I run and get some logs."

"*Don't* try to run," I said. "And by the way, do you come through the pantry on the way up?"

"Why?" he asked.

"In some ways, Ben," I said, "you're fairly bright, but in others you're just plain dull. The joy of creating may be meat and drink to you; but as for me, a bit of cheese —"

He was gone before I finished, but when he came back with the logs he did have a fine slab of cheese, a loaf of rye bread, and a good big tankard of ale.

We put in some kindling and logs and lit her up. She drew fine, and Ben was so proud and excited that I had to be rather sharp with him before he would settle down to food. Even then he was up every minute, to admire it from a new angle.

Before we'd finished even one sandwich, the room had warmed up like a summer afternoon.

"Amos," says he, "we've done it!"

"Thanks for the WE," I said. "I'll remember it."

Author

Robert Lawson is considered one of America's finest authors and illustrators of children's books. He began his career as an illustrator. *Ben and Me* was the first book that he both wrote and illustrated. It was so well-liked that it was made into a cartoon by Walt Disney. Lawson is the only person to have won both the Caldecott Medal and the Newbery Medal.

Concord Hymn
by Ralph Waldo Emerson

SUNG AT THE COMPLETION OF THE BATTLE MONUMENT,[1]
JULY 4, 1837

By the rude bridge that arched the flood,
   Their flag to April's breeze unfurled,
Here once the embattled farmers stood
   And fired the shot heard round the world.

The foe long since in silence slept;
   Alike the conqueror silent sleeps;
And Time the ruined bridge has swept
   Down the dark stream which seaward creeps.

On this green bank, by this soft stream,
   We set to-day a votive stone;
That memory may their deed redeem,
   When, like our sires, our sons are gone.

Spirit, that made those heroes dare
   To die, and leave their children free,
Bid Time and Nature gently spare
   The shaft we raise to them and thee.

---

[1]Commemorating the battles of Lexington and
Concord, April 19, 1775.

Taming the West

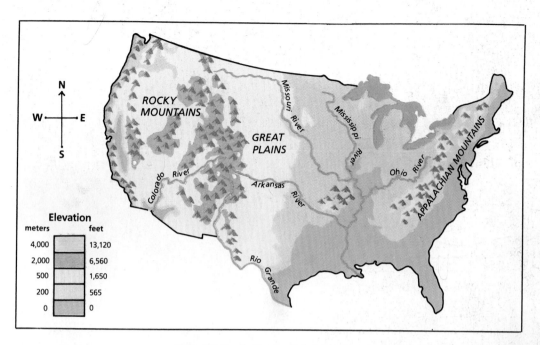

Elevation

meters	feet
4,000	13,120
2,000	6,560
500	1,650
200	565
0	0

The United States of America

The Last West

When people from Europe first migrated to North America, they established colonies in the East, along the Atlantic Coast. To the west lay the frontier, the edge of the territory where Europeans had not yet settled. This area was vast, but the early colonists paid little attention to it. Their ties were still with Europe.

In the mid-1700's, the frontier began to shift westwards. First, settlers pushed into the Appalachian Mountains. By the early 1800's, pioneers were staking out claims as far west as the Missouri River. When gold was discovered in California in 1848, thousands of people rushed to the Pacific Coast. Many followed the overland trails that had been blazed by early explorers. To get to the West Coast, they had to cross an "ocean of grass" — and most of them were glad to get across it.

If you look at the map, you will see that for a long time a vast area of our country — from the Missouri River to the Rocky Mountains — was left empty. The last frontier was not the Pacific Coast. It was the central plains of North America.

The Great American Desert

The plains were unlike anything Americans had seen before. This was not an environment that made new settlement easy. Winter winds tore across the flat grasslands, bringing icy cold and raging blizzards.

In the summer, the winds were very hot. The few rivers became shallow and muddy. The winds brought lightning, hail, and violent tornadoes that twisted across the open land.

Although the plains were covered with grass, few trees grew there. Without trees, there was no wood to build houses or fences, and no fuel to cook or keep warm with. No shade shielded the plains from the summer sun. No barrier broke the force of the constant winds. People called the treeless plains the Great American Desert.

Expansion of Settled Area by:

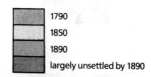

1790
1850
1890
largely unsettled by 1890

U.S. Settlement: 1790–1890

Wagon Trains

How, you may wonder, was this region ever settled? For one thing, the trip to the Pacific Coast was long and hard. Wagons broke down; horses and oxen died. People got sick or ran out of food. Some could simply go no farther and decided to stop where they were. They settled on the plains.

Former Civil War soldiers and freed slaves came too, looking for a new life. Immigrants from Europe came to find land that would be their own. These first settlers took up all the acreage near the few rivers and streams where cottonwood trees grew. For the thousands who came after 1870, there were only the arid plains left. At least by then there was a railroad, and that made the trip easier.

A Transcontinental Railroad

By the 1860's there were railroad lines throughout most of the eastern part of the United States and in California. After the Civil War, the government chartered two companies to construct a railroad that reached all the way across the country. With the transcontinental railroad, a journey that had once taken months could now be made in weeks.

Millions of Acres

Together, the two railroad companies had laid almost 1,800 miles of track. For each mile of track, the government had given the railroad companies ten square miles of land to sell. The companies advertised all over the East for settlers. They sent agents to Europe to spread news of cheap land for sale in America. Many thousands came. The rush to settle the plains had begun.

In 1862, Congress passed the Homestead Act. Under this law, any person could have 160 acres of land free if he or she built a house on the land and lived there for five years. This brought thousands of people from the East and from Europe. As these people soon found out, life on the vast and windswept plains was far from easy.

The daring men and women who settled the plains had to find new ways to:

— build houses
— find water
— farm the land
— protect their crops
— plow the soil

New inventions helped the pioneers solve some of their problems. The pioneers had to find the solutions to other problems for themselves.

Sodbusters

The grass that covered the dry plains had long, strong roots that reached deep into the earth. (This top layer of soil and grass is called *sod*.) When the farmers started to prepare the soil for planting, they found that they could not cut through the tangled mass of grass, roots, and soil. Their iron plowshares either stuck or broke.

173

A sodbuster family

Back East, one person and a horse could plow a field. On the plains, teams of six horses found it hard to pull a plow through the tough sod. Only when the homesteaders could afford to buy the newly invented steel plow could they turn the soil easily.

As homesteaders wrestled with the tough sod, however, they soon realized that it would make good building material. There was a seemingly endless supply of sod. It could be plowed up in long strips, and then cut into "bricks."

Sod Houses

Many of the first homesteaders lived in dugouts — caves dug into the side of a bank. These often had a dirt floor, three dirt walls (a canvas wagon made a fourth), and a roof of earth. A dugout was a dark and dusty place.

Once they learned to prepare sod bricks, some homesteaders built houses of sod.

Sod houses had their drawbacks. Snakes, mice, and insects were often part of the household. Dirt filtered down from the roof and walls. However, there were also advantages. The thick walls were fireproof and kept the family cool in summer and warm in winter.

Water and Windmills

In the East water was plentiful, but for the plains settlers getting water was a major problem.

Homesteaders without access to wells had to load their wagons with barrels and drive to the nearest river or stream to fill

A prairie windmill

them. This could mean a trip of many miles and many hours by wagon. The water they brought back would have to suffice for drinking, cooking, bathing, and washing clothes until another trip could be made.

Under these conditions, people were naturally eager to have wells on their own land. Digging wells was no easy task for the homesteaders, however. They might have to go down three hundred feet to reach water. Even after drilling rigs were invented, most wells were dug by hand — shovelful by shovelful. It was a back-breaking, dangerous task.

Even with a well, bringing up the water was a slow and tedious job. It had to be done one bucketful at a time. The homesteaders solved this problem with the help of the wind and technology. The wind was something they always had with them, a ready source of free energy. They learned to build windmills to harness this energy — and soon there were windmills everywhere.

Fences

Another problem facing homesteaders was protection of their crops. Stray cattle and wild animals often trampled the wheat growing in the field. They ate or crushed everything in the vegetable garden. There was no wood or stone available, which people used in the East for building enclosures. There was wire, but no one had yet designed a wire fence that could keep cattle out.

Then in 1873 Joseph Glidden solved the problem with the invention of barbed wire. Glidden had been thinking about the thorned shrub. He took two long strands of wire and twisted them together. Between these strands, he twisted short pieces of wire with sharp ends, which stuck out like the thorns on the shrub.

The points, or barbs, discouraged cattle or other animals from pushing against the wire and breaking the fence. Glidden's barbed wire was a real boon to the plains farmers, enabling them to keep stray animals out of their fields. At first, the barbed-wire fences caused serious trouble between the farmers and the ranchers, who wanted their animals to be able to graze freely on the open range. However, as more and more settlers came to farm the land and fence the prairies, the vast open range gradually disappeared.

New Ways of Farming

Eventually, the settlers found new and better ways to farm the plains. They planted a hardy kind of wheat that did not need much water. They learned how to preserve moisture in the soil by "dry farming."

Dry farming meant plowing very deeply, and keeping the planted earth broken up so that it did not become hard. The farmers kept a layer of dust over their fields and let some fields lie fallow every other year, giving a two-year supply of moisture for the next crop.

Fortunately for the plains settlers, many new farm implements were being invented. Mechanical reapers, threshers, and binders made the farmers' work easier, and allowed them to plant larger areas.

Prairie farmers

The End of the Great American Desert

In many ways, life on the plains was more primitive than life in the East. In fact, most settlers lived the way Easterners had lived more than a hundred years earlier.

Each family had to provide for most of its own needs. Parents were often the doctors, nurses, and teachers of the family. Candles, soap, and clothing were made at home. The family worked together to build houses and barns, grow food for the table, and raise the crops that were sold for money.

Together, the family shared many experiences — some of them difficult. They lived through droughts that withered their crops. They watched helplessly as hordes of grasshoppers ate every green thing growing. Their endurance was tested, but the settlers who survived those trying early years transformed the "Great American Desert" into the "Breadbasket of the World." They were the true tamers of the West.

An excerpt from

Winter Wheat

by Jeanne Williams

Cobie Lander moved to Harmony, Kansas with her parents and five sisters — Rebecca, the oldest, the twins Liese and Lilibet, Rachel, and four-year-old Gaby. They moved from Russia in 1874 so they would be free to follow their Mennonite religion. Life was harsh on the prairie and because the Landers had little money, they traded work for help and supplies. Cobie helped out by working for their neighbors the Wieses one day a week. The Landers found pleasure in their close family life and in new friendships. Among their friends were Stede Martin, who spoke German, the Mennonites' language, and Bedad, who had lived on the prairie for years. Both helped the Landers with their farming. Prairie life was difficult and unpredictable, though, and danger could appear often.

Cobie's Courage

One cold Friday morning, Rachel went to school alone because the twins had feverish colds. Father was spending the day helping Simon Schmidt make furniture, so he was able to drive Cobie to the Wieses' on his way. It was one of those long, gray bleak days that seemed to stretch on and on, especially since Mrs. Wiese was in bed with an ague that periodically troubled her.

Cobie put the four o'clock tea of bread, butter, zwieback, and tea, out for Heinrich and Elder Wiese, and carried Mrs. Wiese's to her on a tray. As soon as she had cleared away the dishes and set the table for supper, she gave the borscht a final stir and started home through powdery dry snow halfway up to her knees.

It was slow moving and she was exhausted as well as cold when she trudged up to the sodhouse to find Mutti[1] watching anxiously from the window.

---

[1]**Mutti (moo'tē):** a nickname for mother

"You haven't seen little Rachel?"

Cobie stopped working off the sheepskin coat. "Isn't she home yet?"

Mutti shook her head. "I thought perhaps she had waited to walk with you."

Though only a little after four, darkness would fall by six. It had been snowing about the time school let out. Rachel might have lost her way. But the snow had stopped now. She should have come home by this hour even if she had been mixed up for a time by the storm.

"Father's not home yet?"

Mutti shook her head. Cobie pulled the sheepskin back on, wrapped the scarf more securely about her ears and face, which still felt half-frozen.

"Oh, Cobie!" cried Liese, snuffling with her cold and with alarm. "Don't you get lost, too!"

"I won't," said Cobie, more bravely than she felt.

"Child —" began Mutti, and then pressed her hands tight together. Tears showed in her eyes. "Be careful!"

"I'll just go towards school and shout now and then," said Cobie. "I can follow my tracks back. But if I can't find her, I'll go ask Mr. Martin and Bedad to help."

"Can you find their place?"

"Mr. Martin says he can walk right out of the school door and keep going straight east to the tipi," Liese put in. "He's promised to take the whole school there someday when the weather turns fine."

"As if it could ever do that!" sniffed Rebecca. "Don't go, Cobie! Rachel's probably throwing snowballs or idling with the other children. I need help to do the milking and other chores with the twins sick and Father not back."

"If you'll look for Rachel, I'll do the chores," said Cobie. "But one of us has to go — now!"

"Always pretending to be a heroine!" Rebecca scolded.

Cobie shrugged and started out. Rebecca caught her in a tight hug. "I'm sorry, Cobie! Forgive me! Of course, someone must go and I — I'm afraid! I'm afraid to go look for my little sister!"

"There's plenty to do here," Cobie said. She could find only pity in her heart for Rebecca, so beautiful, so unfitted to this raw land. "I don't mind going, truly! I'll be back soon, Mutti, don't worry!"

She plunged into a cold that stung her face, hands, and feet, which had not had a chance to warm thoroughly. How she hoped Father would drive into sight! Sol,[2] who was singly pulling the wagon that day, would scarcely show against the snow except for the brass balls on the end of his horns, but the green wagon would stand out plainly.

It did not come into view though, and Cobie soon had to turn in the opposite direction to reach the school, abandoning the hope of meeting her father. Every hundred yards

---

[2]**Sol** (sōl): the Lander's ox

or so she called Rachel's name, got a sinking feeling when there was no answer. At least it wasn't snowing, and there was no wind to blow over her tracks.

The other schoolchildren lived on the opposite side of the schoolhouse, on farms scattered for several miles. Their families would help search if necessary, yet Cobie's first impulse had been to ask Stede and Bedad.

"Rachel!" shouted Cobie, so loudly that her throat hurt.

How could the child just vanish? There were no thick woods hereabouts, no gorges or ravines. A person could get lost in a blinding storm, but Rachel knew that country well enough so that she should quickly right herself when she could see.

There were coyotes and wolves, but they didn't attack people unless they were hydrophobic, and, of course, in that state, skunks and even squirrels bit. That seemed almost as unlikely as an Indian raid.

But hadn't Bedad warned them about old abandoned wells? He had said discouraged homesteaders often left without bothering to board over such holes, and there were a few abandoned claims near the school. On the way to church, Cobie had glimpsed several caved-in dugouts some distance from the road.

If Rachel had strayed in the snow and *if* there were an open well, she could have fallen into it. Cobie's spine felt colder than her feet as she pictured Rachel lying in a hole, perhaps drowned, perhaps with a broken leg.

Across the white prairie, Cobie saw one of the ruined dugouts. She hurried toward it, shouting, halted some distance from the house. Floundering around in the failing light could pitch her into a well herself.

But what if Rachel were unconscious or — dead? Cobie shuddered, pushed on for where she remembered seeing the other dugout. If she didn't find her sister there, she'd go east of the school and get Stede and Bedad to help her before it was completely dark! And surely, surely, Father would come soon!

But panting and sobbing through the drifts that came above her knees in places, Cobie felt entirely alone and helpless.

"Rachel!" she cried. Her breath turned to frosty smoke. What if her sister were trapped out in such weather? "Rachel!"

Cobie tripped hard, over the skeleton of a cow. Kicking free of the ribs that settled again under the snow, she pushed on. A battered cattle shelter loomed ahead, snow-covered thatch slanting to the ground while the roof pole jutted into the air. Beyond it was the doorless ruin of the other dugout.

Cobie stopped, caught her breath, and cupped her hands.

"Rachel! Rachel!"

Her voice died slowly, seeming to mock her. It was no use. She must get help. It was almost dark, and somewhere on this prairie Rachel might be lying hurt or dead.

For a moment she thought the faint sound was an echo of her own cry. Then it came again, dim, moaning.

"Rachel!" Cobie shouted, running forward. "Where are you?"

"Down here! Be careful — you'll fall, too!"

Cobie moved gingerly toward the voice. "Are you all right?"

"I — I think so. I hurt my knee, but I can stand on it. But Cobie! Help me get out! I'm so cold! I've been so scared!"

Cobie edged near the mouth of the well. Her sister's pale face showed in the darkness from fifteen feet below.

"I don't have a rope," Cobie said. "My scarf's not long enough. Rachel, I'll have to go for help!"

"Don't leave me!" Rachel wailed. "I — I can't stay here anymore! Please, Cobie, get me out!"

"I want to, dearest! Can you climb part way? Is there anything down there to help?"

"I tried to get out. There's a wide casting around the bottom almost as tall as I am and I got on it and worked up a little way, but I fell back down."

"How wide is the well?"

Rachel snuffed, estimated, and said after a moment, "When I stretch out my arms, I can touch both sides."

"Could you find Mr. Martin's from here? It's beginning to get dark."

Rachel began to weep. "Of — of course I could find him if I weren't down here! He's just east of the school. Don't make fun, Cobie! Please get me out!"

"Listen!" Cobie spoke so sharply that Rachel gulped down her sobs. "One of us has to bring help, but if you're afraid to stay here, maybe I can get down and then boost you up on my shoulders. But you've got to make it, Rachel, or we'll both be stuck down there!"

"I — I'll make it if you hold me! Please, Cobie, please don't go off and leave me!"

Cobie hurried over to the falling-down cattle shelter and dragged the roof pole free. It was still sound, it would hold her. She laid it across the well, gripped it and lowered herself, stretching out her legs to feel the sides.

Releasing the pole, she slid till her feet lodged on opposite sides of the casing. "Up with you!" she commanded, leaning to give Rachel a hand. "Get on top of the casing the way you did before. Then I'll bend as much as I can to let you climb up on my shoulders. From there you can reach the pole and scramble out."

"But you'll have to stay in this nasty dark hole!"

"One of us must! So hurry!"

Stubble and earth showered down as Rachel's toes dug into the unlined sides of the pit. Cobie pushed with all her might at her sister's shoes. Gasping, Rachel dragged herself out. A final rain of snow and rubble came down. Cobie shook it out of her face and slid to the bottom. There was no use trying to hold that strained position while Rachel fetched Stede and Bedad.

"I'll run all the way!" Rachel shouted from above.

"Just don't get lost!"

It was too dark to see much of her prison. Rachel had trampled down the snow. There was no water in the well. Perhaps its going dry had been one of the reasons the homesteader had left.

The hours poor Rachel had been trapped here must have seemed an eternity. Even knowing that help would come shortly didn't make it pleasant. Cobie sat down, huddling her arms and face against her knees for warmth.

Rachel was found. She wasn't hurt. But, oh, supposing she had broken her neck in the fall! Or that Bedad's warning hadn't echoed in Cobie's brain and Rachel had frozen to death before she was found!

Thank you, dear God, for helping me find her! Thank you that she wasn't hurt! During the time she waited in the old well, the last of Cobie's grudge toward Rachel for living through the illness that had killed Schatzie melted away. From now on, this younger sister would be especially precious.

It seemed that help would never come. By the time voices roused her, Cobie had almost dozed off in exhaustion. She sprang up eagerly.

"Here we are!" Rachel shouted.

"We'll have you up in a jiffy!" came Stede's reassuring voice. "Slip this loop under your shoulders, hold on to the rope, and we'll haul you out!"

In seconds she stood in the snow, hugged tight in Rachel's arms. Bedad gave her a rough dusting off. "I'll board this well up tomorrow — should have done it long ago!"

"For tonight let's get you girls home to your folks," said Stede, coiling up the rope and tying it to his saddle horn.

He got in the saddle and helped Cobie up behind him on Raven. Bedad and Rachel occupied Belshazzer, who snorted at the burden and shambled through the snow as if utterly disgusted.

It was now dark, but the snow shone underfoot and let one see dark shapes at a distance. Halfway home, Stede said, "There's someone coming!"

"Cobie!" came the faint sound. "Is that you?"

"Yes!" cried Stede. "She found Rachel!"

In minutes Rachel tumbled off Belshazzer to embrace her father, and shortly after that they were all in the sodhouse warming themselves and eating supper.

That night, when Rachel snuggled up to Cobie, Cobie held her with grateful love.

Author

Jeanne Williams, who grew up in the Midwest, became interested in the history of the frontier while at college. In her books, she drew upon her study of history and her grandparents' tales of their homesteading days. *Winter Wheat,* from which the excerpt you have read was taken, was a Notable Children's Trade Book in the Field of Social Studies.

Night Journeys

written by Avi

Houghton Mifflin Literature

In the selections you have just read from *Building a Nation,* the struggle to establish new lives in a new land took a variety of forms. Courage, persistence, good judgement, and faith were common ingredients in each.

The determination found in these stories will now be echoed in *Night Journeys* by Avi, the story of two runaway servants during the late 1700's. Their experience leads them to understand what human beings are willing to pay in return for their dignity.

3

Confronting Nature

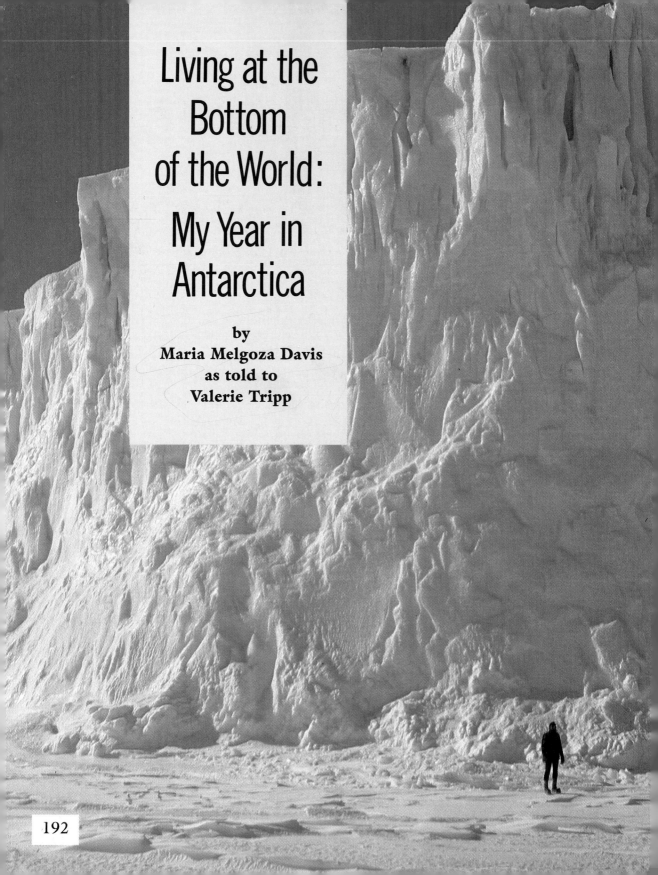

Living at the
Bottom
of the World:

My Year in
Antarctica

by
Maria Melgoza Davis
as told to
Valerie Tripp

192

Imagine a world white with snow all year, where it can be so quiet you can hear your heart beat and so cold metal will freeze to your skin. That's where Maria Melgoza Davis and her husband Randy lived for a year — one of the wildest, windiest, coldest, snowiest places on Earth — Antarctica.

In Antarctica the seasons are reversed, with summer in January and winter in June. There are no cities, super highways, shopping centers, schools, or office buildings. It seems an unlikely place for Maria Melgoza Davis, who grew up in bustling towns in Mexico and Southern California. Why was she there?

Maria and Randy went to Antarctica to study the behavior of the Weddell seals. It is believed that these unique seals were named for James Weddell, the British navigator who explored Antarctica in the 1800's. Weddell seals are the only seals known to survive under shorefast ice, ice that is attached to land. Maria and Randy wanted to find out how the seals keep warm and what they eat during the long cold season. This kind of information may someday help humans survive in cold places.

What was it like for Maria to live at the bottom of the world? This is her story of her year in Antarctica.

January

I'll never forget landing at McMurdo Station, the largest United States base in Antarctica. It was January, the Antarctic summer, a bright blue day. I had never seen snow on the ground before. It was lovely, bright, and white. I couldn't wait to get outside and touch it, but when the door of the plane opened, the air was so cold it felt like a solid wall. I wondered how I would make it to the airport building without freezing.

If the cold was a small shock, the landscape was a big surprise. Antarctica is spectacular! Most people think it is a desolate place, just barren stretches of white snow, but that's wrong. It is one of the most beautiful places on Earth. There are dark purple and black mountains looming on the horizon and brown beaches at the shore. When the sun comes out, it bathes the snow in a golden glow. As it reflects off the ice crystals, it makes rainbows in the sky.

By the end of January, Randy and I were settled in our camp, about twelve miles south of McMurdo, at the foot of White Island. Our camp wasn't actually *on* White Island but rather on the permanent ice shelf that surrounds it. This shelf is so thick and hard that airplanes can land on it. Yet it floats on the water; it is not solid land.

We had two small rectangular huts, one for living and one for working. They were connected by a passageway that served as a wind

shelter and storage area. We also had a Quonset hut for our electric generator and our vehicles. We had snowmobiles for short trips. For longer trips we had a heavy, orange, land vehicle, with treads like a tank.

What a great day it was when we first saw the seals! They are graceful creatures, with sleek, torpedo-shaped bodies. Adults can be seven feet long and weigh a thousand pounds. They have huge dark eyes and short soft fur that is brown or black with white spots. They have small flippers on their sides and a big hind flipper. When their jaws are closed, the seals look as if they are smiling. When they yawn, their jaws open wide to show a big pink mouth.

We counted twenty-five seals on White Island and made a chart for each seal, noting its size, color, sex, and approximate age and weight. This was summer, and we observed that the seals seemed to take it easy. They lay around on the ice as if they were working on a suntan. They dozed, then dove into the water to catch a fish, and then dozed some more.

I could tell by the bones and shell fragments I sometimes found that the seals ate fish and krill. Krill are tiny shrimplike creatures that are food for whales, penguins, fish, and squid. The fact that the Weddell seals stayed strong and healthy eating krill was important. As people take up more of the earth's space, and less land is available for farming, people may have to turn to other food sources — such as krill from the ocean.

The seals had no fear of us, so we could get close enough to attach time-depth recorders to their hind flippers. The recorders registered how frequently the seals dove, how long they stayed underwater, and how deep they dove. The seals' more frequent dives lasted for ten or twenty minutes and were about four hundred feet deep. However, we were surprised to learn that the seals were capable of holding their breath for an hour and of diving to a depth of almost two thousand feet. The deepest dive ever made by a human wearing scuba equipment is only 437 feet. To avoid lung damage, the seals expel air gradually as they dive.

February

Once the last supply plane left in February, I knew I was committed to spending the winter in Antarctica. This is called wintering over. Planes can't fly safely in the extreme cold of an Antarctic winter.

Ships can't make their way through the ice-clogged water. Except during extreme emergencies, no one comes in or goes out for at least four months.

March

In March, as autumn began, the surface of the sea froze. The air temperature dropped lower every day. The sun set — and would not rise again until September.

196

To our surprise, the seals disappeared. We knew they could not live in the severe winter weather, but we didn't expect them to vanish into thin air.

We soon learned that they had vanished into the water under the ice. We couldn't see them but we knew they were there because we could hear them. On land, seals bleat and baa like sheep. Underwater, they sing. We stood on the ice and heard the seals peep, chirp, gurgle, and whistle, and knew they were under our feet.

For several weeks we recorded the noises the seals made underwater. We lowered a special underwater microphone, called a hydrophone, into the water and connected the hydrophone to equipment in our hut. Randy and I took turns listening to the seals, and we made tape recordings of their mysterious vocalizations. We think the seals use their chirps, buzzes, and whistles to communicate with each other. Perhaps the sounds are warnings of danger or invitations to share a good fishing spot or a breathing hole.

To avoid the cold, the seals spend the entire winter in water. The water is warmer than the air even though it is under a thick crust of ice. There the seals are protected from the wind and are close to their food source. Their blubber, a thick layer of fat, insulates them against the cold water.

Since seals are mammals, they have to breathe air. How do they get air through the ice? The answer was another surprise. In one place on the Island, the ocean tide had made a crack in the thick ice. Here, where the ice was only a few inches thick, the clever Weddell seals chewed breathing holes. They held onto the ice with their lower teeth and sawed back and forth until they broke through to fresh air. If the breathing hole froze over, we would observe a seal chew through the new ice to open it again. Sometimes a few seals would share a breathing hole. Weddell seals are the only seals who chew breathing holes in the ice this way.

We discovered the breathing holes when we walked along the ice next to the crack and heard the seals puffing out air like a bellows. We watched the breathing holes for hours and learned that the seals usually stayed under for fifteen or twenty minutes and then came up for a breather. When they wanted to sleep, they propped themselves upright, nose in the breathing hole, body under the ice, and slept.

April

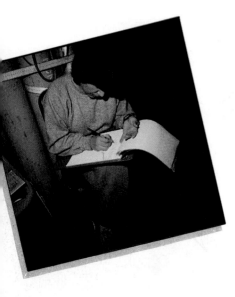

We observed the seals every day during April except when the weather was very stormy and we were hut-bound. Then we listened to our tapes of music, read, played games, or rode our exercise bike. There was also work to do, keeping our logs of weather and activities up to date.

People had warned me about the isolation and cold of the long, dark winter. Some find it terrifying, but I didn't. On calm nights, the brilliant full moon was like a nighttime sun. It seemed huge and close, and three-dimensional. The stars were big and dazzling. Auroras — streamers of light — would dance across the sky like silver dust. I never tired of the winter sky. I always thought, "This is the closest I will ever come to being on another planet."

May

In May, Randy and I moved our camp after it had been buried in snow. Before we had put all the finishing touches on these new quarters, we were hit by a terrible storm. We were sleeping when the storm hit. The shrieking wind woke me. It was completely dark inside the hut. Suddenly, crash! — a shock of frigid air swirling with snow blasted into the hut. I jumped out of my bunk and saw that the wind had ripped the east door off its hinges and blown it into the hut. The torrent through the gaping hole was battering the west wall. The escape hatch in the roof burst open. The chain holding it shut had snapped.

Randy and I struggled to prop the door back in its frame. I held it in place while Randy tried to tie the west door open to relieve the wind's pressure on the wall. With a wham, the west door slammed shut. The knob was frozen, and Randy was outside. Somehow, he managed to pull the door open and get inside. Meanwhile, I leaned against the east door with all my might, but it was like trying to keep a lid on a geyser. Randy came

to help me. Together, we nailed a board across the door. Then we tied the escape hatch shut with a rope. When we finished, I realized I was standing waist-deep in snow. The hut was blown, battered, and full of snow, but we were safe.

June

Every four weeks Randy and I would go to McMurdo. I had a darkroom there because one of my jobs was to develop all our film. During our year in Antarctica I developed over 3,400 pictures, mostly of seals. On these trips we could see movies and go to the library for new books. We also got enough food, fuel, and supplies to last a month. One great treat was freshly baked bread made right at McMurdo.

June 21, the first day of winter, is called the winter solstice. We had a big party in McMurdo to celebrate. Now the sun would get closer to the horizon and the days get longer. The sky is very dramatic as winter ends. Where the sun comes up, the sky appears as red as fire, while on the other horizon, it is black.

July

Earlier we had drilled a hole in the ice. Every day we lowered traps through the hole to catch fish so that we could tell what was there for the seals to eat. We caught sea spiders, isopods, krill, and ice fish.

We also lowered instruments to measure the water currents and temperature.

Sometimes Randy dove into the water through the hole. He wore thick underwear, a dry suit, and two pairs of gloves to protect himself from the cold. With spotlights, he used his underwater camera to take pictures of the under surface of the ice and the seals. The spotlights helped us photograph the seals as they swam through the dark water under the ice — though how the seals navigate in the dark is still a mystery. The hydrophone recordings helped us keep track of our wet friends during those three months, when their only window to the outside world was their breathing hole at the tidal crack.

August–September

One day we drove to the north side of White Island in our land vehicle. It was a gray day. Everything was the same dull color — a condition called white out. It was hard to tell the difference between the snow on the ground and the sky. Randy seemed to be walking in mid-air when he got out of the land vehicle to look for seals. When we were driving home I was suddenly jerked hard against the back of the seat. I looked behind me and saw a huge hole. The back part of the vehicle had fallen into a crack called a crevasse. Randy

gunned the motor, and we pulled out just in time to avoid getting trapped under the ice.

Later, we went back to the crevasse because we thought the seals might be using it. They weren't. The crevasse was eighty feet deep, and beautiful. Inside, it was like an ice palace: a deep, shining blue cave full of huge, sculptured chunks of ice.

October–November

In spring, October and November, the seals came back to the top of the ice. It was a happy occasion, made happier by the births of baby seal pups soon after.

The seal pups were born right on the ice. A newborn seal's fur, called lanugo, is wet and soon freezes into a stiff coat of ice. The pup begins to shiver, which warms it up and makes its furry coat fluff out and dry off.

When a seal pup is only a few days old, its mother starts to teach it to swim. The baby seal starts out making short, five-minute dives. Gradually, the pup dives deeper and longer. After six weeks, the baby is expected to find its own food and make its own air holes. The seal pup is not a helpless baby for long.

December

It was a sad day in December when Randy and I left Antarctica. As I took a last look around, it seemed to me that the snow glittered and sparkled even more than usual, and the sky was a more brilliant blue. It was as if Antarctica had polished itself up to look its very best on my last day.

Our trip was a scientific success. We had lived with the Weddell seals for a year. We learned how they survived the winter, what they ate, and how they behaved in all four seasons.

I learned a lot about myself too. I had tested my endurance to the limit and found I was capable of doing more than just surviving. Like the seal, I had adapted to Antarctica's demanding climate. I could do my share of hard work and stay cheerful in dark isolation.

The adventure of living with the seals and the beauty of Antarctica far outweighed every inconvenience, hardship, and danger of the year. I will always think of my year at the bottom of the world as the most exciting and the best year of my life.

Author

Valerie Tripp, a professional writer for over ten years, especially likes writing for young people. She has visited every state except Alaska. She likes traveling the back roads through small towns. This way she gets to meet and talk with people who often become her friends and sometimes become characters in her books.

HOW DO THEY FIND IT?

by George Sullivan

TWISTER!

THE WORST TORNADO

The Time: Wednesday, March 18, 1925.

The Place: Murphysboro, a small coal-mining town in southern Illinois.

The Setting: It is almost three o'clock in the afternoon. For a March day it has been unseasonably warm — hot, actually — and sticky, very sticky. There are menacing gray clouds in the sky to the west, and the rumble of thunder is beginning to be heard.

At the Joiner Elementary School it is an hour before dismissal. Because of the growing darkness, classroom lights have been put on. Teachers glance out of the windows anxiously at what they believe to be a gathering thunderstorm.

But this is no thunderstorm. A nearby cloud has become heavy and black, and from beneath it stretches a column of whirling air in the shape of a long funnel. Heavy rain is falling and some hail. Brilliant flashes of lightning brighten the sky. Strong winds have begun to blow.

Now a strange, hissing sound is heard. It grows to a loud roar that sounds like a flight of passenger planes at rooftop level. The eerie funnel-shaped cloud, whirling madly, has touched the ground at the outskirts of Murphysboro. Soon it is raging through the very heart of the city, ripping trees up by their roots, lifting people bodily, tearing off rooftops and causing explosions.

Darkness descended on Murphysboro not long after the storm had swept on to the northeast. Survivors clambered over the great masses of debris in search of missing loved ones. From the jumble of metal and timber, the cries of the trapped and injured could be heard.

The Sisters Hospital, the Masonic Temple, the Elks Home, and any other large buildings that had escaped damage were turned into hospitals and morgues. The grisly business of identifying bodies was performed by illumination that came from candles and flashlights.

Because the telegraph lines were toppled, Murphysboro's

pleas for help were slow in reaching the outside world. The nearby town of Carbondale, miraculously untouched by the storm, was the first to respond, and by nightfall the hospitals there were filled to overflowing with the injured.

The tornado was only part of Murphysboro's ordeal. Around midnight the rescuers had to halt their work to fight fires that had broken out. Because the water mains were ruptured, the fires raged out of control. During the siege, a Mobile & Ohio train bound for St. Louis paused outside the city limits to pick up refugees.

A train passenger described what he saw: "It was a city completely in flames. People by the hundreds were running frantically through the streets, some clad only in blankets.

"Some were bleeding. Others wore bandages. Lifeless bodies lay in the streets. It was horrible."

The tornado that struck Murphysboro, Illinois, that spring day in 1925 was the worst in history. It began in eastern Missouri early in the afternoon, virtually wiping out the town of Annapolis. It tore its way across the Mississippi River into Illinois, rising in characteristic fashion and spreading out like a river delta. It then descended on Murphysboro and also De Soto, the town just to the northeast, laying both to waste.

It lifted again, then returned to earth to bludgeon West Frankfort, Parrish (where only one house was left standing), Crossville, and Mt. Carmel, a town close to the Indiana border. Princeton, Indiana, was yet another victim. After striking Princeton, the storm died out.

That tornado covered a path 220 miles long and, in some places, a mile wide. "A turbulent, boiling mass of blackness," is what one witness called it.

It took 689 lives, including 284 in Murphysboro. More than 100 dead and injured were counted at the Joiner Elementary School. Of the 11,000 people that lived in Murphysboro, more than 8,000 were rendered homeless.

Could such a terribly tragic storm occur today?

Tornadoes are not uncommon. In any given year, about 1,000 strike the United States. Some recent years have seen enormous tornado devastation. The U.S. National Weather Bureau called 1973 "The Year of the Tornado" because there were so many of them, and 1974, in terms of tornado severity, was even worse. So it is possible that a storm equaling the 1925 tornado in terms of size and destructive force could occur again.

But things are much different nowadays. Weather scientists are better able to locate tornadoes as they are beginning to form, and so, in many cases, to predict their arrival.

No matter where you live, you undoubtedly have heard broadcasts of a tornado watch or even a tornado warning. A tornado watch informs the public that conditions are ripe for a tornado to form. A tornado warning is more serious, telling the public that a tornado has actually been spotted or indicated by radar.

In its account of the storm that devastated Murphysboro in 1925, *The New York Times* made this observation: "The storm struck without warning, increasing in intensity as it progressed." "The storm struck without warning. . . ." That cannot happen today.

HOW TORNADOES BEHAVE

No storm is more violent than a tornado. None so little understood.

A tornado is much different from a hurricane. A hurricane is characterized by spiraling rain clouds that swirl about a comparatively calm eye. Its winds blow at about 100 miles an hour. Rarely do they reach as much as 150 miles an hour. Compare this to the death-dealing winds of the tornado, which have been measured at up to 300 miles an hour.

As for the matter of frequency, there are about 150 days a year when tornadoes occur in the United States. Hurricanes don't affect the mainland more than six or seven days a year on the average. And there are many states that never experience a hurricane, but every state has been struck by a tornado at one time or another.

Cyclone is a general term used to designate any type of rotary wind motion. Hurricanes are cyclones; so are tornadoes. Northeasters, those storms or gales which come roaring out of the northeast and which are very common to New England, are cyclones too.

In the Midwest, one hears the term "cyclone cellar," referring to the underground shelter a family uses for protection in severe storms. "Tornado cellar" would probably be a more precise term.

One misconception about tornadoes is that they are more common to the Midwest than to any other part of the country. They do often strike the Midwest, but they occur about as frequently in the South, in the broad, flat basin of the Mississippi and its tributaries.

There is also the area that one weather scientist calls the "Dixie tornado alley," a wide swath that begins in Louisiana and cuts through central Mississippi, north-central Alabama, and northern Georgia. This area has been the scene of some of the most devastating tornadoes in the nation's history, including the Mississippi Delta tornado of 1971 in which 130 lives were lost. It is a matter of fact that the highest death tolls over the years have been in the South, not in the Midwest.

Scientists have several theories explaining how tornadoes are formed. The two most frequently heard declare that tornadoes arise from either thermal forces or

Below: The ten-minute life history of one tornado

mechanical forces. Both sets of theorists agree that tornado formation requires layers of air in which there are sharp differences in temperature, moisture, density, and wind force.

The theorists who support thermal formation believe that as the imbalances become more acute, a mass of cold air overrides a warm-air layer. When this happens, nature tries to equalize conditions, and updrafts of warm air are the result. These upward-streaming currents begin to flow in a rotating pattern, leading to the familiar funnel-shaped cloud column.

Scientists who support the mechanical theory believe that the two currents of air are already in a state of rotation. The heavier, moisture-laden air works to restrict the diameter of the rotating column. As the diameter is decreased in size, the speed of the rotation increases.

"Imagine that you've got a rock on a string tied to your finger," says one meteorologist. "When you twirl the rock around your finger, it goes faster and faster as the radius of the string gets shorter and shorter."

Still other scientists hold that neither the thermal nor the

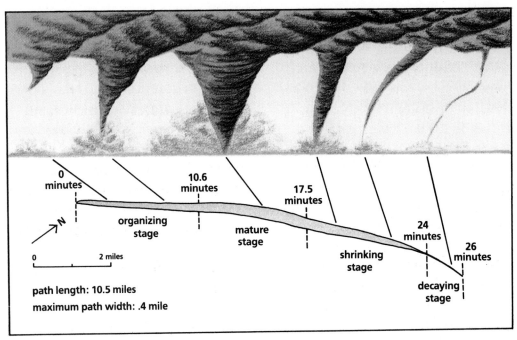

Above: Path and life stages of a typical tornado, lashing 26 minutes

mechanical process operates independently. Tornadoes, they say, are produced by the combined activity of the two forces.

Whatever mechanism produces them, it is well known that the Gulf of Mexico is the perfect breeding ground for tornado activity. Warm, moisture-laden air from the Gulf is carried northward to become wedged up against the Rocky Mountains. Cold, dry currents come gusting northeastward off the Rockies to collide with the warm, moist air from the South. Troublesome weather conditions are the result.

The warm, humid, unstable conditions that bring tornadoes into existence are the same as those which cause thunderstorms. Indeed, tornadoes often develop in conjunction with thunderstorms. As the thunderstorm moves, tornadoes may form at intervals along its path, traveling for a few miles, then dying out.

The tornado funnel usually appears as an extension beneath the thunderstorm's dark, heavy clouds. Often the funnel stretches downward toward the ground, whirling and twisting as it moves. This is known as the storm's vortex. Sometimes the funnel never quite reaches the earth's surface. Other times it touches down briefly, then rises.

On the average, the tornado path is a quarter of a mile wide and 16 miles long. But there have been occasions when tornadoes have caused heavy destruction for a distance of 200 or 300 miles. The forward speed of the tornado is about 40 miles an hour, although speeds of up to 70 miles an hour have been observed.

The destruction that tornadoes do is a result of the combined action of their strong rotary winds and a partial vacuum that is created with the center of the vortex. The winds, believed to reach a speed of 300 miles an hour and perhaps more, twist and rip everything within their path. At the same time, the low pressure area within the twister's "eye" has an explosive effect on any structure it happens to touch. Walls collapse or topple outward; rooftops are sent flying. Heavy objects such as automobiles or machinery can be carried for considerable distances.

PREDICTING TORNADOES AND WARNING THE PUBLIC

Because of the relatively small size and short life-span of tornadoes, it is extremely difficult for meteorologists to detect them and predict where they are going to occur. What they try to do is watch for areas where tornadoes can be expected to develop.

The headquarters for tornado detection in the United States is the National Severe Storms Forecast Center in Kansas City, Missouri. Here specialists are on duty around the clock, constantly monitoring the atmospheric conditions of the forty-eight mainland states. They include forecasters, communicators, radar analysts, and computer operators.

A flood of data pours in to be evaluated, including information from hundreds of weather stations equipped with instruments to observe and record the state of sky, that is, the amount of cloud cover and the height of the clouds, and also such information as temperature, wind speed and direction, atmospheric phenomena that might be of importance. A vast radar network also provides data, and continuous photographic coverage of the United States is provided by satellites.

Radar is not the great blessing that many people believe, not when it comes to finding tornadoes. "Radar doesn't say exactly where, when, and for how long the tornado will occur," says Allen D. Pearson, head man at the Severe Storms Forecast Center. "Radar only gives the operator a clue, so that he may suspect that a given thunderstorm is big enough and tall enough to have definite potential for a tornado."

Information from satellites has only limited value too. "The satellite has been very helpful in some situations in the springtime," Mr. Pearson says, "but as you get into the summer, there tends to be more and more cloudiness over the country, making it nearly impossible to locate all the thunderstorms that have tornado potential."

What experts at the Forecast Center do is look for conditions that are likely to produce severe thunderstorms. In other words, they seek to find masses of unstable air, areas where there is a wide range in temperature between warm surface air and cold upper air. There must also be a certain amount of moisture available in the lower atmosphere and the right kind of wind conditions. Once an area has been identified as one of possible danger, a SKY-WARN system of watches and warnings goes into effect.

When the Forecast Center issues a tornado *watch*, it is alerting people in a given area that a severe storm is likely to occur. Tornado watches are teletyped to local offices of the National Weather Service, and the public hears of them by means of radio and television.

"During a watch, people can go about their business as usual," says Mr. Pearson. "But they should keep tuned in to a radio or television for storm bulletins. They should also keep a weather eye on the sky, scanning the horizon occasionally for low, threatening clouds, what we call a squall line. These often produce tornadoes."

At the same time, the tornado watch serves to alert emergency forces within the area. These include volunteer spotters, men and women recruited by local Weather Service offices and trained to watch for severe storms and tornadoes. "The human eye," says Mr. Pearson, "is still the best means we have for detecting tornadoes."

What do spotters look for? The funnel cloud, which is the trademark of the tornado, is often obscured by dust or driving rain, or the storm may occur at night. So observers, in daytime, watch for a sudden darkening of the sky, which is often accompanied by heavy winds, pounding rain, hail, and much lightning and thunder. At night they listen for a howling wind. "A tornado's wind sounds like fifty freight trains going through your living room," says one veteran spotter.

A tornado *warning* is much more serious than a tornado watch. A tornado warning is issued by the Forecast Center when a tornado has actually been sighted or when one is indicated by radar. Sometimes a volunteer observer will spot the tornado and alert the local office of the Weather Service or the community warning center. The local agency then issues the warning.

A tornado warning tells the precise location of the storm, the time it was detected, and the path it is expected to travel. A person in an office building at the time should go to the designated shelter area, or to an interior hallway on a low floor. To a person at home the basement usually offers the most safety. In schools, students are often led to an interior hallway on the lowest floor. "Stay out of auditoriums, gymnasiums, and structures with wide, free-span roofs," says a bulletin from the Weather Service.

WARNING SYSTEMS SAVE LIVES

When all these elements are put together, the result can be a dramatic saving of lives. Take what happened in the case of a tornado outbreak that struck north-central Kansas on September 25, 1973. It consisted of more than a dozen different twisters, the worst occurrence of a storm of this type in more than fifty years.

Most of the damage that day was caused by two long-track tornadoes, each a potential mass killer. One of these covered 72 miles; the other, about parallel to the first, 158 miles.

Most Kansans were first made aware that tornado conditions existed that morning soon after they awakened. The first warning went out from the National Severe Storms Forecast Center at seven o'clock, alerting all Weather Service offices and Civil Defense units in the area.

Information continued to funnel into the Forecast Center, and by midafternoon there was sufficient evidence to issue a tornado watch for an area south of Salina, Kansas. Another watch was sent out at five o'clock, and this one included Salina itself. Members of the state highway police, local police and fire departments, Civil Defense units, and all other volunteers began scanning the sky for threatening clouds.

Weather Service offices began to receive excited reports. At 5:10 P.M., the Kansas City Highway Patrol spotted a funnel cloud just north of Salina; it was moving north-northeast at about 30 miles an hour. At 5:15 P.M., after receiving several reports from spotters, Concordia issued the first tornado warning of the day. At 5:47 P.M., when another tornado was sighted, Concordia issued a second warning.

Salina braced itself. Spotters never took their eyes from the

In weather stations like the one pictured below, meteorologists keep a careful watch on developing storms.

twister as it bore down on the town. The Salina police chief was monitoring the skies southeast of the city, and when debris began falling around him, he ordered the city's sirens to begin their warning wail. It was 5:50 P.M.

Radio and television began to give minute-by-minute coverage of the twister's approach. Shoppers in supermarkets heard the warning on store public-address systems. And police officers in squad cars covered city streets and back roads, with loudspeakers bellowing. "Take cover to the nearest shelter! This is no drill!"

Salina, a city of 38,000, looked like a ghost town by the time the tornado arrived. The storm unleashed its greatest fury upon a mobile-home park on the city's southeastern fringe. Residents there had watched the storm's approach, and when it had veered their way, they hurried to a thick-walled shelter built of reinforced concrete that had been provided for them. As they huddled in the darkness, their trailers were reduced to a twisted mass of knee-high junk and their belongings were scattered over the Kansas countryside.

About the time the dazed survivors were emerging from the trailer-park shelter, the tornado was lashing out at towns to the northeast. Clay Center was a prime target, with the twister tearing through the heart of the city, destroying or damaging hundreds of structures. But Clay Center, like Salina, had plenty of advance warning, and when the tornado exploded through, its residents had taken shelter. Not one death was recorded in Clay Center that night.

And so it was along the path of both tornadoes. Hundreds of homes and commercial structures were destroyed, and thousands were damaged. Losses totaled well up in the millions. Yet despite the widespread destruction, the death toll was low — 3 persons. Had it not been for the watches and warnings, hundreds might have died.

A CONTINUING CHALLENGE

Some people grumble that the National Weather Service, in its program of tornado watches and warnings, has become *too* efficient. During the times of the year when tornadoes are most likely to occur, alerts are broadcast and telecast so frequently in

Kansas, Oklahoma, Nebraska, and other tornado-prone states, that some residents grow weary of hearing them.

One meteorologist answers complaints he gets by telling the story of an elderly woman who, upon hearing the announcement of a tornado watch, rushed into the cellar and hid under a work-bench, trembling with fear. When no tornado appeared, the woman telephoned the local weather forecaster and scolded him for upsetting her, brushing aside his explanation that a tornado watch is merely an alerting message.

A few weeks later, a second tornado watch was issued. The woman scurried into the basement and hid. When nothing happened, she called the forecaster and reprimanded him again.

A month went by. A third watch was issued. The woman hid again, with much grumbling.

This time a tornado did strike, demolishing the woman's house. Nothing escaped destruction but the basement. When all was silent, the woman fought her way up out of the wreckage, paused only a moment to survey the rubble, then stumbled and staggered down the road to a neighbor's house, where she asked to use the telephone. She dialed the forecaster, and when he picked up the telephone she proclaimed, "Well, now! That's more like it!"

Despite the thoroughness and efficiency with which the tornado watch and warning system now functions, no one is saying that it is not without its shortcomings. Further improvement is possible.

Author

George Sullivan taught nonfiction writing at Fordham University for many years. He says he is curious about many subjects, as young people are. His many books include *How Do They Find It?*, from which this article was taken.

An excerpt from

The Black Pearl

by Scott O'Dell

Ramón Salazar grew up in the town of La Paz, in Baja California. His father was a prosperous pearl dealer, and Ramón had dreamed of learning to dive for pearls himself one day. However, his father had forbidden him to learn to dive because he said the waters of the Vermilion Sea, where the pearls could be found, were occupied by a dangerous manta ray called the Manta Diablo. The ray was said to be larger than a ship, with seven rows of teeth. Ramón did not really believe such a thing existed. He still wanted to learn to dive. Finally his chance arrived when his father left on a week-long trip. Ramón struck a deal with an old Indian, Soto Luzon, a master pearl diver. In exchange for teaching Ramón how to dive in a hidden lagoon in the Vermilion Sea, Soto would receive any pearls that Ramon found.

The lagoon where the old man lived was about seven leagues from La Paz and we should have reached it by midnight. But the currents and the wind were against us, so it was near dawn before we sighted the two headlands that marked the lagoon's hidden entrance.

You could pass this entrance many times and think that it was only an opening in the rocks that led nowhere. As soon as you passed the rocks, however, you came to a narrow channel that wound like a snake between the two headlands for a half mile or farther.

The sun was just rising when the channel opened out and suddenly we were in a quiet oval-shaped lagoon. On both sides of the lagoon steep hills came down to the water and at the far end lay a shallow beach of black sand. Beyond were two scraggly trees and beneath them a cluster of huts where breakfast fires were burning.

It was a peaceful scene that lay before me, much like

many other lagoons that dot our coast. But there was something about the place that made me feel uneasy. At first I thought it must be the barren hills that closed in upon the lagoon and the coppery haze that lay over it, and the beach of black sand and the quiet. I was soon to hear that it was something else, something far different from what I thought.

The old man paddled slowly across the lagoon, carefully raising and lowering the paddle, as if he did not want to disturb the water. And though he had talked most of the time before we reached the lagoon he now fell silent. A gray shark circled the canoe and disappeared. He pointed to it, but said nothing.

Nor did he speak again until we beached the canoe and were walking up the path to the huts. Then he said, "It is well to hold the tongue and not to talk needlessly when you are on the lagoon. Remember this when we go out to dive, for there is one who listens and is quickly angered."

Indians are superstitious about the moon and the sun and some animals and birds, especially the coyote and the owl. For this reason I was not surprised that he wished to warn me.

"Who is it that listens and grows angry?" I asked him.

Twice he glanced over his shoulder before he answered. "The Manta Diablo," he said.

"El Diablo?" I asked, holding back a smile. "He lives here in your lagoon?"

"In a cave," he answered, "a big one which you can see just as you leave the channel."

"The channel is very narrow," I said, "barely wide enough for a canoe. How does a giant like El Diablo swim through it? But perhaps he does not need to. Perhaps he stays here in your lagoon."

"No," the old man said. "He travels widely and is gone for many weeks at a time."

"Then he must swim through the channel somehow."

"Oh, no, that would be impossible, even for him. There is another opening, a secret one, near the place where you enter the channel. When he swims out to sea, it is this one he uses."

We were nearing the huts clustered beneath the two scraggly trees. A band of children came running out to meet us and the old man said nothing more about El Diablo until we had eaten breakfast, slept the morning away, eaten again, and gone back to the lagoon.

As we floated the canoe and set off for the pearling reefs, the old man said, "When the mist goes, that means El Diablo has gone, too."

It was true that the red mist was gone and the water now shone green and clear. I still smiled to myself at the old man's belief in El Diablo, yet I felt a little of the excitement that I had felt long ago when my mother threatened me with the monster.

"Now that he is gone," I said, "we can talk."

"A little and with much care," Luzon replied, "for he has many friends in the lagoon."

"Friends?"

"Yes, the shark you saw this morning and many small fish. They are all friends and they listen and when he comes back they tell him everything, everything."

"When he leaves the lagoon, where does he go?"

"That I do not know. Some say that he takes the shape of an octopus and seeks out those pearlers who have done him a wrong or spoken ill of him. It is also said that he takes the shape of a human and goes into La Paz and seeks his enemies there in the streets and sometimes even in the church."

"I should think that you would fear for your life and leave the lagoon."

"No, I do not fear El Diablo. Nor did my father before

me. Nor his father before him. For many years they had a pact with the Manta Diablo and now I keep this pact. I show him proper respect and tip my hat when I come into the lagoon and when I leave it. For this he allows me to dive for the black pearls which belong to him and which we now go to search for."

Silently the old man guided the canoe toward the south shore of the lagoon, and I asked no more questions for I felt that he had said all he wished to say about the Manta Diablo. In two fathoms of water, over a reef of black rocks, he dropped anchor and told me to do the same.

"Now I teach you to dive," he said. "First we start with the breathing."

The old man lifted his shoulders and began to take in great gulps of air, gulp after gulp, until his chest seemed twice its size. Then he let out the air with a long whoosh.

"This is called 'taking the wind'," he said. "And because it is very important you must try it."

I obeyed his command, but filled my lungs in one breath.

"More," the old man said.

I took in another gulp of air.

"More," the old man said.

I tried again and then began to cough.

"For the first time it is good," the old man said. "But you must practice this much so you stretch the lungs. Now we go down together."

We both filled our lungs with air and slipped over the side of the canoe feet first, each of us holding a sink stone. The water was as warm as milk but clear so that I could see the wrinkled sand and the black rocks and fish swimming about.

When we reached the bottom the old man put a foot in the loop of the rope that held his sink stone and I did likewise with my stone. He placed his hand on my shoulder and took two steps to a crevice in a rock that was covered with trailing weeds. Then he took the knife from his belt and thrust it into the crevice. Instantly the crevice closed, not slowly but with a snap. The old man wrenched the knife free and took his foot out of the loop and motioned for me to do the same and we floated up to the canoe.

The old man held out the knife. "Note the scratches which the burro shell leaves," he said. "With a hand or a foot it is different. Once the burro has you he does not let go and thus you drown. Take care, therefore, where you step and where you place the hand."

We dived until night came, and the old man showed me how to walk carefully on the bottom, so as not to muddy the water, and how to use the knife to pry loose the oysters that grew in clumps and how to get the shells open and how to search them for pearls.

We gathered many baskets that afternoon but found nothing except a few baroques[1] of little worth. And it was the same the next day and the next, and then on the fourth day, because the old man had cut his hand on a shell, I went out on the lagoon alone.

It was on this day that I found the great Pearl of Heaven.

A red haze hung over the water as I floated the canoe on the morning of the fourth day and began to paddle toward the cave where the old man said the Manta Diablo lived.

The sun was up but the haze hung so thick that I had trouble locating the channel. After I found it I searched for almost an hour before I sighted the cave. It was hidden behind a rocky pinnacle and faced the rising sun, and the opening was about thirty feet wide and the height of a tall man,

---

[1]**baroques** (bə **rōks'**): a Portuguese word meaning rough or imperfect pearls.

223

and curved downward like the upper lip of a mouth. I could not see into the cave because of the red mist, so I drifted back and forth and waited until the sun rose higher and the mist burned away.

I had talked to the old man the night before about the cave. We had eaten supper, and the women and children had gone to bed, and the two of us were sitting around the fire.

"You have fished everywhere in the lagoon," I said, "but not in the cave."

"No," he said. "Nor did my father nor his father."

"Big pearls may grow there."

The old man did not answer. He got up and put wood on the fire and sat down again.

"The great one itself, the Pearl of Heaven, may lie there," I said.

Still he did not answer, but suddenly he looked across the fire. It was a fleeting look that he gave me and yet its meaning was as clear as if he had spoken to me and said, "I cannot go to the cave to search for pearls. I cannot go because I fear the Manta Diablo. If you go there, then it is alone. El Diablo cannot blame me."

And that morning when I went down to the beach he did not go with me. "The wound on my hand hurts very much," he said, "so I will stay behind." And the look he gave me was the same I had seen the night before.

At last, about midmorning, the sun burned away the mist and I could see for a short distance into the cave. I paddled through the mouth and soon found myself in a vast vault-like room. The walls of the room were black and smooth and shone from the light that came in through the opening.

Near the mouth of the cave the water was very clear. I picked up my basket and sink stone, took a deep breath, and slipped over the side of the canoe, remembering all that the old man had taught me.

I reached the bottom after about a fathom and a half. I looped my foot in the rope tied to the sink stone and waited until the bubbles that had risen behind me disappeared and I could find the bed of shells I had noticed from above. The bed was five steps away toward the mouth of the cave. I walked carefully in the sand as I had learned to do.

The shells were the largest I had ever seen. They were half the length of my arm and thick through as my body and covered with weed that looked like a woman's hair. I chose the nearest one, which seemed to be easier to get at than the others. I took out my knife and worked quietly, but a school of small fish kept swimming in front of my eyes, so I failed to pry the shell loose before my lungs began to hurt and I had to go up.

On my second dive I had no sooner reached the bottom than a shadow fell across the bed where I was working. It was the shadow of a gray shark, one of the friendly ones, but by the time he had drifted away my breath was gone.

I dived six times more and worked quickly each time I went down, hacking away with my sharp knife at the base of the big shell where it was anchored to the rock. But it had been growing there for many years, since long before I was born, I suppose, and it would not come free from its home.

By this time it was late in the afternoon and the light was poor. Also my hands were bleeding and my eyes were half-blind with salt from the sea. But I sat in the canoe and thought of all the hours I had spent for nothing.

I filled my lungs and took the sink stone and went down again. With the first stroke of my knife, the shell came free. It toppled over on one side, and I quickly untied the rope from the sink stone and looped it twice around the shell and swam back to the surface. I pulled up the shell, but it was too heavy for me to lift into the canoe, so I tied it to the stern and paddled out of the cave.

Across the lagoon I could see the old man standing among the trees. From time to time during the day I had caught glimpses of him standing there with his eyes fixed on the cave. I knew that I could drown and he would not try to save me, and that he was telling El Diablo all the while that he had not wanted me to go to the cave and that he therefore was not to blame. But I also felt that if I found a pearl he would be willing to take his share because he had nothing to do with finding it.

He came out from the trees as I paddled across the lagoon and strolled down to the beach as if he did not care whether I had found a pearl or not. I suppose this was to show El Diablo and his friends the fish and the long, gray shark that Soto Luzon was without blame.

"A big one," he said when I dragged the shell ashore. "In my life I have never seen such a monster. It is the grand-father of all oysters that live in the sea."

"There are many in the cave bigger than this one," I said.

"If there are so many," he answered, "then the Manta Diablo cannot be mad that you have taken only one of them."

"Perhaps a little mad," I said and laughed, "but not much."

The mouth of the oyster was closed and it was hard to put my blade between the tight edges of the shell.

"Lend me your knife," I said. "Mine is blunted from use."

The old man placed his hand on the hilt of his knife and pulled it from the sheath and then slipped it back again.

"I think it is better if you use your own knife," he said and his voice began to tremble as he spoke.

I wrestled a long time with the oyster. At last the hard lips began to give a little. Then I could feel the knife sink through the heavy muscles that held them together and suddenly the lips fell apart.

I put my finger under the frilled edge of the flesh as I had seen my father do. A pearl slid along my finger and I picked it out. It was about the size of a pea. When I felt again, another of the same size rolled out and then a third. I put them on the other half of the shell so they would not be scratched.

The old man came and leaned over me, as I knelt there in the sand, and held his breath.

Slowly I slid my hand under the heavy tongue of the oyster. I felt a hard lump, so monstrous in size that it could not be a pearl. I took hold of it and pulled it from the flesh and got to my feet and held it to the sun, thinking that I must be holding a rock that the oyster had swallowed some-how.

It was round and smooth and the color of smoke. It filled my cupped hand. Then the sun's light struck deep into the thing and moved in silver swirls and I knew that it was not a rock that I held but a pearl, the great Pearl of Heaven.

"Madre de Dios," the old man whispered.

I stood there and could not move or talk. The old man kept whispering over and over, "Madre de Dios."

Darkness fell. I tore off the tail of my shirt and wrapped the pearl in it.

"Half of this is yours," I told him.

I handed the pearl to him, but he drew back in fear.

"You wish me to keep it until we reach La Paz?" I said.

"Yes, it is better that you keep it."

"When shall we go?"

"Soon," he said hoarsely. "El Diablo is away but he will come back. And his friends will tell him then about the pearl."

We did not wait to eat supper. While I dragged the canoe into the water, the old man went up to the huts and came back with a handful of corn cakes. As we passed the cave, he touched his hat and mumbled something to himself, then dug his paddle into the sea. He had brought along another paddle, and this I used though my hands were so sore I could scarcely hold it.

There was a half-moon shining, the currents were good and the wind was at our backs. By midnight we were nearing Pichilinque[2] Bay and the lights of La Paz shone faint on the horizon. It was then that the old man suddenly looked over his shoulder. He had done this several times since we had left the lagoon.

He lifted his arm and pointed. In a quiet voice he said, "El Diablo."

Far astern I looked and saw the ghostly gleam of wing-like fins.

---

[2]**Pichilinque** (pee-che-**leen**-kay)

"A manta," I said, "but not El Diablo. It is one that I have seen around before. Last week . . ."

"It is El Diablo," the old man broke in.

He lifted his paddle and dug hard at the water and the canoe changed direction.

"We go into Pichilinque," he said.

"But La Paz is not far," I said.

"Too far," the old man answered. "We would never reach La Paz."

Furiously he paddled and the canoe leaped forward. There was nothing I could say that would lessen the terror that had seized him. To him El Diablo was real and he was pursuing us to get back the pearl I had stolen. So I fell into the swing of his paddle and thought about the great Pearl of Heaven that I carried inside my shirt. And I wondered what my father would say and all the people of our town.

We were going through the entrance of Pichilinque. The old man said, "Do you see El Diablo?"

"No. I have looked and do not see him anywhere."

At that moment a thunderous sound engulfed the canoe. It was as if the sky had fallen in upon us. Then mounds of water rose on both sides of us and met over our heads and filled the air with spray. There followed a groan, a rending of timbers, and the canoe rose crazily and tipped and I was pitching slowly sidewise into the sea. As I fell my mind raced back to childhood. I heard my mother say, "The Manta Diablo is larger than the largest ship in the harbor. He has seven rows of teeth."

I could not see the old man but from a distance I heard him shout. My first thought was the pearl. I thrust a hand inside my shirt, fumbled around and at last found it, and set out for the shore. The old man was there ahead of me. I crawled out of the water and got to my feet and held up the pearl to show him that it was safe.

"Throw it back," he cried. "El Diablo is waiting for the pearl and he will not rest until he gets it. He is there now."

The bay was quiet. I saw nothing except the splintered canoe drifting away in the moonlight. There was no sign of the manta, and yet I knew it was one of these sea creatures that had wrecked our canoe, by chance or otherwise, for they abound in the Vermilion Sea.

"We have the pearl," I said, "and we are alive, if very wet, and if we go now we can reach La Paz by daylight."

"I do not go there with the pearl," the old man said. "I stay until morning to find the canoe. And the pearl belongs to you. I did not find it and it is not mine."

He drew back from me as if I held a serpent in my hand.

"You will change your mind," I said. "The pearl has great value."

"Never will I change my mind," he answered.

"There are three pearls lying in the shell on the beach," I said. "I forgot them."

"Those I will throw into the sea," he said.

"As you please," I said.

"And the big one you should throw there also," the old man said. "If you do not, señor, someday the Manta Diablo will have it back and your life with it. Of this I warn you."

We said farewell to each other and I started down the shore toward the lights of the town, holding the pearl tight in my hand.

Author

Scott O'Dell, author of almost a score of books for young people, was the first American to win the international Hans Christian Andersen Medal for his work. *Island of the Blue Dolphins,* his first book, received the Newbery Medal.

From Montauk Point
by Walt Whitman

I stand as on some mighty eagle's beak.
Eastward on the sea absorbing, viewing,
 (nothing but sea and sky,)
The tossing waves, the foam, the ships in the distance
The wild unrest, the snowy, curling caps —
 that inbound urge and urge of waves,
Seeking the shores forever.

KON-TIKI

ACROSS THE PACIFIC BY RAFT

From the book by Thor Heyerdahl

It all started with a mystery: the great stone statues, called Tikis, that stood on Easter Island. Where had they come from? Who had brought them there?

Explorer Thor Heyerdahl believed that they had come from Peru — that the ancient Incas had crossed the Pacific to settle the Pacific Islands, bringing with them their sun-king, Kon-Tiki.

Impossible, people said. How could the Incas have crossed thousands of miles of open sea? Heyerdahl was convinced that it was possible, that the Humboldt Current would have carried the Incas' balsa-wood rafts to the Islands.

To prove it could be done, Heyerdahl set out to cross the Pacific on a wooden raft. His companions were Bengt Danielsson, Knut Haugland, Erik Hesselberg, Torstein Raaby, and Herman Watzinger — and one green parrot.

On April 28, 1947, they set sail on the raft Kon-Tiki. *They would travel halfway around the world. The journey would take 101 days.*

SIX AGAINST THE SEA

By the late afternoon the trade wind was already blowing at full strength. It quickly stirred up the ocean into roaring seas, which swept against us from astern. For the first time we fully realized that here was the sea itself come to meet us; it was bitter earnest now — our communications were cut. Whether things went well now would depend entirely on the balsa raft's good qualities in the open sea. We knew that, from now onward, we should never get another onshore wind, and every day would carry us farther and farther out to sea. The only thing to do was to go ahead under full sail. If we tried to turn homeward, we should only drift farther out to sea, stern first. There was only one possible course: to sail before the wind with our bow toward the sunset.

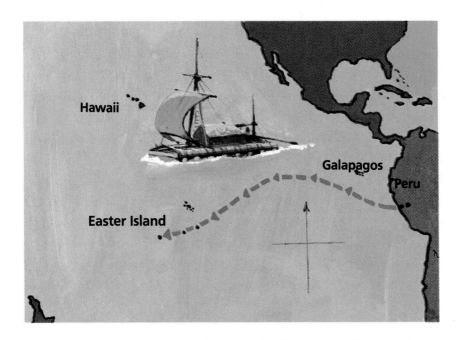

As the troughs of the sea gradually grew deeper, it became clear that we moved into the swiftest part of the Humboldt Current. The water was green and cold and everywhere about us; the jagged mountains of Peru had vanished into the dense cloud banks astern. When darkness crept over the waters, our first duel with the elements began. We were still not sure of the sea; we were still uncertain whether it would show itself a friend or an enemy. When a white crest came groping toward us on a level with the cabin roof, we held on tight and waited uneasily to feel the masses of water smash down over us and the raft.

Every time there was the same surprise and relief. The *Kon-Tiki* calmly swung up its stern and rose skyward, while the masses of water rolled along its sides. Then we sank down again into the trough of the waves and waited for the next big sea.

About midnight a ship's light passed in a northerly direction. At three another passed on the same course. We waved our little paraffin lamp and hailed them with flashes from an electric torch, but they did not see us, and the lights passed slowly northward into the darkness and disappeared. Little did those on board realize that a real Inca raft lay close to them, tumbling among the waves. Just as little did we on board the raft realize that this was our last ship and the last trace of humans we should see till we had reached the other side of the ocean.

The next night was still worse. The seas grew higher instead of going down. So the first sixty hours passed in one continuous struggle against a chaos of waves that rushed upon us, one after another, without cessation. High waves and low waves, pointed waves and round waves, slanting waves and waves on top of other waves.

On the third night the sea went down a bit, although it was still blowing hard. About four o'clock an unexpected deluge came foaming through the darkness and knocked the raft right round before the steersmen realized what was happening. The sail thrashed against the bamboo cabin and threatened to tear both the cabin and itself to pieces. All hands had to go on deck to secure the cargo and haul on sheets and stays in the hope of getting the raft on its right course again, so that the sail might fill and curve forward peacefully. The raft would not right itself. It would go stern foremost, and that was all. The only result of all our hauling and pushing and rowing was that two men nearly went overboard in a sea when the sail caught them in the dark.

The sea had clearly become calmer. Stiff and sore, with skinned palms and sleepy eyes, we were not worth a row of beans. Better to save our strength in case the weather should call us out to a worse passage of arms. One could never know. So we furled the sail and rolled it round the bamboo yard. The *Kon-Tiki* lay sideways on to the seas and took them like a cork. Everything on board was lashed fast, and all six of us crawled into the little bamboo cabin, huddled together, and slept like mummies in a sardine tin.

We did not wake till well on in the day, when the parrot began to whistle and halloo and dance to and fro on its perch. Outside the sea was still running high, but in long, even ridges and not so wild and confused as the day before. The first thing we saw was that the sun was beating down on the yellow bamboo deck and giving the sea all round us a bright and friendly aspect. What did it matter if the seas foamed and rose high so long as they only left us in peace on the raft? What did it matter if they rose straight up in front of our noses when we knew that in a second the raft would go over the top and flatten out the foaming ridge like a steam roller, while the heavy threatening mountain of water only lifted us up in the air and rolled groaning and gurgling under the floor? A cork steam roller — that was what the balsa raft amounted to.

The sea contains many surprises for those who have their floor on a level with the surface and drift along slowly and noiselessly. People who break their way through the woods may come back and say that no wildlife is to be seen. Others may sit down on a stump and wait, and often rustlings and cracklings will begin and curious eyes peer out. So it is on the sea, too. We usually plow across it with roaring engines and piston strokes, with the water foaming round our bow. Then we come back and say that there is nothing to see far out on the ocean.

The very first day we were left alone on the sea, we had noticed fish round the raft, but we were too much occupied with the steering to think of fishing. The second day we went right into a thick shoal of sardines. Soon afterward an eight-foot blue shark came along and rolled over with its white belly uppermost as it rubbed against the raft's stern where Herman and Bengt stood steering.

Next day we were visited by tunnies, bonitos, and dorados. When a big flying fish thudded on board, we used it as bait and at once pulled in two large dorados weighing from twenty to thirty-five pounds each. This was food for several days. On steering watch we could see many fish we did not even know, and one day we came into a school of porpoises that seemed quite endless. The nearer we came to the Equator, and the farther from the coast, the commoner flying fish became. When at last we came out into the blue water where the sea rolled by majestically, sunlit and serene, ruffled by gusts of wind, we could see them glittering like a rain of projectiles that shot from the water and flew in a straight line till their power of flight was exhausted and they vanished beneath the surface.

If we set the little paraffin lamp out at night, flying fish were attracted by the light and, large and small, shot over the raft. They often struck the bamboo cabin or the sail and tumbled helpless on the deck. Unable to get a take-off by swimming through the water, they just remained lying and kicking helplessly. They always came at a good pace and snout first. If they struck us full in the face it burned and tingled, but the attack was quickly forgiven by the injured party — for with all its drawbacks, we were in a land of enchantment where delicious fish dishes came hurling through the air. We used to fry them for breakfast, and whether it was the fish, the cook, or our appetites, they reminded us of fried troutlings once we had scraped the scales off.

Knut was much upset one morning because, when he was standing operating with the frying pan, a flying fish struck him on the hand instead of landing right in the cooking fat.

It was a few nights later. It was overcast and pitch dark, and Torstein had placed the paraffin lamp close by his head so that the night watches could see where they were treading when they crept in and out over his head. About four o'clock Torstein was awakened by the lamp tumbling over and something cold and wet flapping about his ears. "Flying fish," he thought and felt for it in the darkness to throw it away. He caught hold of something long and wet, which wriggled like a snake, and let go as if he had burned himself. The unseen visitor twisted itself away and over to Herman, while Torstein tried to get the lamp lighted again. Herman started up, too, and this made me wake, thinking of the octopus which came up at night in these waters.

When we got the lamp lighted, Herman was sitting in triumph with his hand gripping the neck of a long thin fish, which wriggled in his hands like an eel. The fish was over three feet long, as slender as a snake, with dull eyes and a long snout with a greedy jaw full of long sharp teeth. The teeth were as sharp as knives and could be folded back into the roof of the mouth to make way for what was swallowed.

Bengt, too, was awakened at last by all the noise, and we held the lamp and the long fish under his nose. He sat up drowsily in his sleeping bag and said solemnly, "No, fish like that don't exist," with which he turned over quietly and fell asleep again.

Bengt was not far wrong. It appeared later that we six sitting round the lamp in the bamboo cabin were the first to have seen this fish alive. Only the skeleton of a fish like this one had been found a few times on the coast of South America and the Galapagos Islands; ichthyologists called it *Gempylus,* or snake mackerel, and thought it lived at the bottom of the sea at a great depth because no one had ever seen it alive.

On May 24, we were lying drifting on a leisurely swell in exactly 95° west by 7° south. It was about noon, and we had thrown overboard the guts of two big dorados we had caught earlier in the morning. I was up on the edge of the raft looking at a fish as it passed quietly, when I heard a wild war whoop from Knut, who was sitting aft behind the bamboo cabin. He bellowed, "Shark!" till his voice cracked. As we had sharks swimming alongside almost daily without creating such excitement, we all realized that this must be something extra-special and flocked to Knut's assistance.

Knut had been squatting there, washing his pants in the swell, and when he looked up for a moment he was staring straight into the biggest and ugliest face any of us had ever seen in the whole of our lives. The head was broad and flat like a frog's, with two small eyes right at the sides, and a

toadlike jaw that was four or five feet wide and had long fringes drooping from the corners of the mouth. Behind the head was an enormous body ending in a long thin tail with a pointed tail fin that stood straight up and showed that this sea monster was not any kind of whale. The body looked brownish under the water, but both head and body were thickly covered with small white spots.

The monster came quietly, lazily swimming after us. It grinned like a bulldog and lashed gently with its tail. The large round dorsal fin projected clear of the water, and sometimes the tail fin as well, and the water flowed about the broad back as though washing around a submerged reef. In front of the broad jaws swam a whole crowd of pilot fish in fan formation, and large remora fish and other parasites sat firmly attached to the huge body and traveled with it through the water, so that the whole thing looked like a

curious zoological collection crowded round something that resembled a floating deep-water reef.

When the giant came close up to the raft, it rubbed its back against the heavy steering oar, which was just lifted up out of the water. Now we had ample opportunity of studying the monster at the closest quarters — at such close quarters that I thought we had all gone mad, for we roared stupidly with laughter and shouted overexcitedly at the completely fantastic sight we saw. Walt Disney himself, with all his powers of imagination, could not have created a more hair-raising sea monster than the one that suddenly lay with its terrific jaws along the raft's side.

The monster was a whale shark, the largest shark and the largest fish known in the world today. It is exceedingly rare, but scattered specimens are observed here and there in the tropical oceans. The whale shark has an average length of fifty feet and weighs fifteen tons. It is said that large specimens can attain a length of sixty feet. One harpooned baby had a liver weighing six hundred pounds and three thousand teeth in each of its broad jaws.

Our monster was so large that when it began to swim in circles round us and under the raft, its head was visible on one side while the whole of its tail stuck out on the other. Again and again it described narrower and narrower circles just under the raft, while all we could do was to wait and see what might happen. When it appeared on the other side, it glided amiably under the steering oar and lifted it up in the air, while the oar blade slid along the creature's back.

In reality the whale shark went on encircling us for barely an hour, but to us the visit seemed to last a whole day.

We were visited by whales many times. Sometimes they passed like ships on the horizon, now and again sending a cascade of water into the air, but sometimes they steered straight for us. We were prepared for a dangerous collision the first time a big whale altered course and came straight toward the raft in a purposeful manner. As it gradually grew nearer, we could hear its blowing and puffing, heavy and long drawn, each time it rolled its head out of the water. It came straight toward our port side, where we stood gathered on the edge of the raft, while one man shouted that he could see seven or eight more making their way toward us.

The big, shining, black forehead of the first whale was not more than two yards from us when it sank beneath the surface of the water, and then we saw the enormous blue-black bulk glide quietly under the raft right beneath our feet. It lay there for a time, dark and motionless, and we held our breath as we looked down on the gigantic curved back of a mammal a good deal longer than the whole raft. Then it sank slowly through the bluish water and disappeared from sight. Meanwhile the whole school were close upon us, but they paid no attention to us. The whole morning we had them puffing and blowing round us in the most unexpected places without their even pushing against the raft or the steering oar. They quite enjoyed themselves, gamboling freely among the waves in the sunshine. About noon the whole school dived as if on a given signal and disappeared for good.

The marine creature against which the experts had begged us to be most on our guard was the octopus, for it could get on board the raft. The National Geographic Society in Washington, D.C., had shown us reports and photographs from an area in the Humboldt Current where monstrous octopuses had their favorite resort and came up onto the surface at night. They had arms that could do away with a big shark and set ugly marks on great whales, and a beak like an eagle's hidden among their tentacles. We were reminded that they lay floating in the darkness and that their arms were long enough to feel about in every small corner of the raft, if they did not care to come right on board. We did not at all like the prospect of feeling cold arms round our necks, dragging us out of our sleeping bags at night, and we provided ourselves with machete knives, one for each of us.

For a long time we saw no sign of octopuses, either on board or in the sea. Then one morning we had the first warning that they must be in those waters. When the sun rose, we found an octopus on board, in the form of a little baby the size of a cat. It had come up on deck unaided in the course of the night and now lay dead with its arms twined round the bamboo outside the cabin door.

Young octopuses continued to come aboard. One sunny morning we all saw a glittering shoal of something that shot up out of the water and flew through the air like large raindrops, while the sea boiled with pursuing dolphins. At first we took it for a shoal of flying fish, for we had already had three different kinds of these on board. When they came near, and some of them sailed over the raft at a height of four or five feet, one ran straight into Bengt's chest and fell slap on the deck. It was a small octopus. Our astonishment was great. When we put it into a sailcloth bucket, it kept on taking off and shooting up to the surface, but it did not develop speed enough in the small bucket to get more than half out of the water.

It is a known fact that the octopus ordinarily swims on the principle of the rocket-propelled airplane. It pumps sea water with great force through a closed tube alongside its body and can thus shoot backward in jerks at a high speed. Our experience showed that young octopuses, which are a favorite food of many large fish, can escape their pursuers by taking to the air in the same way as flying fish. They pump sea water through themselves till they get up speed, and then they steer up at an angle from the surface by unfolding pieces of skin like wings. Like the flying fish, they make a glider flight over the waves for as far as their speed can carry them. After that, when we had to begin to pay attention, we often saw them sailing along for fifty to sixty yards, singly and in twos and threes. The fact that they can "glide" has been a novelty to all the zoologists we have met.

The closer we came into contact with the sea and what had its home there, the less strange it became and the more at home we ourselves felt. We learned to respect the old primitive peoples who lived in close converse with the Pacific and therefore knew it from a quite different standpoint from our own. True, we have now estimated its salt content and given tunnies and dolphins Latin names. They had not done that. Nevertheless, I am afraid that the picture the primitive peoples had of the sea was a truer one than ours.

We no longer had the same respect for waves and sea. We knew them and their relationship to us on the raft. Even the shark had become a part of the everyday picture; we knew it and its usual reactions. We did not even move away from the side of the raft if a shark came up alongside. On the contrary, we were more likely to try and grasp its back fin as it glided along the logs. This finally developed into a quite new form of sport — tug of war with shark without a line.

We began quite modestly. We caught all too easily more dorados than we could eat. To keep a popular form of amusement going without wasting food, we hit on comic fishing without a hook for the mutual entertainment of the dorados and ourselves. We fastened unused flying fish to a string and drew them over the surface of the water. The dorados shot up to the surface and seized the fish. Then we tugged, each in our own direction, and had a fine circus performance, for if one dorado let go another came in its place. We had fun, and the dorados got the fish in the end.

Then we started the same game with the sharks. We had either a bit of fish on the end of a rope or often a bag with scraps from dinner, which we let out on a line. Instead of turning on its back, the shark pushed its snout above the water and swam forward with jaws wide to swallow the morsel. We could not help pulling on the rope just as the shark was going to close its jaws again, and the cheated animal swam on with an unspeakably foolish, patient expression and opened its jaws again for the offal, which jumped out of its mouth every time it tried to swallow it. It ended by the shark's coming right up to the logs and jumping up like a begging dog for the food, which hung dangling in a bag above its nose. It was just like feeding a gaping hippopotamus in a zoological gardens.

But our respect for the five or six rows of razor-sharp teeth that lay in ambush in the huge jaws never altogether disappeared.

The last stage in our encounter with sharks was that we began to pull their tails. Pulling animals' tails is held to be an inferior form of sport, but that may be because no one has tried it on a shark. For it was, in truth, a lively form of sport.

To get hold of a shark by the tail we first had to give it a real tidbit. It was ready to stick its head high out of the water to get it. Usually it had its food served dangling in a bag. For, if one has fed a shark directly by hand once, it is no longer amusing. If one feeds dogs or tame bears by hand, they set their teeth into the meat and tear and worry it till they get a bit off or until they get the whole piece for themselves. If one holds out a large dorado at a safe distance from the shark's head, the shark comes up and smacks its jaws together, and without one's having felt the slightest tug, half the dorado is suddenly gone, and one is left sitting with a tail in one's hand. We had found it a hard job to cut the dorado in two with knives, but in a fraction of a second the shark, moving its triangular saw teeth quickly sideways, had chopped off the backbone and everything else like a sausage machine.

When the shark turned quietly to go under again, its tail flickered up above the surface and was easy to grasp. The shark's skin was just like sandpaper to hold on to, and inside the upper point of its tail there was an indentation that might have been made solely to allow a good grip. If we once got a firm grasp there, there was no chance of our grip's not holding. Then we had to give a jerk, before the

shark could collect itself, and get as much as possible of the tail pulled in tight over the logs. For a second or two the shark realized nothing, but then it began to wriggle and struggle with the fore part of its body. Without the help of its tail a shark cannot get up any speed. The other fins are only for balancing and steering. After a few desperate jerks, during which we had to keep a tight hold of the tail, the surprised shark became quite crestfallen and apathetic. As the loose stomach began to sink down toward the head, the shark at last became completely paralyzed.

When the shark had become quiet and, as it were, hung stiff awaiting developments, it was time for us to haul in with all our might. We seldom got more than half the heavy fish up out of the water; then the shark, too, woke up and did the rest itself. With violent jerks it swung its head round and up onto the logs, and then we had to tug with all our might and jump well out of the way, and that pretty quickly, if we wanted to save our legs. For now the shark was in no kindly mood. Jerking itself round in great leaps, it thrashed at the bamboo wall, using its tail as a sledge hammer. Now it no longer spared its iron muscles. The huge jaws were opened wide, and the rows of teeth bit and snapped in the air for anything they could reach.

The parrot was quite thrilled when we had a shark on deck. It came scurrying out of the cabin and climbed up the wall at frantic speed till it found itself a good, safe lookout post on the roof. There it sat shaking its head or fluttering to and fro along the ridge, shrieking with excitement. It had at an early date become an excellent sailor and was always bubbling over with humor and laughter. We reckoned ourselves as seven on board — six of us and the green parrot. At night the parrot crept into its cage under the roof of the

cabin. In the daytime it strutted about the deck or hung on to guy ropes and stays and did the most fascinating acrobatic exercises.

We enjoyed the parrot's humor and brilliant colors for two months, till a big sea came on board. When we discovered that the parrot had gone overboard, it was too late. We did not see it, and the *Kon-Tiki* could not be turned or stopped. If anything went overboard, we had no chance of turning back for it—numerous experiences had shown that.

The loss of the parrot had a depressing effect on our spirits the first evening; we knew that exactly the same thing would happen to ourselves if we fell overboard on a solitary night watch. We tightened up on all the safety regulations, brought into use new life lines for the night watch, and frightened one another out of believing that we were safe because things had gone well in the first two months. One careless step, one thoughtless movement, could send us where the green parrot had gone, even in broad daylight.

On July 21, the wind suddenly died away. It was oppressive and absolutely still, and we knew from previous experience what this might mean. Right enough, after a few violent gusts from east and west and south, the wind freshened up to a breeze from southward, where black, threatening clouds had rushed up over the horizon. Suddenly Torstein's sleeping bag went overboard. What happened in the next few seconds took a much shorter time than it takes to tell it.

Herman tried to catch the bag as it went, took a rash step, and fell overboard. We heard a faint cry for help amid the noise of the waves and saw Herman's head and a waving arm, as well as some vague green object in the water near him. He was struggling for life to get back to the raft through the high seas that had lifted him out from the port side. Torstein, who was at the steering oar aft, and I myself, up in the bow, were the first to perceive him, and we went cold with fear. We bellowed "Man overboard!" at the top of our lungs as we rushed to the nearest lifesaving gear. The others had not heard Herman's cry because of the noise of the sea, but in a trice there was life and bustle on deck. Herman was an excellent swimmer, and though we realized at once that his life was at stake, we had a fair hope that he would manage to crawl back to the edge of the raft before it was too late.

Torstein, who was nearest, seized the bamboo drum round which was the line we used for the lifeboat. It was the only time on the whole voyage that this line got caught up. Herman was now on a level with the stern of the raft but a few yards away. His last hope was to crawl to the blade of the steering oar and hang on to it. As he missed the end of the logs, he reached out for the oar blade, but it slipped away from him. There he lay, just where experience had shown we could get nothing back. While Bengt and I launched the dinghy, Knut and Erik threw out the life belt. Carrying a long line, it hung ready for use on the corner of the cabin roof, but today the wind was so strong that when it was thrown it was simply blown back to the raft. After a few unsuccessful throws, Herman was already far astern of the steering oar, swimming desperately to keep up with the raft, while the distance increased with each gust of wind. He realized that the gap would simply go on increasing, but he set a faint hope on the dinghy, which we had now got into the water. Without the line, which acted as a brake, it would perhaps be possible to drive the rubber raft to meet the swimming man. Whether the rubber raft would ever get back to the *Kon-Tiki* was another matter. Nevertheless, three men in a rubber dinghy had some chance; one man in the sea had none.

Then we suddenly saw Knut take off and plunge headfirst into the sea. He had the life belt in one hand and was heaving himself along. Every time Herman's head appeared on a wave back Knut was gone, and every time Knut came up, Herman was not there. Then we saw both heads at once; they had swum to meet each other and both were hanging on to the life belt. Knut waved his arm, and as the rubber raft had meanwhile been hauled on board, all four of us took hold of the line of the life belt and hauled for dear life, with our eyes fixed on the great dark object that was visible just behind the two men. This same mysterious beast in the water was pushing a big greenish-black triangle up above the wave crests; it almost gave Knut a shock when he was on his way over to Herman. Only Herman knew then that the triangle did not belong to a shark or any other sea monster. It was a corner of Torstein's watertight sleeping bag. The sleeping bag did not remain floating for long after we had hauled the two men safe and sound on board. Whatever dragged the sleeping bag down into the depths had just missed a better prey.

"Glad I wasn't in it," said Torstein and took hold of the steering oar again.

Otherwise there were not many wisecracks that evening. We all felt a chill running through nerve and bone for a long time afterward, but the cold shivers were mingled with a warm thankfulness that there were still six of us on board.

We had a lot of nice things to say to Knut that day — Herman and the rest of us too.

There was not much time to think about what had already happened, for as the sky grew black over our heads the gusts of wind increased in strength, and before night a new storm was upon us.

For five whole days the weather varied between full storm and light gale. Then on the fifth day, the heavens split to show a glimpse of blue, and the malignant, black cloud cover gave place to the ever victorious blue sky as the storm passed on. We had come through the gale with the steering oar smashed and the sail rent. The centerboards hung loose and banged about like crowbars among the logs, because all the ropes that had tightened them up under water were worn through — but we ourselves and the cargo were completely undamaged.

As early as July 3, when we were still one thousand sea miles from Polynesia, Nature was able to tell us, as it was able to tell the primitive raftsmen from Peru in their time, that there really was land ahead somewhere out in the sea. When we were a good thousand sea miles out from the coast of Peru we had noted small flocks of man-o'-war birds. They disappeared at about 100° west, and after that we saw only small petrels, which have their home on the sea. On July 3 the man-o'-war birds reappeared, at 125° west, and from now onward small flocks of them were often to be seen. As these birds did not come from America astern of us, they must have their homes in another country ahead.

On the night before July 30, there was a new and strange atmosphere about the *Kon-Tiki*. Perhaps it was the deafening clamor from all the sea birds over us that showed that something fresh was brewing. The screaming of birds with many voices sounded hectic and earthly after the dead creaking of lifeless ropes, which was all we had heard above the noise of the sea in the three months we had behind us. The moon seemed larger and rounder than ever as it sailed over the lookout at the masthead. In our fancy it reflected palm tops; it did not shine with such a yellow light over the cold fishes out at sea.

At six o'clock Bengt came down from the masthead, woke Herman, and turned in. When Herman clambered up the creaking, swaying mast, the day had begun to break. Ten minutes later he was down the rope ladder again and was shaking me by the leg.

"Come out and have a look at your island!"

His face was radiant, and I jumped up, followed by Bengt, who had not quite gone to sleep yet. Hard on one another's heels, we huddled together as high as we could climb, at the point where the masts crossed. There were many birds around us, and a faint violet-blue veil over the sky was reflected in the sea as a last relic of the departing night. Over the whole horizon away to the east, a ruddy glow had begun to spread, and far down to the southeast it gradually formed a blood-red background for a faint shadow, like a blue pencil line, drawn for a short way along the edge of the sea.

Land! An island! We devoured it greedily with our eyes and woke the others, who tumbled out drowsily and stared in all directions, as if they thought our bow was about to run on to a beach. Screaming sea birds formed a bridge across the sky in the direction of the distant island, which stood out sharper against the horizon as the red background widened and turned gold with the approach of the sun and the full daylight.

The long journey did not end with the first sight of land. For several days, the winds and currents carried the Kon-Tiki *past one island after another. Finally, on the 101st day at sea, the* Kon-Tiki *ran aground on a coral reef near a small, uninhabited island. The voyagers waded ashore to radio news of their arrival and to await the ship that would take them home again.*

Author

Thor Heyerdahl, the noted Norwegian explorer, adventurer, and author, shared his voyage to Polynesia in the book *Kon-Tiki*. His account of this adventure became a best-seller and was acclaimed throughout the world. It has been translated into sixty-four languages and was made into a documentary film, which received an Academy Award.

Thor Heyerdahl was awarded a doctorate by the University of Oslo, in Norway. Other scientific trips, and books about them, brought him further fame. He now lives in Italy, where he has restored a medieval village by the sea.

HEROES & Villains

Rikki-Tikki-Tavi
Rudyard Kipling

The Reluctant Dragon
Kenneth Grahame

Houghton Mifflin Literature

In the selections you have just read from *Confronting Nature,* the forces of nature placed people in situations that demanded an immediate response.

The next set of stories explores the theme *Confronting Nature* from a slightly different perspective. In *Rikki-Tikki-Tavi* by Rudyard Kipling one of nature's creatures (a mongoose) is forced into a deadly confrontation with a cobra; while in *The Reluctant Dragon* by Kenneth Grahame, a mythical creature seeks to *avoid* a confrontation at all costs.

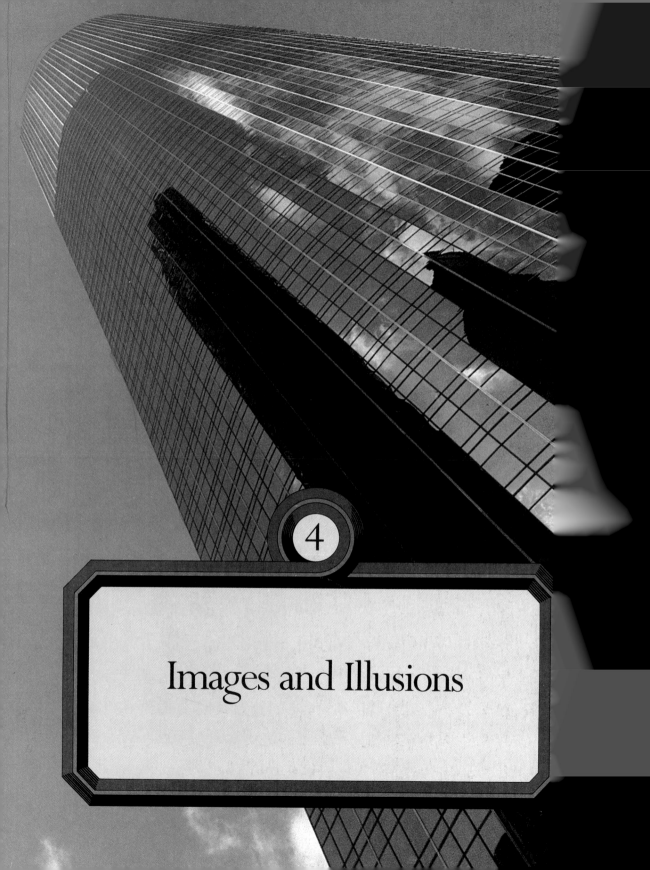

4

Images and Illusions

The Doubtful Guest

by Edward Gorey

When they answered the bell on that wild winter night,
There was no one expected — and no one in sight.

Then they saw something standing on top of an urn,
Whose peculiar appearance gave them quite a turn.

All at once it leapt down and ran into the hall,
Where it chose to remain with its nose to the wall.

It was seemingly deaf to whatever they said,
So at last they stopped screaming, and went off to bed.

It joined them at breakfast and presently ate
All the syrup and toast, and a part of a plate.

It wrenched off the horn from the new gramophone.
And could not be persuaded to leave it alone.

It betrayed a great liking for peering up flues,
And for peeling the soles of its white canvas shoes.

At times it would tear out whole chapters from books,
Or put roomfuls of pictures askew on their hooks.

Every Sunday it brooded and lay on the floor,
Inconveniently close to the drawing-room door.

Now and then it would vanish for hours from the scene,
But alas, be discovered inside a tureen.

It was subject to fits of bewildering wrath,
During which it would hide all the towels from the bath.

In the night through the house it would aimlessly creep,
In spite of the fact of its being asleep.

It would carry off objects of which it grew fond.
And protect them by dropping them into the pond.

It came seventeen years ago — and to this day
It has shown no intention of going away.

The Sandhill Crane

by Mary Austin

Whenever the days are cool and clear
The sandhill crane goes walking
Across the field by the flashing weir
Slowly, solemnly stalking.
The little frogs in the tules hear
And jump for their lives when he comes near,
The minnows scuttle away in fear,
When the sandhill crane goes walking.

The field folk know if he comes that way,
Slowly, solemnly stalking,
There is danger and death in the least delay
When the sandhill crane goes walking.
The chipmunks stop in the midst of their play,
The gophers hide in their hole away
And hush, oh, hush! the field mice say,
When the sandhill crane goes walking.

In Search of a Sandhill Crane

by Keith Robertson

When Lincoln Keller's mother decided to take a summer computer course in another state, his own summer plans had to change. Before he knew it, Link had committed himself to a summer in Michigan with his Aunt Harriet, whom he barely knew. Reluctantly, he agreed to take with him his Uncle Albert's expensive camera in order to get a picture of a rare bird, the sandhill crane.

On his second morning in Michigan, Link drove with his Aunt Harriet to her log cabin in the wilderness, where he had promised to spend at least two weeks. Its isolation and the lack of any modern conveniences were a shock to city-bred Link, and suddenly the summer began to look unbearably boring.

The cabin had only three rooms. Most of the space was taken up by one large room that served as the kitchen, dining, and living area. An old-fashioned kitchen range stood near one corner, and a big stone fireplace occupied the middle of the opposite wall. There was a cedar plank table, four straight chairs, several easy chairs that looked worn but comfortable, some built-in cupboards, and a worktable near the stove. Two doors led to the two smaller rooms. Each contained a bed, with what appeared to be a new mattress, a straight chair, an old bureau, and a small closet.

The floors were of worn planks, and the inside of the log walls had been paneled with boards. Inside, the cabin was much cozier and inviting than Link had expected. It was clean and had none of the musty smell that houses usually have after being closed for a long time.

"Charley and his wife did a good job cleaning the place," Harriet said approvingly. "He has looked after the cabin for years — kept the roof tight, repaired the windows, things like that. When I wrote him that I was coming up this summer, he said that the squirrels and mice had got in and had ruined the mattresses. So I sent up two new ones. He's put new screens on the windows, and I noticed before we came in that he'd set out some tomato plants for us. He's a wonderful man. You'll like him."

"What is Charley's last name?" Link asked.

"Horse."

"You're not serious?"

"His real name is Running Horse," Harriet said. "He's a Chippewa Indian. He used to work in the lumber camps as a young man, and someone called him Charley and he's kept the name ever since. He knows more about the woods than anyone I've ever known. He's an expert guide."

Link unloaded the station wagon while his aunt put things away. Then he went to the pile of wood that Charley Horse had left near the edge of the clearing and brought in wood for the kitchen stove.

"We used to have an outdoor fireplace," Harriet said. "It was built of stones stacked together. If we can find the metal grill, we can rebuild it. Then we can cook out of doors part of the time. In the middle of the summer it's too hot to build a fire in the stove. We usually didn't unless it rained."

"What about a refrigerator?" Link asked, looking at the boxes of food he had carried in from the car.

"I've talked about getting one of those gas refrigerators for years," Harriet said. "But I just haven't bothered. There's a spring not very far away. We used to use it for our drinking water when your father and I were children. Later we drilled a well. But I still use the spring to keep things cold, like butter. We put whatever we want in one of those metal pails and put the pail in the water. As for the bottles of milk, just tie a string around the necks and lower them into the water. You'll be surprised how cold they'll get."

They had lamb chops, canned peas, and baking powder biscuits for dinner. Then Harriet got her cane, and with

Link carrying the large metal pail full of perishables, they walked through the gathering gloom down an overgrown path to the spring. It was not far. The trail sloped downward for a short distance and then wound around a small hillock. Water gushed out of a low ledge of rock and trickled down into a pool about ten feet in diameter. A tiny stream led the overflow away into the darkness of the woods.

"I think the water is perfectly safe to drink," Harriet said. "The real reason Dad had the well put in was that he and your father liked to come down here to take baths. Mother objected to that. She said she wasn't going to drink bath water even if it was running."

Link leaned over and put his hand in the water. "It's ice cold," he said.

"Much too cold to bathe in, I always thought," she

agreed. "Mother and I carried water and took a bath with warm water in a tub."

Link found a flat rock ledge in the pool, placed the pail on it, and then weighted it down with another rock.

"That will do fine unless some bear gets too inquisitive," Harriet said. "One year I had real trouble. Charley put a rope up over that limb, and I suspended the pail out in the middle of the pool. I had to use a long stick with a hook on the end to reach out and get it."

"Are there many bears around here?" Lincoln asked, looking back into the thick depths of the woods.

"Lots of them. But if you leave them alone, they'll usually leave you alone."

It was dark by the time they returned to the cabin. Harriet lighted a kerosene lamp and showed Link how it worked. "I imagine you're tired," she said. "Up here you'll find you just naturally get up with the light and go to bed with the dark."

Link went outside and brushed his teeth at the pump and then went to bed. When he blew out the lamp, complete darkness descended. There were no distant street lights outside his window and no occasional flash of headlights. The room was so totally black that it bothered him. He glanced at his watch just to be certain that nothing had happened to his eyes. After about ten minutes he was able to make out the square of his window, a slightly grayer shade of black in the black wall.

Suddenly he heard something rustling around outside. It sounded enormous. Charley Horse had put new screens on the windows, but would a screen discourage a bear? He tried to convince himself that if iron bars had been needed, they would have been put on. The rustling was suddenly replaced by a gnawing sound as though a rat the size of a bear were gnawing down a big tree. There were lots of trees, he decided, one more or less would make no difference as long as it didn't fall on him. He had just become resigned to the gnawing, when suddenly the night was pierced with a blood-chilling screech: *"Oouuoooouuuoo, oh oh oh!"* This brought him bolt upright in bed. Then he lay back down again. He'd read of screech owls. The screech was repeated, and then in the distance he heard a high-pitched barking, like a dog but still not a dog. The peace and quiet of the deep woods! he thought disgustedly. What he needed was a few trucks or cement mixers driving down the street so he could get to sleep. He covered his ears with his pillow and closed his eyes.

He drifted off to sleep in spite of the strange noises, and the next thing he knew it was light and he was awake. He got dressed, went out to the pump, and sloshed cold water over his face. On his way back he noticed the broom that had been left beside the door. It had fallen to the ground, and something had gnawed the handle half through. He carried it inside and held it up for Harriet to see.

"Porcupine," she said with a laugh. "I think it's the salt in the perspiration from your hands that they're after. They'll sometimes gnaw a hoe handle in two in a night. Did you hear that owl screeching last night?"

"I heard lots of animals, and I see signs of them, but I don't see them," Link objected.

"Once in a while you will just stumble onto an animal, but usually they are very wary and cautious. So you have to be even more wary and quiet. If you stand quietly any place long enough, you'll be surprised at what you'll see."

While they ate breakfast, Harriet drew a rough map of the surrounding area, pointing out what she thought might interest him.

"It's always a good idea to carry a compass if you go very far into the woods," she cautioned. "It's not so much that a compass will keep you from getting lost, but if you do get lost, you can then keep going in one direction. Eventually, even up here, you will come to a road."

She produced a small compass, which Link stuck in his pocket before he went exploring. He found the swamp that Harriet had indicated, and the sizable stream of dark brown water that led away from it through the trees to the Manistique (Man'-uh-steek') River. He located the old beaver dam and a pond above it. And he visited the remains of what Harriet had said was an old stagecoach station. They were interesting, he admitted, but you couldn't stand around for hours and look at a beaver dam or a tumble-down log cabin. By the middle of the afternoon he had seen practically everything on Harriet's crude map. He was on his way back to the cabin when he passed by the spring. Walking through the woods was much warmer work than he had expected, and the water looked inviting. He stripped off his clothes and stepped into the edge of the pool.

The water was icy. It was so cold that his feet felt numb in a matter of seconds. He looked out at the center of the pool. The water was at least four feet deep. His father used to take a bath here, he told himself. He could at least take a quick dip. Holding his breath, he made a shallow dive toward the center. The water was deeper than he had expected; when he stood up it came to his chin. He had never been so cold in his life. With his teeth chattering he waded as quickly as possible to the edge and climbed out.

He found a spot of sunshine and stood shivering in it for several minutes while he tried to brush off some of the water from his body. He was covered with goose pimples. He put on his clothes and then sat down by the pool for a while. He felt wonderful. That quick dip had been the most fun of anything since his arrival in Michigan. But that was only a minute. What was he going to do with an entire summer?

The next day he went into Germfask[1] with his aunt to buy some milk and a few other staples. They visited the Seney Wildlife Refuge Headquarters and looked at the exhibits, and Link watched some Canada geese on the pond just outside the main building. When they returned to the cabin, he wrote several letters and took several short aimless walks into the woods. The following morning he weeded the area around the tomato plants and then thumbed aimlessly through one of his aunt's bird books.

"You're bored, aren't you?" Harriet asked in the middle of lunch.

---

[1] a town nearby

The sudden question caught Link unprepared. "Well, I don't know what you find to do all summer up here," he admitted finally. "What did my dad do when he was a boy?"

"He was like me. He could lie hidden in the underbrush and watch a beaver or a heron all day long. You have to love the creatures of the wild to like it here I guess. I find New York City terribly dull." She reached out a hand and touched him on the arm. "I suppose in a way the whole idea of coming up here was selfish. Now that I am partially crippled I don't feel up to staying here alone the way I once did. So I told myself that you would enjoy it so that I could come. I love it here. I can hobble outside and just sit watching and have a wonderful time. And of course there *was* the chance that you might like it too. Would you like to leave?"

"Well, I haven't really given it a trial yet," Link said, reluctant to hurt her by saying that he would.

"You've run out of things to do," Harriet observed. "I suppose you ought to try to get that picture your uncle wanted before you leave."

"Yes, I'd forgotten that," Link agreed. "Where would I go to find sandhill cranes?"

"Lakes, marshes, wet areas," Harriet said. "There are a number of these around within a few miles. Why don't we leave it that you will stay long enough to get your pictures. Then we'll pack up and leave."

"That's fair enough," Link said, feeling much better.

"I want to go pay Charley Horse for his work here and see several other people," Harriet said, getting up from the table. "You don't mind being left here alone?"

"Not at all," Link said.

He went to his room, got out his Uncle Albert's camera, and picked a 105 mm. lens. There were only four exposures left on the roll of film, so he went outside and used them up taking pictures of the cabin. Then he reloaded the camera, tucked his aunt's bird guide in his pocket, and started off through the woods. There might be a sandhill crane at the old beaver pond. "Wet areas," Harriet had said. He might be lucky and get his pictures right away. If he did, he wouldn't say anything but wait until he got the developed slides back. He could put up with another week or so buried in the woods. Then Harriet wouldn't feel she had completely wasted her money having the cabin repaired.

He spent the next hour crouched beside the pond, trying to sit quietly, but it was almost impossible. Tiny insects buzzed around his face, crawled down his collar, and generally made him miserable. At first he tried to swat them but decided this was a waste of time. Finally he crawled underneath a low shrub and, with the leaves almost brushing his face, managed to find a little peace.

He waited as patiently as he knew how, but he saw nothing that either resembled a crane or a crane's nest. According to his bird book they didn't build much of a nest — just a shallow cluster of sedge grass and twigs on the ground. The trouble was that the edges of the pond were thick with sedges, reeds, and cattails, and it would have been difficult to see a standing crane, much less a nest. He was about to give up and move on, when suddenly, almost in front of him in the middle of the pond there was a floating bird. It looked slightly like a small duck with a long, slender neck. Its back was gray-brown, and it had a white bill. Link raised his camera to his eyes and looked through the telescopic lens. There was a black band around the whitish bill. He snapped pictures and then put his camera down gently. He began thumbing through the book trying to find a picture of the floating bird. He made a slight sound as he turned the pages and when he looked up the bird was slowly sinking into the water. It sank lower and lower until finally just its eyes were above the water. He watched fascinated as it disappeared

entirely. He waited and waited until he decided that something must have pulled it under and eaten it. Then suddenly it popped to the surface about twenty feet farther away. Link watched as the bird dived several times. It could disappear in a flash or sink slowly and then reappear fifteen or twenty feet away. He wished that he could swim like that underwater. Finally it disappeared for a much longer period of time. His eyes searched the surface of the pond looking for it. Then, entirely by chance, he saw its head slowly emerging in the reeds, not very far from where he sat. It came up slowly, its neck turning cautiously like a submarine periscope. Suddenly it hopped onto what seemed to be a floating pile of reeds. It scratched away some covering reeds and sat down on a nest.

Slowly and cautiously, Link raised his camera and took several pictures. He had been sitting within a few yards of

the nest for some time without seeing it. He understood now what Harriet had meant when she said if he sat still long enough he would see things.

After ten minutes of thumbing through his book, he decided that the strange bird that could impersonate a submarine was a pied-bill grebe. He sat quietly for another hour. He saw blue jays and several songbirds that he could not identify and then — for a few hopeful minutes — he thought he saw a sandhill crane. An enormous bird flew high overhead on slow, flapping wings. Link looked at it through his camera lens. It was blue-gray, but it had no red crown on its head. His Uncle Albert had warned him not to confuse the great blue heron with the sandhill crane.

"A crane flies with his neck stretched out straight and a heron curves his in an *S* curve," Albert had said.

He was growing stiff and restless, and buzzing insects continued to plague him, so he decided to call it a day, go back, and have a quick dip in the spring. He took a slightly different route and passed through a small natural clearing that he had not visited before. He was partway across when he realized that several birds, including a particularly noisy blue jay, were screaming excitedly about something. He stopped and looked around carefully, searching for the cause of all the fuss. He looked first at the ground and then at the lower branches of the trees. Suddenly he saw an animal about eighteen inches long up in a maple tree at the edge of the clearing. Whether it was the cause of the birds' alarm or not he had no idea, but it was so grotesque-looking that he forgot about the birds. He raised his camera to use the lens as his binoculars. The animal had sort of yellowish tinged hair and a back and tail covered with white spikes. It was a porcupine! It seemed to be staring straight at him.

He moved slowly toward the tree. The porcupine made no move to run away or even to hide behind the tree trunk.

That would make quite a picture, he thought, as he watched the animal with its ratlike face and eyes. The trouble was that a branch partially blocked his view. He circled trying to get a clear shot. Either maple leaves or the feathery branches of a nearby spruce kept him from getting a good picture. The porcupine still showed no sign of being afraid.

He looked at a low branch thoughtfully. If he climbed up about level with the animal he could get a beautiful shot. There would be nothing in the way, and he could take the picture from the correct angle as far as the light was concerned. What a story that would make when he got back home! "I was in the same tree as the porcupine when I took this shot," he would say casually.

He slung the camera over his shoulder so that it hung against his back. Then he reached up, grabbed the lowest

limb, and began climbing. It was not difficult, but he went slowly and cautiously, keeping a wary eye on the porcupine. He got up about ten feet, just slightly below the porcupine, propped himself in a reasonably secure position, and got his camera. He took several shots and then moved a trifle closer. The porcupine began to show the first signs of nervousness. It retreated along its branch, moving about three feet farther out. The fact that it seemed frightened of him gave Link more courage. He climbed one branch higher and leaned over to get at just the right angle. He snapped one picture and then leaned farther to the left. He was too intent on getting the picture, and his right foot slipped. He began to topple. He grabbed frantically for the nearest branch — which was the one on which the porcupine was perched. He caught it. The sudden weight on the small branch shook the porcupine off. Link was too busy to notice or care what happened to the porcupine. His right foot slipped off the branch completely, throwing most of his weight on his left foot. The branch on which it was resting was small, and it snapped. That left him with only his right hand grasping one branch. His left hand still held the precious camera. The branch was too big around to hold properly, and it was doubtful if he could have held himself by one hand anyway. He did manage to hold on long enough to allow his feet to swing over so that he was dangling upright. Then he let go and dropped.

It was not a long drop, and he landed on his feet on soft ground. Slightly off balance, he stumbled backward and sat down heavily. There was an instant searing pain. He let out a yelp of agony and dropped the camera. It fell only a few inches to the ground which was carpeted with leaves and pine needles. Link was not much interested whether the camera was safe or not. He was in too much agony. He felt as though he were sitting on a red-hot stove. He rolled over until he was on his hands and knees. Then he reached back and felt the seat of his pants with his hand, half expecting to feel blood. Instead he felt what seemed to be stiff needles. He looked around suddenly for the porcupine. It was gone, but it had left plenty to remember it by. The entire seat of his pants was filled with quills! He had either landed on or beside the porcupine when he sat down.

Slowly and gingerly he got to his feet. Each movement was painful. He reached around and carefully took hold of the nearest quill he could see. He gave a yank. Nothing happened except he felt a sharp pain in his behind.

He picked up the camera and slowly started toward the cabin. Each step was torture. He paused every few feet, but he couldn't sit down. There was nothing to do but to plod onward, trying to move with the least amount of pain. About two thirds of the way he leaned against a tree, sort of half lying on his stomach, and examined the camera. It seemed unharmed. He blew away a few specks of dirt on the lens and got the lens cap from his pocket and put it on. At least he had got some good shots before he fell. And what a story he would have to tell now when he showed the family those slides!

He reached the cabin, went to his room, and lay face down on his bed. Once more he tried pulling a quill. He had no more success than before. Those things were in there to stay! He could see himself being wheeled into a hospital, face down on the stretcher. The doctor would operate while the nurses and everyone stood around laughing.

He was wondering how he would ever get to the hospital when he heard his aunt drive in. He waited until she had entered the cabin.

"Would you come in here, Aunt Harriet?" he called. "I had an accident!"

Harriet came into the room. Link turned to look at her.

She glanced at him without changing her expression and said, "Yes, you certainly did. And I'll bet it's painful! What did you do, sit on him?"

"I guess," he said. "I climbed a tree to take his picture and we both fell."

"Hurt yourself otherwise?" she asked.

"Nope. It was rough walking home though."

"I'll bet it was," she said. "Well, we have to get those quills out. Each quill is covered with dozens of little barbs. That makes them hard to pull out. But if you don't pull them out they work deeper. You can't possibly take off your pants. I'll have to pull the quills out through the cloth. The best way is to take a pair of pliers and give a quick yank. I've got some antiseptic that has sort of a chilling effect, and I'll try to spray you thoroughly with that. Maybe it will soak through your trousers and deaden the pain a little. But I warn you it will hurt."

"Go ahead," Link said, relieved that he wouldn't have to go to the hospital.

Harriet left and returned a few minutes later with a pair of pliers from the car and a can of antiseptic spray. She sprayed Link's posterior thoroughly and then asked, "Ready?"

"I guess as ready as I'll ever be," Link said. He pressed his lips together.

There was a sudden stab of pain, and Harriet said, "That's one! There's quite a few to go!"

"Don't count them," Link said. "I don't want to know how many until it's all over."

"The Indians dyed porcupine quills and used them to decorate deerskin shirts and pouches and moccasins," she said some time later as she yanked out the fifteenth quill.

"I'm going to save these and use them to decorate a poster

that says 'Beware of Porcupines'," Link said. He clenched his teeth as she gave another yank.

She pulled out twenty-two quills altogether. Link was sore and he knew he would be unable to sit comfortably for several days, but at least he could walk without pain.

"You'd better take off your clothes and examine yourself closely to be certain we haven't missed any. And then spray yourself with disinfectant again."

Link followed her suggestion and then dressed. "I'm going down to the spring," he announced as he walked into the main room of the cabin. "The other day when I waded in, my feet were numb by the time I'd gone three feet. Maybe if I sit down for fifteen minutes I can get the same results."

Harriet gave a slight chuckle. "I don't blame you." He had reached the door when she said, "Link."

He turned.

"I want you to know that I realize how painful that was," she said, almost shyly. "No one could have complained less."

She was much more sympathetic than he had thought, he decided, as he went on toward the spring. But she didn't know how to express it. He was beginning to understand her a little, and the more he understood her the better he liked her. She was really quite a good egg.

Author

Keith Robertson says of his boyhood in the Midwest, "I was always very fond of the out-of-doors and spent a great deal of time hiking, fishing, and camping." The book from which this story was taken, *In Search of a Sandhill Crane*, was named an Outstanding Science Trade Book for Children. Mr. Robertson also wrote the Henry Reed books.

FOG

by Carl Sandburg

The fog comes
on little cat feet.

It sits looking
over harbor and city
on silent haunches
and then moves on.

An excerpt from

Portrait of Myself

by Margaret Bourke-White

Margaret Bourke-White was one of the best-known photographers in the world. When she was fresh out of college she began her career as a photographer. At first she was interested in architectural and industrial photographs, though later she expanded her interests to many other types of photography as well. In Cleveland, Ohio, where she was living, she began by taking architectural photographs but then developed an interest in photographing the nearby steel mills. With the help of a camera clerk, Alfred Hall Bemis (Beme), she developed a reputation for her industrial photos. The Union Trust Company, one of the first clients for her industrial photos, would also be her break into photographing the steel mills.

The Enchanted Steel Mills

"Beme, aren't the presidents of banks on the boards of directors of industries, and vice versa?" We were eating goulash in Stouffer's Restaurant. "Someone like the president of the Union Trust, I mean?"

"Listen, child, old John Sherwin is on the board of directors of half the firms in town. More than half, maybe."

"And I photographed Mrs. John Sherwin's garden. Maybe he never saw the picture of the steer in his own bank — that's all public relations — but he must surely know the pictures of his own estate."

"I'd rather do business with the president any day than some whippersnapper down in the aisle," Mr. Bemis said.

"Yes," I said, "especially if it's the president of the bank that you get to introduce you to the president of the steel mill."

And so it turned out. John Sherwin, president of Union Trust, was puzzled that a "pretty young girl should want to take pictures in a dirty steel mill." But he was quite willing to send a letter of introduction to his friend Elroy Kulas at Otis Steel.

Mr. Kulas was forceful, short of stature, able. In the twelve years since he had become president, his company's output of steel ingots had quadrupled.

This of course I did not know, but I knew very well why I wanted to photograph the making of those steel ingots, and Mr. Kulas eyed me kindly while I tried to explain.

I do not remember the words I used, but I remember standing there by his massive carved desk, trying to tell him of my belief that there is a power and vitality in industry that makes it a magnificent subject for photography, that it reflects the age in which we live, that the steel mills are at the very heart of industry with the most drama, the most beauty — and that was why I wanted to capture the spirit of steelmaking in photographs.

He must have been a little surprised at the intensity of this twenty-one-year-old girl, possessed of this strange desire to photograph a steel furnace. And I, too, was a little surprised to find myself talking so fearlessly to the first industrial magnate I had ever faced.

But during my camera explorations down in the Flats among the ore boats and bridges I had done a good deal of thinking about these things. To me these industrial forms were all the more beautiful because they were never designed to be beautiful. They had a simplicity of line that came from their direct application to a purpose. Industry, I felt, had evolved an unconscious beauty — often a hidden beauty that was waiting to be discovered. And recorded! That was where I came in.

As I struggled to express these ideas to Mr. Kulas, I remembered to tell him certain things I had decided in advance I must say — to assure him I was not trying to sell him something, that at this stage I wanted only permission to experiment. And he in turn expressed a polite interest in seeing and perhaps purchasing for the company some of the pictures if they turned out well. I said, "Wait till we see what I get, first." And then of course I heard again about the fainting schoolteacher and about the "dangers": the acid fumes, the overpowering heat, the splashing hot metal. I wasn't the fainting kind, I insisted.

Mr. Kulas turned to the portfolio I had brought, looked at the pictures one by one, and stopped to study a photograph of the Sherwin rock garden. It showed little rills from a spring falling through moss-covered stones, with a little lead figure of a Cupid or nymph guarding each rill.

"I think your pictures of flower gardens are very artistic," said Mr. Kulas, looking up, "but how can you find anything artistic in my mill?"

"Please let me try."

And he did. He called in some vice-presidents and gave the word that I was to be admitted whenever I came to the plant to take pictures. And then he did me the greatest favor of all. He went off to Europe for five months.

I did not know what a long-term task I had taken on, nor did Mr. Kulas and his vice-presidents. I believe the Otis officials expected me to come down once or twice for a few snapshots, and I came nearly every night for a whole winter. If there had been someone, however kindly, asking how I was getting along, asking to see pictures (when for months there was nothing worth looking at), I could never have taken the time I needed to learn all the things I had to learn. Without knowing it, I had picked the hardest school I could have chosen. The steel mills with their extreme contrasts of light and shade make a difficult subject even today, with all our superior techniques and equipment. But then I had no technique, almost no experience. Also my difficulties were more than technical. The theme itself was colossal. Despite

my enthusiasm I needed orientation. I needed to go through a kind of digestive process before I could even choose viewpoints on my subjects.

The mill officials grew impatient. I was doubtless in the way. They were sure I was going to break a leg or fall into a ladle of molten metal. And a girl who came back night after night after night! What kind of pest was that? But the president had given his word. No one could gainsay it. I had my five months.

The first night was sheer heaven. Beme talked about it when we met years later.

"You had a very joyous time watching that steel. We were standing up high someplace and they pulled a furnace, and you were as delighted as a kid with a Fourth of July firecracker. I think you must have pyromania someplace. You grabbed your camera and you were off to a flying start.

"You weren't exactly dressed for the occasion. You had on some kind of a flimsy skirt and high-heeled slippers. And there you were dancing on the edge of the fiery crater in your velvet slippers, taking pictures like blazes and singing for joy."

My singing stopped when I saw the films. I could scarcely recognize anything on them. Nothing but a half-dollar-sized disk marking the spot where the molten metal had churned up in the ladle. The glory had withered.

I couldn't understand it. "We're woefully underexposed," said Mr. Bemis. "Very woefully underexposed. That red light from the molten metal looks as though it's illuminating the whole place. But it's all heat and no light. No actinic value."

So for weeks we struggled with actinic values. We brought in floodlights, laid cables; Earl set off his flashpans. But our illumination was simply gobbled up in the vast inky maw of the steel mill.

One tends to forget how quickly photography has developed as a science. With present-day equipment, steel mills still must be approached with respect, but then, film and paper had little latitude, negative emulsions were slow, there were no flashbulbs, no strobe; the miniature camera was not yet on the market. Stepped-up high-speed developers were unheard-of.

"If only I could go to someone who's been taking steel mill pictures and would be willing to advise me," I said to Beme.

"There isn't anybody like you mean." Mr. Bemis hunted up some shots made by a commercial photographer in the mills in Youngstown, Ohio. "These are the only pictures of the kind that have been taken as far as I know." I turned from them in despair — this was not the way I thought of steel mills, these gray tasteless blotting-paper scenes. "They're what I call map pictures," said Beme. "No drama shown. But probably none called for, kiddo. You're trying to do what nobody's done, to put the artist's touch on what others have thought a very dull mechanical problem."

Each night, Mr. Bemis borrowed some piece of equipment from the store, and we tried it out. "There's no one camera will take every kind of picture," said Beme. "A guy goes out to shoot pictures like you do needs a whole potful of cameras." A lens came in which we thought remarkably "fast" — f/3.5. It would seem quite average today. Beme lent it to me from the store till I saved enough to buy it. We still suffered from meager illumination and from halation; the faster lens helped, but not enough: our shadows were far too dim, our highlights blurred paste. We heard of an exciting new development in film: infrared. I wired to get some, learned from the research department of Eastman Kodak it was made up only for motion picture film.

I tried closer viewpoints, hoping to get more help from the light of the molten steel. The men put up a metal sheet to protect me from the heat while I set my camera in place, slipping the shield away while I made my shots. The varnish on my camera rose up in blisters and I looked as though I had been under a tropical sun. I climbed up the hanging ladder into the overhead crane so I could shoot directly down into the molten steel during the pour. During some shots, bursts of yellow smoke at the height of the pour blotted out everything in front of the lens; during others, the crane cab started trembling during the vital moments, and all my pictures were blurred.

By this time I was living entirely for the steel mills. The jobs I was able to keep going during the daytime just about paid for the films I shot up at night. And those same films, after exposure in the mills and processing in my kitchen sink, filled up my wastebasket — a gluey mass of sick, limping, unprintable negatives. At the end of a developing session Beme would pick up his hat, light one of his endless cigarettes, and start for the door, saying, "I'm going home to read the whole Book of Job. How Job sat in the ashes. Maybe it will do some good."

And apparently it did, for then traveling salesmen came into my life.

The first of these was H. F. Jackson, long-armed and long-legged, with a profile like Abraham Lincoln. Jack was traveling representative for the Meteor Company, which handled "photographic specialties." When he came to town, Beme called me excitedly. "I used to know Jack when we were both sixteen-year-old kids in Springfield, Massachusetts. He's the same age as me. I haven't seen him in all these years, until he turns up out of nowhere with his case full of samples. I told him about your problem, how you couldn't get enough light. Oh, he could get enough light, he says, to light up a hole in Hades. And he drags out these big magnesium flares with wooden handles, like Roman candles. He's on his way to Hollywood to demonstrate them for the movies. I told him if he would come with us he could see the steel mills, and he fell for it."

We had more than our usual red tape at the gate that night — a strange guard who didn't recognize our passes, and then phoned endlessly until he could rouse some higher-up who would admit Jack. And while all this went on in the drafty guardhouse, a wet snow blew up, and through the storm we could watch the rising crescendo of rosy light glowing from the door of the open hearth, which showed us we were missing a "heat" and would have to wait three hours for the next pour.

I know of no colder place than a steel mill in winter between "heats," and no hotter place than a mill during the pour. During our three hours we roamed the windy cat-walks, climbed up and down ladders with the sleet driving through, and planned our shots. I was eager to work out a side lighting which would emphasize the great hulk and roundness of the ladles and molds, and still not flatten and destroy the magic of the place. To do that properly would take two flares for each shot, Jack decided, used at each side and at varying distances from the camera.

At the end of the third hour, Jack made a heroic decision. In his sample case were one dozen flares with which he had set out to conquer Hollywood. He would save one flare to demonstrate to the movie colony. Eleven he would demonstrate in the steel mills.

Then in a great rush the pour began. With the snow at our backs and the heat in our faces, we worked like creatures possessed. The life of each flare was half a minute. During those thirty seconds I steadied my reflex camera on a

crossrail, made exposures of eight seconds, four seconds, two seconds, dashed to a closer viewpoint, hand holding the camera for slow instantaneous shots until the flare died.

In the beginning, Beme stood at one end and Jack at the other, each holding one flare. Then as the metal rose bubbling in the ladle with great bursts of orange smoke shrouding the mill, Jack was afraid we were not getting enough fill-in light. So we took the great gamble: he and Beme held two flares each. The eleventh flare we saved for that last spectacular moment in the pouring of the ingot molds — that dramatic moment when the columns of tall tubular forms are full to bursting, each crowned with a fiery corona of sparks, and the cooling ladle in one last effort empties the final drops of its fiery load and turns away.

The next night we developed the films, and there it all was: the noble shapes of ladles, giant hooks and cranes, the dim vast sweep of the mill. There was one moment of anxiety, when we developed the negative we had taken with the eleventh flare. It was filled with black curving lines, as though someone had scratched it deeply with his fingernails.

Beme couldn't make it out. "The film seems to be damaged in some manner."

"But the marks are so regular," I said, "like looped wire. Each one is a perfect curve."

And suddenly I knew. I had photographed the actual path of the sparks.

Margaret's steel pictures led to a job with Fortune, *a magazine about business and industry. She began to travel all over the United States, taking pictures of buildings and workers. In 1936, Margaret was hired as a photographer for* Life, *which became a very successful magazine. She went to Europe, China, Russia, and the Arctic. She took pictures of kings and queens and presidents. She photographed the daily lives of people everywhere.*

In 1941, when the United States went to war, Margaret Bourke-White became the first woman to work in the battle zones. After the war, she continued to travel all over the world on assignment. She photographed the rich and poor of India, the miners of South Africa, and the war-torn families of Korea. Although she became ill with a disease that affected her body movements, she worked until her death in 1971 at the age of sixty-seven.

photos by
**Margaret
Bourke-White**

opposite: *Log Rafts, 1937*
left: *Herero Women*
bottom: *Coney Island, 1952*

An excerpt from

THE LION, THE WITCH
and
THE WARDROBE

by C. S. Lewis

The Land in the Wardrobe

Once there were four children whose names were Peter, Susan, Edmund and Lucy. This story is about something that happened to them when they were sent away from London during the war because of the air-raids. They were sent to the house of an old Professor who lived in the heart of the country, ten miles from the nearest railway station and two miles from the nearest post office. He had no wife and he lived in a very large house with a housekeeper called Mrs. Macready and three servants. (Their names were Ivy, Margaret and Betty, but they do not come into the story much.) He himself was a very old man with shaggy white hair, which grew over most of his face as well as on his head, and they liked him almost at once; but on the first evening when he came out to meet them at the front door he was so odd-looking that Lucy (who was the youngest) was a little afraid of him, and Edmund (who was the next youngest) wanted to laugh and had to keep on pretending he was blowing his nose to hide it.

As soon as they had said good night to the Professor and gone upstairs on the first night, the boys came into the girls' room and they all talked it over.

"We've fallen on our feet and no mistake," said Peter. "This is going to be perfectly splendid. That old chap will let us do anything we like."

"I think he's an old dear," said Susan.

"Oh, come off it!" said Edmund, who was tired and pretending not to be tired, which always made him bad-tempered. "Don't go on talking like that."

"Like what?" said Susan; "and anyway, it's time you were in bed."

"Trying to talk like Mother," said Edmund. "And who are you to say when I'm to go to bed? Go to bed yourself."

"Hadn't we all better go to bed?" said Lucy. "There's sure to be a row if we're heard talking here."

"No there won't," said Peter. "I tell you this is the sort of house where no one's going to mind what we do. Anyway, they won't hear us. It's about ten minutes' walk from here down to that dining room, and any amount of stairs and passages in between."

"What's that noise?" said Lucy suddenly. It was a far larger house than she had ever been in before and the thought of all those long passages and rows of doors leading into empty rooms was beginning to make her feel a little creepy.

"It's only a bird, silly," said Edmund.

"It's an owl," said Peter. "This is going to be a wonderful place for birds. I shall go to bed now. I say, let's go and explore to-morrow. You might find anything in a place like this. Did you see those mountains as we came along? And the woods? There might be eagles. There might be stags. There'll be hawks."

"Badgers!" said Lucy.

"Snakes!" said Edmund.

"Foxes!" said Susan.

But when next morning came, there was a steady rain falling, so thick that when you looked out of the window you could see neither the mountains nor the woods nor even the stream in the garden.

"Of course it *would* be raining!" said Edmund. They had just finished breakfast with the Professor and were upstairs in the room he had set apart for them — a long, low room with two windows looking out in one direction and two in another.

"Do stop grumbling, Ed," said Susan. "Ten to one it'll

clear up in an hour or so. And in the meantime we're pretty well off. There's a wireless and lots of books."

"Not for me," said Peter, "I'm going to explore in the house."

Everyone agreed to this and that was how the adventures began. It was the sort of house that you never seem to come to the end of, and it was full of unexpected places. The first few doors they tried led only into spare bedrooms, as everyone had expected that they would; but soon they came to a very long room full of pictures and there they found a suit of armour; and after that was a room all hung with green, with a harp in one corner; and then came three steps down and five steps up, and then a kind of little upstairs hall and a door that led out onto a balcony, and then a whole series of rooms that led into each other and were lined with books — most of them very old books and some bigger than a Bible in a church. And shortly after that they looked into a room that was quite empty except for one big wardrobe; the sort that has a looking-glass in the door. There was nothing else in the room at all except a dead blue-bottle on the window-sill.

"Nothing there!" said Peter, and they all trooped out again — all except Lucy. She stayed behind because she thought it would be worth while trying the door of the wardrobe, even though she felt almost sure that it would be locked. To her surprise it opened quite easily, and two moth-balls dropped out.

Looking into the inside, she saw several coats hanging up — mostly long fur coats. There was nothing Lucy liked so much as the smell and feel of fur. She immediately stepped into the wardrobe and got in among the coats and rubbed her face against them, leaving the door open, of course, because she knew that it is very foolish to shut oneself into any wardrobe. Soon she went further in and found that there was a second row of coats hanging up behind the first one. It was almost quite dark in there and she kept her arms stretched out in front of her so as not to bump her face into the back of the wardrobe. She took a step further in — then two or three steps — always expecting to feel woodwork against the tips of her fingers. But she could not feel it.

"This must be a simply enormous wardrobe!" thought Lucy, going still further in and pushing the soft folds of the coats aside to make room for her. Then she noticed that there was something crunching under her feet. "I wonder is that more moth-balls?" she thought, stooping down to feel it with her hands. But instead of feeling the hard, smooth wood of the floor of the wardrobe, she felt something soft and powdery and extremely cold. "This is very queer," she said, and went on a step or two further.

Next moment she found that what was rubbing against her face and hands was no longer soft fur but something hard and rough and even prickly. "Why, it is just like branches of trees!" exclaimed Lucy. And then she saw that there was a light ahead of her; not a few inches away where the back of the wardrobe ought to have been, but a long way off. Something cold and soft was falling on her. A moment later she found that she was standing in the middle of a wood at night-time with snow under her feet and snowflakes falling through the air.

Lucy felt a little frightened, but she felt very inquisitive and excited as well. She looked back over her shoulder and there, between the dark tree-trunks, she could still see the open doorway of the wardrobe and even catch a glimpse of the empty room from which she had set out. (She had, of course, left the door open, for she knew that it is a very silly thing to shut oneself into a wardrobe.) It seemed to be still daylight there. "I can always get back if anything goes wrong," thought Lucy. She began to walk forward, *crunch-crunch,* over the snow and through the wood towards the other light.

In about ten minutes she reached it and found that it was a lamp-post. As she stood looking at it, wondering why there was a lamp-post in the middle of a wood and wondering what to do next, she heard a pitter patter of feet coming towards her. And soon after that a very strange person stepped out from among the trees into the light of the lamp-post.

He was only a little taller than Lucy herself and he carried over his head an umbrella, white with snow. From the waist upwards he was like a man, but his legs were shaped like a goat's (the hair on them was glossy black) and instead of feet he had goat's hoofs. He also had a tail, but Lucy did not notice this at first because it was neatly caught up over the arm that held the umbrella so as to keep it from trailing in the snow. He had a red woolen muffler round his neck and his skin was rather

reddish too. He had a strange, but pleasant little face with a short pointed beard and curly hair, and out of the hair there stuck two horns, one on each side of his forehead. One of his hands, as I have said, held the umbrella: in the other arm he carried several brown paper parcels. What with the parcels and the snow it looked just as if he had been doing his Christmas shopping. He was a Faun. And when he saw Lucy he gave such a start of surprise that he dropped all his parcels.

"Goodness gracious me!" exclaimed the Faun.

"Good evening," said Lucy. But the Faun was so busy picking up his parcels that at first he did not reply. When he had finished he made her a little bow.

"Good evening, good evening," said the Faun. "Excuse me — I don't want to be inquisitive — but should I be right in thinking that you are a Daughter of Eve?"

"My name's Lucy," said she, not quite understanding him.

"But you are — forgive me — you are what they call a girl?" asked the Faun.

"Of course I'm a girl," said Lucy.

"You are in fact Human?"

"Of course I'm human," said Lucy, still a little puzzled.

"To be sure, to be sure," said the Faun. "How stupid of me! But I've never seen a Son of Adam or a Daughter of Eve before. I am delighted. That is to say —" and then he stopped as if he had been going to say something he had not intended but had remembered in time. "Delighted, delighted," he went on. "Allow me to introduce myself. My name is Tumnus."

"I am very pleased to meet you, Mr. Tumnus," said Lucy.

"And may I ask, O Lucy, Daughter of Eve," said Mr. Tumnus, "how you have come into Narnia?"

"Narnia? What's that?" said Lucy.

"This is the land of Narnia," said the Faun, "where we are now; all that lies between the lamp-post and the great castle of Cair Paravel on the eastern sea. And you — you have come from the wild woods of the west?"

"I — I got in through the wardrobe in the spare room," said Lucy.

"Ah!" said Mr. Tumnus in a rather melancholy voice, "if only I had worked harder at geography when I was a little Faun, I should no doubt know all about those strange countries. It is too late now."

"But they aren't countries at all," said Lucy, almost laughing. "It's only just back there — at least — I'm not sure. It is summer there."

"Meanwhile," said Mr. Tumnus, "it is winter in Narnia, and has been for ever so long, and we shall both catch cold if we stand here talking in the snow. Daughter of Eve from the far land of Spare Oom where eternal summer reigns around the bright city of War Drobe, how would it be if you came and had tea with me?"

"Thank you very much, Mr. Tumnus," said Lucy. "But I was wondering whether I ought to be getting back."

"It's only just round the corner," said the Faun, "and there'll be a roaring fire — and toast — and sardines — and cake."

"Well, it's very kind of you," said Lucy. "But I shan't be able to stay long."

"If you will take my arm, Daughter of Eve," said Mr. Tumnus, "I shall be able to hold the umbrella over both of us. That's the way. Now — off we go."

And so Lucy found herself walking through the wood arm in arm with this strange creature as if they had known one another all their lives.

They had not gone far before they came to a place where the ground became rough and there were rocks all about and

little hills up and little hills down. At the bottom of one small valley Mr. Tumnus turned suddenly aside as if he were going to walk straight into an unusually large rock, but at the last moment Lucy found he was leading her into the entrance of a cave. As soon as they were inside she found herself blinking in the light of a wood fire. Then Mr. Tumnus stooped and took a flaming piece of wood out of the fire with a neat little pair of tongs, and lit a lamp. "Now we shan't be long," he said, and immediately put a kettle on.

Lucy thought she had never been in a nicer place. It was a little, dry, clean cave of reddish stone with a carpet on the floor and two little chairs ("one for me and one for a friend," said Mr. Tumnus) and a table and a dresser and a mantelpiece over the fire and above that a picture of an old Faun with a grey beard. In one corner there was a door which Lucy thought must lead to Mr. Tumnus' bedroom, and on one wall was a shelf full of books. Lucy looked at these while he was setting out the tea things. They had titles like *The Life and Letters of Silenus* or *Nymphs and Their Ways* or *Men, Monks and Gamekeepers; a Study in Popular Legend* or *Is Man a Myth?*

"Now, Daughter of Eve!" said the Faun.

And really it was a wonderful tea. There was a nice brown egg, lightly boiled, for each of them, and then sardines on toast, and then buttered toast, and then toast with honey, and then a sugar-topped cake. And when Lucy was tired of eating the Faun began to talk. He had wonderful tales to tell of life in the forest. He told about the midnight dances and how the Nymphs who lived in the wells and the Dryads who lived in the trees came out to dance with the Fauns; about long hunting parties after the milk-white Stag who could give you wishes if you caught him; about feasting and treasure-seeking with the wild Red Dwarfs in deep mines and caverns far beneath the forest floor; and then about summer when the woods were green and old Silenus on his fat donkey would come to visit them, and sometimes Bacchus himself, and then the streams would run with wine instead of water and the whole forest would give itself up to jollification for weeks on end. "Not that it isn't always winter now," he added gloomily. Then to cheer himself up he took out from its case on the dresser a strange little flute that looked as if it were made of straw and began to play. And the tune he played made Lucy want to cry and laugh and dance and go to sleep all at the same time. It must have been hours later when she shook herself and said, "Oh Mr.

Tumnus — I'm so sorry to stop you, and I do love that tune — but really, I must go home. I only meant to stay for a few minutes."

"It's no good *now,* you know," said the Faun, laying down his flute and shaking his head at her very sorrowfully.

"No good?" said Lucy, jumping up and feeling rather frightened. "What do you mean? I've got to go home at once. The others will be wondering what has happened to me." But a moment later she asked, "Mr. Tumnus! Whatever is the matter?" for the Faun's brown eyes had filled with tears and then the tears began trickling down his cheeks, and soon they were running off the end of his nose; and at last he covered his face with his hands and began to howl.

"Mr. Tumnus! Mr. Tumnus!" said Lucy in great distress. "Don't! Don't! What is the matter? Aren't you well? Dear Mr. Tumnus, do tell me what is wrong." But the Faun continued sobbing as if his heart would break. And even when Lucy went over and put her arms round him and lent him her handkerchief, he did not stop. He merely took the handkerchief and kept on using it, wringing it out with both hands whenever it got too wet to be any more use, so that presently Lucy was standing in a damp patch.

"Mr. Tumnus!" bawled Lucy in his ear, shaking him. "Do stop. Stop it at once! You ought to be ashamed of yourself, a great big Faun like you. What on earth are you crying about?"

"Oh — oh — oh!" sobbed Mr. Tumnus, "I'm crying because I'm such a bad Faun."

"I don't think you're a bad Faun at all," said Lucy. "I think you are a very good Faun. You are the nicest Faun I've ever met."

"Oh — oh — you wouldn't say that if you knew," replied Mr. Tumnus between his sobs. "No, I'm a bad Faun. I don't suppose there ever was a worse Faun since the beginning of the world."

"But what have you done?" asked Lucy.

"My old father, now," said Mr. Tumnus, "that's his picture over the mantelpiece. He would never have done a thing like this."

"A thing like what?" said Lucy.

"Like what I've done," said the Faun. "Taken service under the White Witch. That's what I am. I'm in the pay of the White Witch."

"The White Witch? Who is she?"

"Why, it is she that has got all Narnia under her thumb. It's she that makes it always winter. Always winter and never Christmas; think of that!"

"How awful!" said Lucy. "But what does she pay *you* for?"

"That's the worst of it," said Mr. Tumnus with a deep groan. "I'm a kidnapper for her, that's what I am. Look at me, Daughter of Eve. Would you believe that I'm the sort of Faun to meet a poor innocent child in the wood, one that had never done me any harm, and pretend to be friendly with it, and invite it home to my cave, all for the sake of lulling it asleep and then handing it over to the White Witch?"

"No," said Lucy. "I'm sure you wouldn't do anything of the sort."

"But I have," said the Faun.

"Well," said Lucy rather slowly (for she wanted to be truthful and yet not to be too hard on him), "well, that was pretty bad. But you're so sorry for it that I'm sure you will never do it again."

"Daughter of Eve, don't you understand?" said the Faun. "It isn't something I *have* done. I'm doing it now, this very moment."

"What do you mean?" cried Lucy, turning very white.

"You are the child," said Mr. Tumnus. "I had orders from the White Witch that if ever I saw a Son of Adam or a Daughter of Eve in the wood, I was to catch them and hand them over to her. And you are the first I ever met. And I've pretended to be your friend and asked you to tea, and all the time I've been meaning to wait till you were asleep and then go and tell *her*."

"Oh but you won't, Mr. Tumnus," said Lucy. "You won't, will you? Indeed, indeed you really mustn't."

"And if I don't," said he, beginning to cry again, "she's sure to find out. And she'll have my tail cut off, and my horns sawn off, and my beard plucked out, and she'll wave her wand over my beautiful cloven hoofs and turn them into horrid solid hoofs like a wretched horse's. And if she is extra and specially angry she'll turn me into stone and I shall be only a statue of a Faun in her horrible house until the four thrones at Cair Paravel are filled — and goodness knows when that will happen, or whether it will ever happen at all."

"I'm very sorry, Mr. Tumnus," said Lucy. "But please let me go home."

"Of course I will," said the Faun. "Of course I've got to. I see that now. I hadn't known what Humans were like before I met you. Of course I can't give you up to the Witch; not now that I know you. But we must be off at once. I'll see you back to the lamp-post. I suppose you can find your own way from there back to Spare Oom and War Drobe?"

"I'm sure I can," said Lucy.

"We must go as quietly as we can," said Mr. Tumnus. "The whole wood is full of *her* spies. Even some of the trees are on her side."

They both got up and left the tea things on the table, and Mr. Tumnus once more put up his umbrella and gave Lucy his arm, and they went out into the snow. The journey back was not at all like the journey to the Faun's cave; they stole along as quickly as they could, without speaking a word, and Mr. Tumnus kept to the darkest places. Lucy was relieved when they reached the lamp-post again.

"Do you know your way from here, Daughter of Eve?" said Tumnus.

Lucy looked very hard between the trees and could just see in the distance a patch of light that looked like daylight. "Yes," she said, "I can see the wardrobe door."

"Then be off home as quick as you can," said the Faun, "and — c-can you ever forgive me for what I meant to do?"

"Why, of course I can," said Lucy, shaking him heartily by the hand. "And I do hope you won't get into dreadful trouble on my account."

"Farewell, Daughter of Eve," said he. "Perhaps I may keep the handkerchief?"

"Rather!" said Lucy, and then ran towards the far-off patch of daylight as quickly as her legs would carry her. And presently instead of rough branches brushing past her she felt coats, and instead of crunching snow under her feet she felt wooden boards, and all at once she found herself jumping out of the wardrobe into the same empty room from which the whole adventure had started. She shut the wardrobe door tightly behind her and looked around, panting for breath. It was still raining and she could hear the voices of the others in the passage.

"I'm here," she shouted. "I'm here. I've come back, I'm all right."

Author

C. S. Lewis, born as Clive Staples Lewis in Belfast, Ireland, was a poet, a writer, and a professor at Cambridge University in England. He was a well-known writer both for children and adults. *The Lion, the Witch and the Wardrobe* is the first book in his seven-volume series written for young readers about the magic land of Narnia. Among the many honors and awards he has won are the Lewis Carroll Shelf Award in 1962 for *The Lion, the Witch and the Wardrobe,* and the Carnegie Award in 1956 for the final book in the series, *The Last Battle.* Once when asked how he knew what to write for children he answered, "I put in what I would have liked to read myself as a child and what I still like reading now that I am in my fifties."

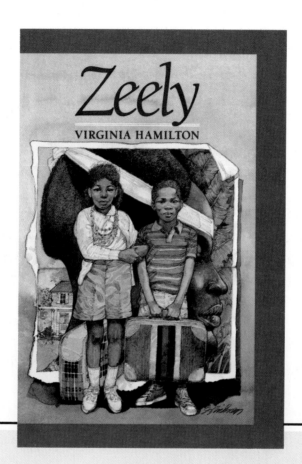

Zeely

VIRGINIA HAMILTON

In the selections you have just read from *Images and Illusions,* images and illusions played with your sense of what is real. Looking, and then looking again; seeing in *another* way became important in these selections.

Now you will read *Zeely* by Virginia Hamilton, a story about appearances, this time concerning human beings. In it, "Geeder" and her brother go to their uncle's farm and meet Zeely. But who *is* Zeely? Is she what she seems to be?

5

Living
With
Change

Grandpa's Miracle

by Eve Bunting

Saturday, April 3

"Do you want to come to the park with me?" I asked Grandpa today. Our park is terrific; it has lots of space, and there's even a river that runs through it. That's where Grandpa taught me to skip rocks when I was little.

"I don't want to go to the park," Grandpa said, and he turned his head away.

So I went with my best friend, Laura, who lives in my building. We decided to go for a run along the river path.

As we jogged along at an easy pace, I thought about Grandpa and how he'd changed.

Laura stopped to tie her shoelace. I knew she really stopped to rest because she was huffing and puffing like a train. I decided to tell her about my problem.

"Grandpa's no fun at all these days," I told her. I wanted Laura to talk about him. I wanted her to help me understand why he was suddenly the way he was.

"Aw, he's not so bad," Laura said. What does Laura know — she's not even *related* to him.

Grandpa lives with Mom and me. He used to be my friend. Every night when he came home from work, we talked or we did something, such as building a model of the space shuttle. Grandpa helped Mom too. He did the supper dishes, and sometimes he made the best spaghetti and meatballs. His Saturday morning special breakfasts weren't so bad, either.

Since January, Grandpa doesn't go to work anymore. They told him he had to retire because he's too old. It's strange — when they told Grandpa that, he turned all moody and gloomy. I didn't tell him he was too old to do things with me, and Mom sure didn't tell him he was too old to help around the house; but all of a sudden he believes he is. All he does now is sit and sit and sit — and complain.

Wednesday, April 7

Today Judy Spencer asked Laura and me to try out for the girls' softball team. When I told Grandpa that tryouts were next week, he didn't even offer to help us practice.

"Are you sure you're good enough?" he asked.

I didn't let that get to me; I tried one more time. "Want to hit some balls to us?" I asked. "We need practice catching Texas leaguers."

"I don't play games anymore," Grandpa said. "Just leave me alone."

I'll leave him alone all right.

What has happened to him? Grandpa is the one who taught me to play all kinds of games. I still have the moonstone marble he gave me when I was eight. It's there in my secret box, all pink and blue and orange as fire.

When Mom came home from work, I helped her fix a tuna and rice casserole. When she asked me how Grandpa was, I didn't answer.

"Cathy," Mom said, "Grandpa has always been such a proud man, so independent. It's going to take him time to get accustomed to being retired. Right now he feels depressed because he thinks life is over for him."

"Well, that's stupid," I said. I felt as gloomy as Grandpa.

Saturday, April 10

Laura and I went to the park today. We took our gloves and ball so we could practice to get on the softball team. I want to make pitcher. Laura caught for me even though she wants to play first base. Instead of just crouching and catching, she kept jumping up and shouting, "Pitch it in the glove, Cathy! Get it down! Wow, is your eye ever off!"

"I just need practice," I muttered.

Laura shook her head. "You're never going to make it."

Sometimes Laura gives me an enormous pain.

We decided to visit the ducks before we left. When we were little, we used to bring bread to feed them, but we haven't done that since the third grade.

We counted eleven ducks on the river, and we were just about to go when Laura said, "Look!"

She pointed, and I saw a mother duck with her four little ducklings starting off from the river bank. They glided downstream in a row. The little ones were trying to imitate their mother, and they were adorable.

Then I saw the nest. It was by the bank close to where we were standing. I saw something else too; the mother duck had abandoned one light tan egg. It was lying there, all sparkly and shiny, and when I gently picked it up, it was as smooth as glass. It was as smooth as my moonstone, only bigger.

"She'll be back to get it," Laura said; but I knew about mallards, and I knew this family was gone for good.

"You can't keep it anyway," Laura said. "Pretty soon it's going to get smelly."

"No, it won't." I figured Laura was miffed because she hadn't found the egg first. Very carefully, I wrapped it in my flannel shirt.

We ran all the way home and found Grandpa sitting in the courtyard.

"Look!" I held the egg on my hand and imagined the baby curled inside, its head under its dark little wing. "It's a mallard's egg," I said. "The mother left it." I don't know why I said what I said next. The words just popped out. "I'm going to hatch it."

"Just how do you propose to do that?" asked Grandpa.

I hadn't thought about it yet, but quickly I said, "Well, I'll wrap it in something — maybe in a towel — and hold it all day."

"What about school?" asked Grandpa. "You going to take an egg in a towel to school?"

"I'll think of something," I said. No way was I going to let Grandpa spoil my idea.

"Here, let me see it." Grandpa took the egg and cradled it in his big hand and stared off into the distance for a long time. I tried to figure out what he was staring at, but there is just our courtyard and the fence between our building and the next one. There are trees and the TV aerials on the roofs and the ECONO GAS sign above the corner service station.

"Cathy," he said, "if this egg hatches, it will be a miracle."

I waited but he didn't say anything else. He just sat there, holding the egg.

"Are you going to just sit there, holding that egg?" I asked him.

Grandpa nodded. "Maybe. Somebody has to monitor it if the baby is to make it. Besides, who else is there who has the time and the patience and the know-how?"

"Nobody but you, Grandpa," I said.

Grandpa asked me to get his old woolen cap. He put the egg inside and held the cap warm in his hand. Then he started making phone calls. "Better find out for sure how to hatch a duck egg," he muttered.

I guess he found somebody who knew for sure. They talked and talked. Then Grandpa said, "That was the county agricultural agent. He gave me some suggestions. You hold the egg carefully in the cap, Cathy. I'm going to get that old aquarium from the basement."

Grandpa set up the tank with lights, a towel, and a pan of hot water.

"The water supplies humidity," Grandpa explained. He put the egg in the tank and propped a thermometer in the corner. "We can't let this water drop below 99 degrees," he said.

"Hatching a baby duck is tricky stuff," I said.

Grandpa smiled. "We can do it."

When he went to bed tonight, Grandpa put the tank on the nightstand next to his bed. He didn't seem to mind sleeping with the lights on. I guess having a baby duck is going to be worth it.

Sunday, April 11

Grandpa monitored the egg off and on all day. Once he carefully turned it.

I'm getting worried. What if that old egg is rotten? I keep hearing Grandpa say, "If this egg hatches, it will be a miracle." What if Grandpa hatches a dud? What if it *never* hatches?

Mom kids Grandpa a lot. "That little duck will be convinced you're its daddy because you'll be the first thing it sees when it breaks out of that shell. That happens with a lot of orphaned baby animals. It's called imprinting."

"Huh," Grandpa said. "I never figured on being a duck's daddy." But he didn't say it in the old, dreary way.

Grandpa crooked his finger at me. "Come here, Cathy," he said. He put the egg in my hand, all moonstone smooth, and I felt the tiniest of taps against my palm. Tap, tap, tap.

"It's in there all right," I said, "and it feels as if it's trying to get out."

"A couple more days," Grandpa said.

Tuesday, April 13

When Laura and I came home from school, we had a duckling.

It had just happened. There were little pieces of tan shell on Grandpa's pants and sticking to his sweater. The duckling was perched on Grandpa's knee, staring at him. It was a little ball of dandelion fluff with button eyes. When Grandpa put it on the floor, it walked splayfooted around his shoes.

"Oh, it's so pretty," I said.

Grandpa touched the fluffy head with the tip of his finger. "It's going to take a lot of care and attention. It's going to need feeding and . . ."

I interrupted. "I bet it would love your spaghetti and meatballs. Everybody does."

Grandpa half smiled. "For now it needs chick mash. Want to accompany me to the pet shop, girls?"

Mom duck-sat while Grandpa and Laura and I were gone. Laura and I talked a lot on the way there — and Grandpa listened. It was the first time in ages he really listened.

"Cathy's not getting the ball into the strike zone when she pitches," Laura told him.

"You have to bend your back more, Cathy," Grandpa said. "We'll work on it."

Laura nudged me and grinned. "OK," she whispered.

As soon as we got back with the duck chow, the little duck ran peep-peep-peeping straight for Grandpa.

"Duck's daddy," Mom teased, and Grandpa shook his head; but I could tell he was pleased. He got the heating pad and made a warm bed for the baby in the kitchen.

"It's going to be a while before it's self-sufficient," Grandpa said. "Till it is, we can't put it back in the river."

"How long will that be?" I asked. It's such a dear little duck that I want it to stay around. Now there's something else — I like the way Grandpa is these days. I don't want him to turn back into that old gloomy person again.

"It can't go till it's all feathered out," Grandpa said. "The downy feathers are what insulate it in the water. About a month, I'd say."

"How come you always know so much?" Laura asked.

Sometimes Laura asks good questions, especially considering that Grandpa's not even her grandpa.

"It must be a matter of longevity." There was a kind of boasting in Grandpa's voice and in the way he looked at the little duck.

Laura let the duck nip her finger. "What's its name, anyway?"

"Miracle," Grandpa said. "I told Cathy that if this egg hatched, it would be a miracle, and here it is."

Tuesday, April 27

Miracle just keeps eating and growing. For the past few weeks, Grandpa has been taking him into the courtyard of our building so that he can look for bugs in the ground.

"Miracle has to learn to forage for food," Grandpa says. "We don't want him to be dependent on humans."

Grandpa has been learning a lot about ducklings. He went to the library and got a couple of books. He read, and then he told us things he had read.

"Miracle's a male duck, so he's really a drake," he told me.

"But he's so little," I said. "Let's just call him 'duck' for now."

Grandpa talked to the pet store owner. He even made a trip to the zoo and talked to the duck-keeper. When my grandpa does something, he does it well! He wants our little duck to have the right start in life.

When he isn't hunting food, he's following Grandpa around — indoors, outdoors, through our apartment, everywhere — just like Mom said he would.

"Imprinting, remember?" I asked.

"How could I forget?" Grandpa said.

Tonight we sat in the kitchen after dinner. "Such a change," Mom smiled, cradling our duckling in her arms. I think she was talking about Miracle, but she was looking at Grandpa. He was mixing up a batch of bran muffins. We've discovered his muffins are just as delicious as his spaghetti. He puts dates in them.

Saturday, June 9

Today Grandpa said it was time to set Miracle free. "He's big enough and he's strong enough and he knows enough."

I called up Laura, and we walked over to the park with Grandpa and Miracle.

When we got to the edge of the river, Grandpa set Miracle down. Right away that nosy, hungry, little duck began to poke around; but when Grandpa started to edge away, Miracle started to follow him. Grandpa had to shoo Miracle back toward the river. "Go, baby," he said. "It's time to be a duck again."

"Go, Miracle!" I pointed to a bunch of ducks his size that were swimming downstream and gave him a little push.

Miracle just didn't want to go.

Then one of the ducks in the river looked right at him and called, "Quack! Quack!" That must mean something significant in duck talk because Miracle quacked back and rushed straight into the water.

We watched. The other ducks watched too; they seemed to be paddling, just waiting.

Miracle sure is a good swimmer. I could see his little orange feet churning below the greenish surface. I watched carefully because he looked just like the other ducks. I knew if I took my eyes off him, I wouldn't be able to tell which one he was. That's sad, but it's nice, too, because it means he'll fit right into a duck family.

Grandpa put his hand on my shoulder. He knew how I felt — and I knew how he felt. Grandpa and I have always known about each other, even when things weren't this good.

He smiled down at me and said, "Everything's going to be all right, Cathy." I know that he was making a promise, and I know that I don't have to worry about him anymore.

"Bye, Miracle," I said. We watched the ducks swim across the river and climb out on the bank. Then I turned to Grandpa and asked, "Want to hit a few fly balls to Laura and me? I could dash home and get my bat."

Grandpa grinned. "Sure. Dash home and get it. I can see you have plans for your old grandpa."

"Old," I said. "You're not old. You're just Grandpa!"

Author

Born in Ireland, Eve Bunting began her writing career after moving to California with her husband and three children. Many of her more than one hundred books have won awards. Her concern for wildlife is portrayed in "Grandpa's Miracle" and in her book *One More Flight*.

An excerpt from

TOOLMAKER

by Jill Paton Walsh

The Boy Who Shaped Stone

Ra was a young man in the Stone Age in a tribe where each man made his own tools and hunted for himself. However, Ra was especially skilled in making tools. The tribe needed the tools that only Ra could make so well; but how could Ra hunt for food and still have time for making tools for the tribe?

Ra was making his summer house when he broke his axe. He was cutting long bendy branches of hazel from the coppice at the edge of the forest, and the axe wedged in the thick bole of the tree. He heaved at it to free it, and it came unstuck so suddenly that it flew out of his hand, and struck a stone lying a little way behind him, and broke. Ra picked up the pieces, and looked at them to see if he could perhaps use them for making something else, but there were milky cracks showing in the dark flint — the pieces were useless. Ra grunted angrily and threw them away. He gathered up the sticks he had already cut, and walked down the hillside, out of the hazel copse, and towards the stream.

On the grassy slopes in the shelter of the wood, and just a little above the stream, his tribe were busy making shelters for the summer, each family building one hut. They dug away the earth of the hillside till they got down to a solid, firm floor; then they made a framework of branches, and stretched over it tents made of skins. There were many skins in a tent, all carefully stitched together with overlapping edges to keep out the wind and rain. Ra had not earned one yet — his hut would be covered in bracken and brushwood. He looked enviously at the others. Nearly all the huts were almost finished, but only the Great-grandmother's was completely ready, for everyone had to help with hers before starting their own. Ra's house was slowest of all because he had nobody helping him. Among the forest tribes, a boy lived with his mother's and grandmother's family; but Ra's mother had died in the snows of the winter which was just passing, and he had not yet gathered enough skins and bones and flint tools to buy himself a wife, and join her family. So for the time being he was alone, and had to live in a hut by himself.

He had scraped an earth floor out of the grassy slope. Now he was making a ring of pliable sticks set upright in the ground all around it. He set to work with the new

bundle. First he made a hole by driving a piece of bone into the ground with a large stone for a hammer. Then he rocked the bone drill to and fro, pulled it out of the ground, and set the hazel branch in the hole, wedging it firmly with a little loose earth. Soon the ring of sticks was finished, with a gap in it for a door. Ra unwound from his waist a long strip of leather, and reaching up he bent the hazel branches down over his head one by one, and tied them into a bundle with his thong.

It was getting dark now, and Ra went hastily down to the stream to find a piece of flint in the pebbles in the water, to make himself a new axe. There was no time now to gather bracken to cover the framework of his hut — that would have to wait till tomorrow. He found a big heavy stone of the right sort, and then went to one of the bright fires which now blazed on the slope.

He bowed to the grandmother of the family, who sat between the fire and the door-hole of the hut, in the place of honour.

"Is there room beside your fire, mother?" he asked her.

"Sit Ra, there is room," she said. Ra sat down a little way outside the family circle, and began to make his new axe, working in the firelight where it fell between the shadows of Brun and Mi, a boy and girl only a little older than Ra. First Ra broke his stone in two against the ground. Then he chose the better half, and wedged it firmly against his bent knee on the ground. Then he took from his leather pouch a short piece of the leg bone of a stag, and placing one end against the axe stone, first here, and then there, he struck the other end with the rejected half of the stone, making flakes of flint fly off in all directions.

Ra was good at making axes, but the light was poor, and he bent closely over his work. Even so he could feel that someone was watching him. Ra glanced up, hoping it was Mi, and his eyes met those of Yul. Yul was a grown man, tall and strong — some said the best hunter in the tribe — and he had hunted with Ra's father long ago. Ra was in awe of him; he looked away quickly. When he had finished his axe, he stood up to go.

"May the hunt be good tomorrow to those who shared fire with me tonight," he said.

In his own unfinished house he lay down to sleep. There was nothing else to do, for the day had gone in travelling, and in hut making; there had been no time to hunt, and so there was nothing to eat. Ra was used to going to bed with an empty stomach, but all winter he had slept in a deep cave in the distant hills, and he was not used to sleeping in the open. The year had only just begun to turn warmer, and the leaves were scarcely breaking bud on the trees when the Great-grandmother had moved them out of the caves. It was still sharply cold, and a wind swept the sloping glade. Shivering, Ra wished he had finished his house. Through the web of sticks over his head he could see the cold stars — the distant camp fires of the spirit folk who hunt the moon.

"May their arrows stray, their spear-shafts break, their traps all fail to spring!" muttered Ra to himself, for the moon was useful to his tribe. Not only the stars disturbed him; unseen creatures moved in the forest and in the grasses all night long. The echoing tapping of dripping water in the cave had gone, and instead there were the quiet movements of living things going about their business, and hunting each other in the dark. And although he slept, Ra slept so lightly all night long that he dimly knew from the sound and smell of them what creatures had come near. No wolf or wildcat came to startle him awake, but he drowsed on the chill earth till the dawn.

When he woke he went to the stream, and drank greedily, lifting the water to his mouth in cupped hands. Cold trickles ran down his forearms, sleeking the thick hair that had grown upon them last summer. And when he returned to his hut he had a visitor. Yul stood there.

"Is there room beside your fire, Ra?" he asked.

"There is no fire yet, but there is room," said Ra.

Yul sat down. "Show me the axe you made at our fireside last night," he said. Ra stared at Yul in surprise. Then he picked up the axe, and held it out to Yul. Yul took it, and turned it over and over in his hands. Then he held it with the thick end in his palm, and tried it, striking it against the ground.

"This is a good axe, Ra," he said.

"It is mine," said Ra, puzzled by all this talk of his axe. "I made it."

"You were quick and deft about making it," said Yul. "I take longer. And when I have an axe to make, I gather several stones, so that I need not stop to look for another when the one I am working splits in the wrong place. You had only one stone with you."

"The stones are good to me, Yul. They almost always break as I wish them to."

"Since that is so, Ra, will you make a new spearhead for me? Hard though I try, I cannot make them balance so that the spear flies really straight. You make me a good one."

Ra was silent. This was a new thing Yul was doing; new things frightened Ra. The men of his tribe each did everything for himself. There were no rules for this sort of asking.

"I must hunt, Yul," he said at last. "I am hungry."

"Today I will bring you food. I will hunt until I have enough for two, and share what I catch with you. You can sit here and make me the spear which I need. Do this for me, Ra."

"I will do it," said Ra, unhappily. Indeed one had no choice but to do what Yul wanted; he was big and strong. He could have knocked Ra down with one hand only. Ra did not dare refuse him.

So that morning Ra stood at his door like a woman, watching the men and dogs go out to hunt. The dogs ran yelping at the hunters' heels, and the men walked away into the forest, carrying spears, and bows, and bundles of arrows. The barking sounded clearly in the cold morning, and echoed faintly from the bare hill above the wooded valley. The sounds came more and more distant to Ra's ears. The quiet of the camp made him uneasy. He wanted to run after the hunt, but instead he went looking for a good piece of flint.

He returned to his hut a while later with two large lumps of flint tucked under each arm. Then he sat down and set to work. First he wedged one of his stones firmly on the ground with a little earth, to make an anvil. Then he chose the best of the stones, and taking it in two hands raised it above his head, and brought it hard down on the anvil stone so that it broke cleanly in two across the middle. He took the larger half, and set it down with the new broken surface upwards. And now he took his bone chisel, and a spare piece of stone to bang it with. He had to get the slant of the chisel exactly right to make the flint split where he wanted it to. First he struck the stone round the rim of the new surface; and at each blow a flake of stone cracked off the side, so that soon all the hard rough surface of the stone had been struck away, and he was left with a block of pure black, unweathered flint.

Now he worked more carefully still. He struck the top surface of his block near the edge, so that a long narrow flake of flint broke off the side. This flake would make a good knife; Ra put it on one side. Then he tried again, and

this time got a shorter, wider chip. Just what he wanted. He put the block aside and started to work on the chip. It was wafer thin at the edges, and thick in the middle. Ra tapped the edges gently, and broke off little pieces until he had rounded it into a leaf shape. Then he trimmed it, holding a stick at a slant on his anvil, laying the edge of the spearhead against the stick, and pressing the stick upwards under the thin edge of the stone blade until a little flake dropped off. These tiny flakes left a beautiful rippled surface on the flint, like a light wind on dark water. They also left a wavy, bitter-sharp edge. Ra was pleased. He had never made a better one.

But now it was finished he had time to feel hungry. He wondered about the hunt, and felt uneasy. All his instincts, all the ways of his tribe, told him that when he was hungry he must hunt. He shook his head, and took up the long flake of flint he had laid aside before. This had flat straight edges already, because of the way it had split from the block. Ra took careful aim, and sharpened the end of it with a single blow which nicked a diagonal chip from the end. Then he took it, and went up to the forest to cut more brushwood for his hut.

Ra finished his roof, and tied it down securely, and gathered a pile of pebbles for a hearth. All day the women and children stared at him curiously, for it was a new thing for man or boy to stay away from the hunt. And all day Ra's ears were pricked for any sound of the men returning.

At last he heard them. Down the valley, from among the trees, came the sound of singing — a low droning song. The hunt had been good. The hungry families gathered at the hut doors to watch the hunters come. They marched out of the woods, and scrambled up the slope to the camp, bringing the carcasses of deer and rabbits across their shoulders. Ra looked at them hungrily, and licked his lips. He was apprehensive — what if Yul did not keep his unheard-of bargain? The night would be cold, and the cramps of hunger in his stomach would keep him awake. But Yul brought him the flank of a young doe, and half a rabbit, and exclaimed in delight when he saw the spearhead Ra had made for him.

"This bargain is good," he said.

Ra gathered firewood, and stacked it on his hearth of stones, and went to the Great-grandmother's house to get fire; for all the fires of his tribe were lit from hers, and hers had been carried on torches of pine wood all the way from the winter caves. He roasted his meat on a spit over the fire, not taking long about it, for he liked it still red and raw in the middle. He grunted with pleasure as he sunk his teeth into it, and when he had finished and sat sleepily beside his fire, the good, well-fed feeling spread through his limbs. He just sat enjoying this feeling for a long time, and then he built up his fire so that it would last the night, for it is not only men who hunt for food, and Ra knew that he did not wake quickly when he was not hungry. Then he crept into his hut to sleep. He did not fall asleep at once. He felt odd. Never in all his life before did he remember sleeping well-fed, and yet not tired from running in the hunt all day. But although the strange feeling was a new thing, he liked it.

The next morning, when Ra was collecting his arrows, and tightening the thong on his bow, Brun came to him, and said, "Make with me today the bargain you made with Yul yesterday. I need more arrowheads, and a scraper, and my sister, Mi, wants this little bone worked into a harpoon for fishing the deep pools."

So Ra stayed at home that day too, and worked stones beside his fire. He worried a little about his food, but not as much as he had the day before. And he discovered that making a whole lot of arrowheads all together instead of one by one as he needed them, was in a way easier. He got defter and quicker with each one. The little grunts he made as he worked ran together into a jerky, gruff sort of song, the beat keeping time with the sharp cracking noise of the breaking flints. Ra was happy.

In the afternoon, when Ra was using his new knife to cut little notches in Mi's bone, to make it into a harpoon for her, his thoughts took a new turn. The bone had to be notched to make it catch in the fishes' flesh; a smooth point just slipped out. Ra remembered how often he had lost a rabbit or a deer because the arrow with which he had hit it had dropped out of the wound as the beast ran. Why shouldn't the arrowhead be notched too? Of course, it would be very hard to make notches in stone. But the thought was good; trembling with excitement, Ra took up one of the completed arrowheads, and tried to notch the back, so that it would pierce smoothly, and then lodge securely. It broke. He tried again. And again. It was hard, but before evening he had succeeded in making one tiny triangular blade, with two deep notches cut in the broad end, so that it had two barbs, and a little stem by which it could be tied to the shaft.

He gave it to Brun with the others, in return for a hunk of wild boar, and Brun went round the whole tribe, showing everyone what he had got, until Ra was surrounded by men asking him to work for them the next day, and the day after that, and even promising to pay him with the skins of their catch as well as the flesh, to make himself a better hut with.

"This is a new thing we are doing," said Ra. "We must ask the Great-grandmother." He said this because he was becoming alarmed. Surely the Great-grandmother would keep them to the old, well-tried ways, for it was she who knew how things had always been, and how they ought to be.

The Great-grandmother listened while one after another of her children told her that they wanted the tools that Ra knew best how to make.

"Tell him to work for us, and we will feed him," they said. She took the arrowheads he had made for Brun between her stick-like fingers, and stroked them, learning what they were like from touch, since she had no eyes. She was very old; nobody in the tribe could remember a time when she had not been Great-grandmother over them, and since long before Ra's birth she had been blind with age.

"What is this?" she asked when she felt the barbed arrow. Ra told her how he had thought of it, and how it worked. She was silent for a time, her head tilted back on her

shoulders as though she were looking at the sky, and her fingers turned the barbed arrowhead over and over. At last she said, "If Ra makes better tools it is good that he should make them for us all."

"I am afraid," said Ra. "If I do not hunt, what will happen to me when food is short? I shall starve as soon as the hunt is bad. I am afraid."

"No matter how little is brought home, you shall share what there is," said the Great-grandmother. "The tribe promises this. It shall be one of our ways."

And so Ra, who had been a hunter, became a toolmaker instead. And in Ra's tribe there were good tools for the doing of many things. The summer was good that year. There were many warm days, and the hunt did not fail. Ra made great axes from large stones, and the men cut down full-grown trees from the forest and built dams and fish traps across the stream, and the children's limbs rounded and plumped with the plentiful food. Several groups of strangers came trading for Ra's tools; everyone prospered and everyone was content.

Author

A native of England, Jill Paton Walsh was a teacher before turning to writing. Her interest in ancient history contributed to the settings of many of her books, including *Children of the Fox* and *Toolmaker,* from which this excerpt was taken.

An excerpt from

HOMESICK

My Own Story

by Jean Fritz

Jean had waited for twelve long years to go to America. She had been born and raised in China, but her parents were from Washington, Pennsylvania. Her grandmother and relatives were waiting for her there. Though she loved certain things about China, she had always felt that she was on the wrong side of the globe. Finally the time had come for Jean and her family to take the 28-day ship voyage from Shanghai, China to the United States.

When they arrived in Pennsylvania Jean was so excited. Now she was finally home. Grandmother's farm seemed so familiar after all those years of hearing about it. However, some things weren't familiar at all. As a matter of fact, they weren't at all what she had expected.

When Aunt Margaret took me to the back of the house to show me around, I found everything so familiar I didn't need to be told what was what. "Here's the grape arbor," I said, and I ran through the long archway that led from the back door to what was once the stable but was now a garage for my grandfather's truck.

"Oh, and there's the pump!"

"We have running water now," Aunt Margaret explained, "so we don't use the pump much."

"But I can pump if I want to, can't I?"

"Sure you can."

Running up the hill on one side of the house was the cornfield. Running down the hill on the other side was the vegetable garden, the rhubarb plot, the dahlia beds. At the bottom of the hill was my grandfather's greenhouse.

"Where are the chickens?" I asked.

"Around the corner."

As we went to the other side of the house, a brown-and-white-speckled rooster came strutting to meet us.

"That's Josh," Aunt Margaret said. "He's such a serious-minded rooster, he can't stand to hear anyone laugh. He ruffles up his feathers and cusses his head off."

I squatted down and tried to force a laugh. "Ha ha-ha ha."

"No," Aunt Margaret said, "he knows you're just pretending."

Not far behind Josh was the chicken house with a big fenced-in yard around it. I ran over and looked at the hens, teetering like plump little ladies on spike heels.

"What are their names?" I asked.

"They don't have names."

"How come?"

"We don't want to become too fond of them."

I'd never heard anything so silly. If I was going to feed them, I ought to know their names. "Why not?" I asked.

"Well, Jean," Aunt Margaret explained, "you know that this is a farm. In the end we eat every one of those chickens."

I felt dumb not to have known. I decided that when I fed the chickens, I'd try not to even look them in the eye.

As we went inside, Aunt Margaret pointed to a pair of roller skates on the back porch. "I dug those out of the attic," she said. "I thought you'd like them." She looked at my legs. "But you can't roller-skate in silk stockings."

"That's O.K.," I grinned. "I have socks."

Of course I wanted to try the roller skates right away but my mother's family was due to arrive for a welcome-home party and all of us had to get dressed up.

"Are we going to have flannel cakes?" I asked.

Aunt Margaret laughed. "That was just a joke. We're going to have potato salad and smearcase[1] and cold chicken and apple pie and lots of other good things. We've been cooking ever since your father called."

[1]**Smearcase:** cottage cheese

My mother's family arrived all at once: Aunt Blanche, Aunt Etta, Aunt Mary L., Aunt Sarah and Uncle Welsh, Uncle George and Aunt Edith, and my four cousins — Elizabeth and Jane who were much older and Katherine and Charlotte who were about three years younger. There were a couple of extra girls, but I couldn't figure out where they fit in. The family parked their cars at the top of the hill, stopped to pull on galoshes, and then picked their way down the grassy side of the road which was fairly dry. When my mother saw them, she ran up the hill, her arms out, and I watched one of her sisters run ahead of the others, her arms out too. I knew it must be Aunt Blanche. They stood beside the road, hugging, stepping back to make sure who they were, then hugging again. When the whole family got to the bottom of the hill where my father and I were waiting, everyone began crying and laughing and kissing and hugging at the same time. I never saw such carrying-on. Not just one kiss apiece, but kiss after kiss while I was still trying to figure out which aunt was which.

My youngest cousin, Charlotte, who was watching all this, suggested that we clear out until the excitement had died down. Those two other girls tagged along as we went to the back of the house where we all sat down on the platform surrounding the pump.

"I can't stand all that kissing business," Charlotte said. "Can you?"

"No," I agreed. "They wouldn't even let me get my breath."

"Let's make a pact," she suggested. "I'll never kiss you if you promise never to kiss me."

We shook on it. But I still wondered about those other two girls, so I whispered to Charlotte, asking if they were related. She said no, they were neighbor kids who had begged to come along because they wanted to see the girl from China. "This is Ruth and this is Marie," she said, but I could tell she wished they were someplace else.

Up to this time Ruth and Marie had just stared at me, but now Ruth nudged Marie and whispered, "You ask."

Marie giggled. "We want to know if you ate rats in China and what they tasted like."

"And if you ate their *tails* too," Ruth added.

Rats! "No one in China eats rats," I said stiffly.

"Oh, you don't need to pretend." Ruth was smuggling her laughter behind her hands. "Everyone knows that people in China eat queer things. Snakes, birds' nests . . ."

"They do not."

The girls were looking at me as if I were some kind of a freak in a circus. As if maybe I had two heads.

"Did you use sticks to eat with?" Marie asked.

"Chopsticks, you mean. Sometimes. Of course."

Both girls lay back on the platform, shrieking with laughter. Josh came tearing around the house, scolding, ruffling his feathers, and I didn't blame him. He wasn't any madder than I was.

"Quit it," I told the girls. "You're upsetting the rooster."

This only set them off again. When they finally got control of themselves, they asked if I could speak Chinese and I said yes, I certainly could.

I turned to Marie and said in Chinese, "Your mother is a big turtle." ("Nide muchin shr ega da wukwei.") Then I looked at Ruth and told her that her mother was a turtle too. I knew that in English it wouldn't sound so bad but in China this was an insult.

The girls were rolling all over the platform in spasms of laughter while Josh croaked and flapped. "Oh, it sounds so funny, say it again," Ruth begged.

So I did. And I added that they were worthless daughters of baboons and they should never have been born.

"What does it mean?" they asked. "Tell us what it means."

"You wouldn't understand," I said coldly. "Come on, Charlotte, let's go back to the party."

That night after everyone had left, I told my mother and father about the crazy questions Ruth and Marie had asked.

"Well, Jean," my father said, "some people in Washington don't know any better. China seems so far away they imagine strange things."

I told myself that only little kids like Ruth and Marie could be so ignorant. Eighth graders would surely know better.

But for a while I didn't worry about eighth grade. I spent the summer doing the things I had dreamed about. Charlotte and I roller-skated, and although it didn't take me long to learn, my knees were skinned most of the time. I didn't care. I was proud of every one of my scabs; they showed that I was having a good time. And there were so many ways to have a good time — so many flavors of ice cream to try, so many treasures to choose at the five-and-ten, so many trees to climb, so many books to borrow from the library, so many relatives willing to stop for a game of dominoes or checkers. My grandfather and I played horseshoes, and although I never beat him, he said I was every bit as good as my father had been at my age.

And I helped my grandmother. Sometimes I spent the whole day working beside her: shelling peas, kneading bread dough, turning the handle of the wringer after she'd washed clothes, feeding the chickens, sweeping the porch. In China I'd had nothing to do with the work of the house. It just went on automatically around me as if it could have been anyone's house, but now suddenly I was a part of what went on. I had a place. For instance. My grandmother might ask me if we had enough sugar in the house or should she get some, and likely as not, I would know.

"The sugar bin is getting low," I would say. "Maybe you should buy another bag."

Then my grandmother would add "sugar" to her shopping list and she'd say she didn't know how she'd ever got along without me. I loved to hear her say that even though I knew she'd done fine without me. But I did have a lot of new accomplishments. I wrote to Lin Nai-Nai and described them to her. I could even do coolie work, I told her. I could mow grass. I could mop floors.

Still, I thought about school. I'd always supposed I knew exactly what an American school would be like, but as the time came near, I wasn't sure. Suppose I didn't fit in? Suppose I wasn't the same as everyone else, after all? Suppose I turned out to be another Vera Sebastian?[1] Suppose eighth graders thought I was a rat eater?

I couldn't forget the first Sunday I'd gone to church in Washington. The other kids in church had poked each other when I'd walked in. "There's the girl from China." I knew by their faces that's what they were thinking. The woman who sat behind me had made no bones about it. I overheard

---

[1] A girl in Jean's class at the British school in China

her whispering to her husband. "You can tell she wasn't born in this country," she said. How could she tell? I wondered. If just looking at me made people stare, what would happen when they heard me talk? Suppose I said something silly? I remembered the rainy afternoon at my grandmother's when we were all sitting around reading and I had come to a word that I didn't know.

"What's a silo?" I asked.

The way everyone looked up so surprised, it was as if they were saying, "How on earth did she live this long without knowing what a silo is?" Of course when my father explained, I realized I'd seen silos all over the country; I just hadn't known what they were called. But suppose I had asked that question in school!

I kept pestering Aunt Margaret to tell me if there was anything about eighth grade that I should know and didn't.

"It doesn't matter," she would say. "Not everyone in eighth grade is going to know exactly the same things."

Aunt Margaret had a new beau and I suspected that she wasn't giving my eighth-grade problems enough serious thought, but one day she did ask me if I knew the Pledge of Allegiance.

"What Pledge of Allegiance?"

So she explained that every morning we'd start off by pledging allegiance to the flag and she taught me how to say it, my hand over my heart. After that, I practiced every day while I was feeding the chickens. I'd clap my hand over my heart and tell them about "one nation indivisible." It gave me courage. Surely if the whole class felt strongly about the American flag, I'd fit in all right.

My mother and father would be away when school started. Toward the end of the summer they had begun to give lectures in order to raise money for the Y.M.C.A. and now they were going to Canada for two weeks. Before they left, my mother called the school principal to notify him that I'd be entering eighth grade. She gave Aunt Margaret money to buy me a new dress for school. When she kissed me good-bye, she smoothed out my eyebrows.

"Be good," she whispered.

I stiffened. I wondered if she'd ever forget goodness. Probably the last thing she'd say to me before I walked up the aisle to be married was "Be good."

The next day Aunt Margaret took me to Caldwell's store on Main Street and bought me a red-and-black-plaid gingham dress with a white collar and narrow black patent leather belt that went around my hips. She took me to a beauty parlor and I had my hair shingled.

When I got home, I tried on my dress. "How do I look?" I asked my grandmother.

"As if you'd just stepped out of a bandbox."

I wasn't sure that was the look I was aiming for. "But do I look like a regular eighth grader?"

"As regular as they come," she assured me.

The day before school started, I laid out my new dress and stockings and shoes so I'd be ready. I put aside the loose-leaf notebook Aunt Margaret had given me. I pledged allegiance to the chickens and then I sat down on the back steps next to my grandmother who was shelling peas. I reached into her lap, took a bunch of peas, and began shelling into the pan.

"I wish my name were Marjorie," I said. "I'd feel better starting to school with the name Marjorie."

My grandmother split a pea pod with her thumbnail and sent the peas plummeting into the pan.

"Do you like the name Marjorie?" I asked.

"Not much. It sounds common."

"But that's the idea!" I said. "It would make me fit in with everyone else."

"I thought you were going to be a writer."

"I am."

"Well, my stars! Writers do more than just fit in. Sometimes they don't fit in at all." My grandmother quit shelling and looked straight at me. "You know why I like the name *Jean?*" she asked.

"Why?"

"It's short and to the point; it doesn't fool around. Like my name — Isa. They're both good, strong Scottish names. Spunky."

I'd never known my name was Scottish. I surely had never thought of it as strong.

"Grandma," I said, "do you worry about whether I'm good or not?"

My grandmother threw back her head and hooted. "Never. It hasn't crossed my mind." She gave my knee a slap. "I love you just the way you are."

I leaned against her, wanting to say "thank you" but thinking that this wasn't the kind of thing that you said "thank you" for.

The next morning my grandmother and grandfather watched me start up Shirls Avenue in my new outfit, my notebook under my arm.

"Good luck!" they called. I held up my hand with my fingers crossed.

The school was about four blocks away — a big, red-brick, square building that took care of all grades, kindergarten through the eighth. So, of course, there were all ages milling about, but I looked for the older ones. When I'd spotted some — separate groups of girls and boys laughing and talking — I decided that I didn't look any different, so I went into the building, asked in the office where the eighth grade was, and went upstairs to the first room on the right.

Others were going into the room, and when I saw that they seemed to sit wherever they wanted, I picked a desk about halfway up the row next to the window. I slipped my notebook into the open slot for books and then looked at the teacher who was standing, her back to us, writing on the blackboard. She had a thick, straight-up, corseted figure and gray hair that had been marcelled into such stiff, even waves I wondered if she dared put her head down on a pillow at night.

"My name is Miss Crofts," she had written.

She didn't smile or say "Good Morning" or "Welcome to eighth grade" or "Did you have a nice summer?" She just looked at the clock on the wall and when it was exactly nine o'clock, she tinkled a bell that was like the one my mother used to call the servants.

"The class will come to order," she said. "I will call the roll." As she sat down and opened the attendance book, she raised her right index finger to her head and very carefully she scratched so she wouldn't disturb the waves. Then she began the roll:

Margaret Bride (*Here*). Donald Burch (*Here*), Andrew Carr (*Present*). Betty Donahue (*Here*).

I knew the G's would be coming pretty soon.

John Goodman (*Here*), Jean Guttery.

Here, I said. Miss Crofts looked up from her book. "Jean Guttery is new to our school," she said. "She has come all the way from China where she lived beside the Yangs-Ta-Zee River. Isn't that right, Jean?"

"It's pronounced *Yang-see,*" I corrected. "There are just two syllables."

Miss Crofts looked at me coldly. "In America," she said, "we say Yangs-Ta-Zee."

I wanted to suggest that we look it up in the dictionary, but Miss Crofts was going right on through the roll. She didn't care about being correct or about the Yangtse River or about me and how I felt.

Miss Crofts, I said to myself, your mother is a turtle. A big fat turtle.

I was working myself up, madder by the minute, when I heard Andrew Carr, the boy behind me, shifting his feet on the floor. I guess he must have hunched across his desk, because all at once I heard him whisper over my shoulder:

"Chink, Chink Chinaman

Sitting on a fence,

Trying to make a dollar

Out of fifteen cents."

I forgot all about where I was. I jumped to my feet, whirled around, and spoke out loud as if there were no Miss Crofts, as if I'd never been in a classroom before, as if I knew nothing about classroom behavior.

"You don't call them Chinamen or Chinks," I cried. "You call them *Chinese.* Even in America you call them *Chinese.*"

The class fell absolutely silent, all eyes on me, and for the first time I really looked at Andrew Carr. I think I had expected another Ian Forbes,[2] but he was just a freckle-faced

---

[2]A mean boy in Jean's class at the British school in China

kid who had turned beet-red. He was slouched down in his seat as if he wished he could disappear.

Miss Crofts stood up. "Will someone please explain to me what all this is about?"

The girl beside me spoke up. "Andrew called Jean a Chinaman."

"Well, you don't need to get exercised, Jean," she said. "We all know that you are American."

"But that's not the *point!*" Before I could explain that it was an insult to call Chinese people *Chinamen,* Miss Crofts had tapped her desk with a ruler.

"That will be enough," she said. "All eyes front." Obediently the students stopped staring and turned their attention to Miss Crofts. All but one boy across the room. He caught my eye, grinned, and put his thumb up, the way my father did when he thought I'd done well. I couldn't help it; I grinned back. He looked nice, I thought.

"We will stand now and pledge allegiance," Miss Crofts announced. Even though I still felt shaky, I leaped to attention. I wasn't going to let anything spoil my first official pledge. As I placed my hand on my heart, I glanced around. The girl next to me had her hand on her stomach.

"I pledge allegiance to the flag of the United States of America." The class mumbled, but maybe that was because of the flag. It was the saddest-looking flag I'd ever seen, standing in the corner, its stars and stripes drooping down as if they had never known a proud moment. So as I pledged, I pictured the American flag on the Bund,[3] waving as if it were telling the world that America was the land of the free and the home of the brave. Maybe I made my pledge too loud, because when I sat down, the boy across the room raised his thumb again. I hoped he wasn't making fun of me but he seemed friendly so I smiled back.

---

[3] The grandest street in Hankow, China

When I looked at Miss Crofts, she had her finger in her hair and she was daintily working her way through another wave.

After the commotion I had already made in the class, I decided to be as meek as I possibly could the rest of the morning. Since this was the first day at school, we would be dismissed at noon, and surely things would improve by then.

Miss Crofts put a bunch of history books on the first desk of each row so they could be passed back, student to student. I was glad to see that we'd be studying the history of Pennsylvania. Since both my mother's and father's families had helped to settle Washington County, I was interested to know how they and other pioneers had fared. Opening the book to the first chapter, "From Forest to Farmland," I skimmed through the pages but I couldn't find any mention of people at all. There was talk about dates and square miles and cultivation and population growth and immigration and the Western movement, but it was as if the forests had lain down and given way to farmland without anyone being brave or scared or tired or sad, without babies being born, without people dying. Well, I thought, maybe that would come later.

After history, we had grammar and mathematics, but the most interesting thing that I learned all morning was that the boy across the room was named Donald Burch. He had sandy-colored hair combed straight back and he wore a sky-blue shirt.

The last class was penmanship. I perked up because I knew I was not only good at penmanship, but I enjoyed making my words run across a page, round and neat and happy-looking. At the British School we had always printed, so I had learned to make my letters stand up straight and even, and when I began to connect up my letters for handwriting, I kept that proud, straight-up look.

I took the penmanship workbooks from the girl in front of me, kept my copy, and passed the rest to Andrew Carr. The workbook was called *The Palmer Method,* but the title was not printed; it was handwritten in big, oversized, sober-looking letters, slanting to the right. If you pulled one letter out of a word, I thought, the rest would topple over like a row of dominoes.

"Jean," Miss Crofts said after the workbooks had been distributed, "I expect you have not been exposed to the Palmer method of penmanship. The rest of the class will work on Exercise One, but I want you to come up to my desk while I explain the principle of Palmer penmanship."

Slowly I dragged myself to the front of the room and sat down in the chair that Miss Crofts had pulled up beside her own.

"You see," Miss Crofts said, "in the Palmer method you really write with the underside of your forearm. The fleshy part." She pointed to her own forearm which was quite fleshy and then she put it down on the desk. "You hold your fingers and wrist stiff. All the movement comes from your arm. You begin by rotating the flesh on your arm so that your pen will form slanting circles." She filled a line on the paper with falling-down circles. "When you have mastered the circles," she said, "your arm will be ready for the letters."

As Miss Crofts looked at me to see if I understood, she made a quick dive with her index finger into her waves.

I folded my hands in my lap. "I have very good penmanship," I said. "No one has trouble reading it. I really do not care to change my style."

Miss Crofts pushed a pen and a pad of paper in front of me. "The Palmer method has been proved to be the most efficient system." She had so many years of teaching behind her I could see she wasn't going to fool around. "Just put your arm on the desk, Jean," she said, "and try some circles."

"I don't think I have enough flesh on the underside of my arm," I whispered. "I'm too skinny."

Miss Crofts reached over, picked up my arm, put it on the desk, and pushed a pen in my hand. "Just roll your arm around but keep your fingers stiff. Let your arm do the work."

Sitting in front of the room with everyone peeking up at me from their workbooks, I was afraid I was going to cry. How could I stand to let my letters lean over as if they were too tired to say what they wanted straight out? How could I ever write a poem if I couldn't let the words come out through my fingers and feel their shape? I glanced at Donald Burch who, like everyone else, must have seen how miserable I was. He tapped his forehead to show how crazy Miss Crofts was. Then he shrugged as if he were saying, "What can you do with a nitwit like that?"

I moved my arm halfheartedly and produced a string of sick-looking circles.

"I think you have the idea," Miss Crofts said. "You may go to your seat and practice."

So I went to my seat but I didn't make a single circle unless I saw Miss Crofts watching me. I just hunched over my workbook, promising myself that I would never use the Palmer method outside the classroom. Never. I wouldn't even try hard in the classroom and if I flunked penmanship, so what? I kept looking at the clock, waiting and waiting for the big hand to crawl up and meet the little hand at *Twelve*. When it finally did, Miss Crofts tinkled her bell.

"Class — attention!" she ordered. We all stood up. "First row, march!" Row by row we marched single file out the door, down the stairs, and into the free world where the sun was shining.

Donald Burch was standing on the sidewalk and as I came up, he fell into step beside me.

"She's a real bird, isn't she?" he said.

"You said it!" I glanced up at him. He was two inches taller than I was. "Where do you suppose she dug up the Palmer method?"

"It's not just here," Donald said. "It's all over. Every school in the country uses it."

I stopped in my tracks. "All over *America?*"

"Yep."

I had a sudden picture of schools in every one of the forty-eight states grinding out millions and millions of sheets of paper covered with leaning letters exactly alike. "But what about liberty for all?" I cried. "Why do they want to make us copycats?"

Donald shrugged. "Search me. Grown-ups don't write all the same. Dumb, isn't it?"

As we walked on together, I began to feel better, knowing that Donald felt the same way as I did. Besides, I'd had a good look at him now. When he grew up, he might look a little like Charles Lindbergh, I decided, especially if he wore goggles.

"I guess you never had anyone as bad as Miss Crofts in your school in China, did you?" he asked.

"Well, I had one teacher who was pretty bad, but I think Miss Crofts has her beat."

"Did you like living in China?" Donald asked.

"Yes." (*Oh, please, I prayed, please don't let him ask me if I ate rats.*)

"I bet it was nice. But you know something?"

"What?"

"I'm sure glad you came back to America." He squinted at the sky as if he were trying to figure out the weather. "How about you? Are you glad you came back?"

"And how!" I didn't say it; I breathed it. At the same time I began mentally composing a letter to Andrea.

Dear Andrea: I started school today and there's this boy in my class. Donald Burch. He is the CAT'S!

We had come to Shirls Avenue now. I pointed down the hill. "That's where I live," I said. "That's my grandparents' farm down there. Where do you live?"

Donald pointed over his shoulder. "Back there a few blocks."

He had come out of his way.

"O.K. if I walk with you again tomorrow?" he asked.

I'm sure I said it would be O.K., although all I remember as I ran down the hill was thinking: Oh, I'm in love, I'm in love, and I think it's requited!

When I came to the bottom of the hill, I called out that I was home and my grandmother yoo-hooed from the vegetable garden. I found her among the carrots, standing up in her long white, starched apron, waiting for me, smiling.

"My, you look happy," she said.

I grinned. "I made a friend," I explained.

"Good! That's the best thing that could happen. And how about school?"

I came down to earth with a thump. There was no way I could look happy with a question like that to answer. I just shook my head.

"So it wasn't one-hundred-percent," my grandmother said. "Few things are."

"It was a flop."

"Who's your teacher?"

"Miss Crofts."

"My stars!" My grandmother put her hands on her hips. "Don't tell me she's still hanging around? Why, Margaret had her."

"She's still hanging around," I said.

My grandmother's face took on a sly, comical look. She put her index finger to her head and scratched carefully. "Still scratching, is she?"

Her imitation was so perfect, I burst out laughing.

"Still scratching," I said.

My grandmother and I laughed together and once started, we couldn't seem to stop. We'd let up for a second, then look at each other, and one of us would scratch, and we'd break out again. In fact, it felt so good to laugh, I didn't want to stop.

"She must have cooties," I gasped.

"She ought to have her head examined." And off we went again!

By this time Josh, who had joined us at the first explosion, was throwing himself about in an outrage, but I couldn't let a rooster spoil the fun. Coming to the surface from my last spasm, I told my grandmother about the Palmer method.

"We're supposed to write with the underside of our arms." I showed her where. "We can't move our fingers or our wrists."

At first my grandmother couldn't believe me, but as I went on about the workbooks and circles, she dissolved into another round of laughter. She turned toward the greenhouse where my grandfather was working. "Will," she called. "Oh, Will! Come and hear this!"

Well, I decided, the only thing a person could do about the Palmer method was to laugh at it. And listening to my grandmother telling it, making up bits as she went along about the imaginary Mr. Palmer who was so set on exercising the underside of children's forearms, I had to laugh again. We all laughed until we were laughed out.

My grandmother turned serious. "You can't move your

fingers at all?" she asked, as if she might not have heard right the first time.

"Not at all."

My grandmother shook her head. "They must be preparing you for a crippled old age." She leaned down to comfort Josh. "Sh, sh, sh," she said, smoothing out his feathers. "It's all right, Josh. It's all over. You don't know how funny the world can be, do you? Maybe even a little crazy. There are times when people just *have* to laugh."

"Times when they have to eat too," my grandfather added. "What are we having?"

My grandmother said she'd fixed apple dumplings, and together the three of us walked to the house. Past the cabbages and beans, down the path lined with gold and orange chrysanthemums. We stopped to admire the grapes, dangling in heavy clusters from the vines, fat and purple.

Then I ran ahead to put the plates on the table.

Author

Jean Fritz was born and raised in China until the end of the seventh grade. It was in China, at age five, that she announced to her father her desire to be a writer. When asked what kind of stories she would write she answered, "Stories about Americans," and that is exactly what she has done. She is best known for her historical novels about famous people of the American Revolution. *Homesick* is the story of her own life in China. Throughout the years many of her books have been named ALA Notable Books. She has also won the American Book Award for many of her works.

Photos
from
China

Change

by Charlotte Zolotow

The summer
still hangs
heavy and sweet
with sunlight
as it did last year.

The autumn
still comes
showering gold and crimson
as it did last year.

The winter
still stings
clean and cold and white
as it did last year.

The spring
still comes
like a whisper in the dark night.

It is only I
who have changed.

An excerpt from

THE
LONER

by Ester Wier

For as long as he could remember, the boy had lived among the crop pickers, moving from camp to camp with the harvest. No one could remember whether he had ever had a family. He did not even have a name — he was just "Boy."

His friend, Raidy, had promised to think of a name for him, but she had been killed in an accident. Overcome with grief, the boy left the pickers' camp and set out on his own to find a better life in California. The winter was already beginning, and he'd better get there as fast as he could.

To Find a Name

The boy stood in the middle of the road, gazing up at the wedge of wild geese high in the sky above him. Their noisy honking broke the immense quiet that lay like a blanket, spread from the mountains beyond to the endless plains far below. He turned slowly, watching the birds disappear to the south, thinking how Raidy would have liked seeing them. She would have made up something about them, like saying they were an Indian arrowhead flung across the sky by some unseen arm behind the mountains.

He shook his head dully, pushing Raidy out of his mind, and looked down at his feet. There was little left of the sneakers now, only the ragged canvas around his ankles, the raveled strings which held them on, and what had not been gouged from the soles on the long walk from the highway many miles behind him now.

A late afternoon wind was rising, biting into his legs through the threadbare dungarees and into his body under the worn flannel shirt. The crack in his lower lip opened again and his tongue, touching it, tasted blood. He put a chapped hand against his lip and pressed hard. Every inch of his body ached, ached with weariness and hunger and the terrible emptiness of losing Raidy.

Beyond him the road climbed another hill, and upon the crest, spruce trees bent in the wind, and shadows spread like dark water seeping from the mountainside. The ruffled edges of the clouds had turned gold, and for a moment it seemed that the whole world had become golden, the dried slopes about him reflecting the coming sunset. He was used to being out of doors at all hours, but he had never seen anything like this, and he stood, swaying wearily, caught by its splendor. In the distance off to his right, a herd of deer driven from the higher ridges by the first signs of winter, moved slowly across the bronze grass. Except for birds, they were the first signs of life he had seen in days of struggling through this country, and suddenly the enormity of the space around him and the loneliness of its silence became more than he could stand, and he found himself running toward the animals, leaving the road and scrambling over sun-scorched pasture land in a fury of haste.

"Wait!" he called, fighting through bushes and over hillocks. "Wait!" he shouted foolishly with all his strength, his voice carrying through the thin air. The deer poised for a moment and then faded into the landscape. He watched them go, still calling frantically and running toward them. They were alive and at this moment he needed to be near something living, something besides endless stretches of hills and plains.

When he realized they were gone, his breath began to come in long shaking sobs. The reserve strength he had called on in trying to reach them left him, and he fell headlong on the earth beside a cluster of pale-gold serviceberry bushes. The impact knocked the air out of him, and he lay without moving, his tear-streaked face pressed into the rough dry grass.

A Montana mountain rat, busy on an errand of nest making, paused and sat on her haunches looking at him before scurrying on across the fields, and a flock of crows flew above him, seeking their roost for the night.

Finally the boy tried to raise his body, his shaggy brown hair falling over his eyes. He couldn't go any farther. He was through, finished, beaten. How long had it been since he left the potato fields and started off on his own across this unfamiliar country? How many rides had he hitched on the highway? Which way was he headed now? How many meals had he made on berries and the raw potatoes he carried in his pockets? He didn't know. He didn't care. Nothing mattered now.

He lay quietly until the sobs began again, deep and racking. Above him the sky turned from gold to dark blue and the clouds drifted to the south. He burrowed deeper into the earth, rolling his body into a ball against the bushes, the weariness spreading through him like a soothing syrup. He cried himself out and slowly his hands relaxed and his eyes closed. Like a small animal seeking the warmth of the earth, he pressed his face against the grass and slept.

The woman waiting on the rise of the hill stood six-foot-two in her boots. They were sturdy leather boots, laced to the knee. Above them she wore wool trousers and a heavy wool-lined jacket. On her head was a man's old felt hat, pulled down to cover her ears and the gray hair cut short all over her head. From a distance it would have been hard to tell she was a woman, for her body was powerful and she stood with the grace of an athlete, relaxed yet disciplined. She lifted a hand and called, "Come!" and the dog, Jupiter, below the hill beside some serviceberry bushes, raised his head and looked at her. The rough coat of the collie was black with white markings on the chest, the neck, the legs and the feet. He stood thirty inches at the shoulder and his weight was nearly eighty pounds. The bigness of his mistress would have dwarfed most dogs, but not Jupiter. He came from a line of the finest sheep dogs of northern Scotland, and it showed in his deep chest, his remarkable height, his proud balance of body.

He looked at the woman and took a few steps toward her, then flung his head high and growled low in his throat. He retraced his steps to the bushes and looked at her again. Barking for a sheep dog was always the last resort in an emergency and one sure to excite the sheep, so he held his voice deep in his throat, and the sound carried no farther than to the woman on the hill.

"What is it, Jup?" she asked, watching him. "If I walk down there and find it's only a rabbit, I'll skin you alive."

The dog, hearing her voice, started toward her again, then stopped and flung his head high.

"All right, all right," she said, "I'm coming."

He met her halfway and led her back to the bushes where the boy lay. There was no surprise on the woman's face. She had lived too long in this vast and unpredictable land to question what happened here. Although her son's death two years before had shaken the very foundations on which her life was built, she still held to her belief in a wisdom greater than man's. "God moves in a mysterious way His wonders to perform," she marveled now. How else had the boy been led here, a stone's throw from the only human being within miles?

"Well," she said at last, "if it were a sheep and as scrawny as this, I'd say it was hardly worth the finding. How do you suppose he got here, Jup? Where does he belong? Hardly enough clothes or flesh on him to cover his bones. You found a real stray this time."

The wind from the mountains carried the icy threat of snows soon to come. The sunset was over and night blue had spread across the sky. The first stars appeared and the chill turned to raw cold.

"Back to the sheep, Jup," the woman said. "I'll handle this." The collie hesitated for a moment in leave-taking, then sped off toward the bed-ground, the white tip of his tail moving through the fast-falling darkness.

The woman bent over the sleeping boy. Traces of tears were on his face, streaks through the dust and dirt. His thin body was curled against the cold, and the straight brown hair hung ragged against his neck. "What a miserable little critter," she said softly. "I wouldn't let a sheep get into such a wretched condition." She studied for a while how to move him and decided against awakening him. Carefully she placed an arm underneath and slowly raised him so that he lay against her, reminding her of stray lambs she had so often carried back to the fold. He stirred, a long convulsive shudder running through his body, then lay quietly in her arms.

She carried him up the hill and across the hundred yards to the sheep wagon. Jup was waiting for her, his head turned toward her, yet his senses alert for any movement among the sheep on the bed-ground. They lay, over 900 of them, close together on a slanting rise beside the wagon. Around the bed-ground, several feet apart, stood the flags to scare off marauding animals.

The other dog, Juno, sniffed daintily, her nose pointed up at the boy. Her rough white coat moved in the wind and her dark mahogany-colored ears stood three-quarters erect, with the ends tipping forward.

"It's all right," the woman assured her. "Now you two get back to your posts and keep a sharp lookout for coyotes. If they get a sheep tonight, I'll skin you both alive." Jup whined softly and moved toward the sheep, Juno following a parallel course on the opposite side of the flock.

Smoke curled from the stovepipe atop the sheep wagon, drifting south with the wind. The woman mounted the steps to the door, pulling it open carefully so as not to disturb the boy. Once in, she shut it behind her and looked about. The benches on either side of the long narrow room were hard and bare, so she carried the boy to the end where her bed was built crosswise into the wagon. She pushed aside the soogan, the heavy square comforter, and laid him on top of the blankets. The room was warm and the boy sighed as he turned over and adjusted himself to the softness.

The woman took off her heavy coat and old felt hat and went to the kerosene stove, which stood to the right of the door. Taking a kettle, she poured water into it from a bucket, salted it, and set it on the flame. She seemed to fill the end of the wagon, her head clearing the ceiling by only a few inches. While the water came to a boil, she raised a trapdoor in the long bench on the left and pulled out two wool sacks stuffed with straw, two blankets, and another soogan. She made up a bed quickly on the bench, then returned to the stove and poured cornmeal into the boiling

water. When the mush was ready, she put it into a bowl and punctured a can of milk. She looked at the sugar and hesitated. She didn't hold with spoiling children with sweets. Even her own son had never been allowed sugar on his mush. Life was a hard business and indulgences led only to softness, and softness to weakness. She didn't believe in weakness. She left the bowl on the stove to keep warm and went back to the bed where the boy lay.

"Come," she said, rousing him. The boy's eyes flew open and he lay staring up at her. Confusion was on his face and a wary look about his eyes. "Here's some food," she said. "You look as if you could stand it." She went back to the stove and picked up the bowl.

The boy sat up and backed into a corner of the bed. He looked around the strange room and then up at the woman again. "Who're you?" he asked.

The woman handed him the bowl and poured milk on the mush. "Eat," she said. "I'll talk while you fill your stomach." She wanted to wash his hands and face before he ate, but she knew at the moment his need was more for nourishment than for cleanliness.

"Eat!" she said again. The boy stared at her, then dropped his eyes to the bowl. Picking up the spoon, he began to eat, placing the hot mush in his mouth and swallowing hungrily.

"Take it slow," she said. "There's more if you want it." She sat on the bench and leaned forward. "My dog found you a while ago, and I carried you here and put you to bed. I figured you must be hungry so I fixed you something to eat. And I wanted you to know where you were so that when you woke up in the morning you wouldn't be scared to find yourself here."

The boy listened as he ate. "Who're you?" he asked again.

"You can call me Boss, I guess. It's been years since

anyone called me anything else. I've got a flock of sheep outside and this is my wagon, and it's resting on the winter range."

The boy finished the mush and raising the bowl to his mouth licked it clean. The woman refilled it for him.

"Now, suppose you tell me what to call you," she said.

The boy looked at her silently for a long time. Distrust and caution played over his face, and Boss had the notion that if he could squirm out of the corner and past her, he would make a dash for the door.

"This ain't a home for children?" he asked.

Boss laughed. "It's a home for me; that's what it is. Now, what's your name?"

The boy's eyes narrowed. "Boy," he said. "That's what folks call me, unless they're mad at me."

The woman knew she had been right about his being a stray. He was underfed, uncared for, and didn't even have a name. Right now he looked like a hunted animal, a lonely animal fighting for its life in a world where nobody cared about it. It made her mad all over.

"All right," she said, "I'll call you Boy for now." She knew there was no use asking him questions. Let him settle down and relax first. There would be time enough to find out where he belonged and decide what to do with him later.

She took the bowl back to the stove and filled a pan with water from the kettle. In a corner of the dish cupboard beside the stove she found a towel. She got some soap and carried it all back to him.

"Wet a corner of the towel and wash your face. Then scrub your hands," she said. "And use the soap! I'll find something for you to sleep in."

The boy looked at the water and soap. "Is it Saturday?" he asked. In the crop-pickers' camps no one ever bathed except on Saturday evening.

"No, it isn't Saturday but I want you clean because I'm letting you sleep in my bed tonight. I won't have it messed up with a lot of dirt. Now, get to washing!"

She turned her back on him, lifted the bed she had made to get to the trapdoor of the bench again. When she found the garment she wanted, she came back to him and dropped it on the bed. He had rubbed the wet towel across his face, leaving his neck and ears grimy with dirt. She saw that the palms of his hands were heavily calloused, as though they had blistered and healed again and again, forming heavy pads of thickened skin. "Wipe your hands and get into this shirt."

The boy picked up the nightshirt in surprise. "Take off my clothes? Why?"

"So you'll sleep better," she answered. "Take off everything and put it on. I won't watch you."

She took the pan to the door, opened it, and flung the water out upon the ground. Then she refilled the pan and washed the bowl and spoon he had used. "All right to look now?"

The answer was muffled and she turned to see him struggling into the flannel shirt, his head coming slowly through the open neck.

"It's big," he said. "Is it yours?"

She shook her head. "Belonged to old Bezeleel, who used to live here. I found it when I moved in. It's clean."

He pulled the nightshirt around him. "Take off your shoes," she said, "and don't ask me why again." He did as he was told.

"Where you sleeping?" he asked.

She pointed to the wool sacks on the bench. "I'll sleep here tonight, soon as I get my boots off."

"You going to wash and take off your clothes too?"

"I've already washed. I do that as soon as I come in from the range and get the sheep settled. And I don't undress because a good herder never takes his clothes off at night. He sleeps with one ear on the sheep and the other on the dogs, and never knows from one minute to the next when he'll have to get out there and scare off a coyote or two."

"That why Beze — the other sheepherder ain't here no more? 'Cause he took off his clothes and used this night shirt?"

Boss laughed. He was quick all right . . . "No, that's not why." She stood up and straightened her bed.

"You'd be a good crop-picker," the boy said, studying her. "You're bigger than most men and you could lift a sack of potatoes easy, or even a full hamper of beans."

The woman knew he had paid her a compliment. So

that's where he had come from, she thought. Probably from the potato fields in Idaho. But why is he here, and who does he belong to?

She raised the blankets on his bed and told him to crawl under. "It's going to be cold when I turn off the stove, so dig down deep and keep the potatoes warm." She picked up a sack of potatoes and put them under the covers beside him. "When you sleep in this bed, that chore goes with it."

He looked at her as though she were crazy. "Sleep with potatoes? Why?"

"So they won't freeze. Now, no more questions. I'll leave the stove on in the morning when I start out, and the window over your bed cracked just enough to give you some air. I'll leave biscuits on the stove and a pot of beans, and the rest of the canned milk. Sleep all you can and I'll see you when I get home at sundown. Don't go outside in those thin clothes."

"Where you going?"

"Out with the sheep. They're ready to leave the bed-ground at sunup and they'll graze a few miles from here tomorrow. Now, no more questions. Go to sleep."

She turned off the lamp and lay down on the straw-filled wool sacks, drawing the blankets and soogan over her. She listened for the dogs but heard nothing. Not a sound came from the sheep. The wind was dying down, and she thought gratefully that perhaps tonight she would be able to sleep straight through. Jup or Juno would warn her if the coyotes came near, or if the sheep became restless and decided to look for higher ground, or if the lead sheep felt she hadn't had enough grass and set off to find more, with the rest of the flock following her.

She would think what to do with the boy tomorrow while she was out on the range. Right now she was tired, and sunup was too few hours away.

When the boy awoke in the morning, he was startled by his surroundings. Slowly it came back to him. He lay snug and warm under the blankets, examining the room. Boss had left her bed on the long bench neat, the blankets pulled smooth and the soogan folded lengthwise. The hinged window above his bed was held open a crack by a short stick, and he pulled himself up to look out.

There was no sign of Boss or her sheep, only the hills beyond covered with dried brown grass. He got out of bed and walked the length of the wagon to the window set in the upper half of the door. The view from here was a slope leading down to a stand of trees. A road cut through the middle of them and ended at the foot of the hill on which the wagon stood. There was no sign of life in that direction either, only a light wind bending the trees which stood pale and golden in the thin sunlight. The brush among the trees was a flaming orange, and here and there were wild currant and serviceberry bushes.

He turned to find the beans and a pan of biscuits warm on the stove. There was a note on a piece of paper tacked to the dish cupboard but, since he couldn't read, he only looked at it curiously. Opening a biscuit, he heaped beans into it and ate, standing beside the stove, the long flannel nightshirt dropping in folds upon the floor.

The woman called Boss had told him not to go out in his thin clothes. He turned the handle of the door and sniffed the air outside. It was brittle-cold and he withdrew hurriedly. Next, he examined the stove, opened the dish cupboard, then tested the sliding bracket of the lamp, standing on his toes to reach it. Discovering the table hinged to the bed, he lifted it and placed the leg under it upright on the floor. He found that when raised it rested on the two benches and he lifted and lowered it several times. Seeing the rope ring on the hinged short bench lid, he thrust his finger through it and raised the trapdoor. In the grub box were tins of milk, bags of sugar, beans, coffee, and some dried fruit.

Satisfied, he returned to the bed and slipped under the blankets. It was time to think about where he was and what he should do next. Boss hadn't asked him where he had come from. She wasn't nosy like some of the people who had given him rides along the highway. He had told them all something different, anything that popped into his head, but nothing about Raidy or the digging machine or the pickers' camp. He couldn't talk about that.

He had to be getting on to California before the winter set in. Somehow he must have got turned in the wrong direction, so he would have to go back and find the highway again. He looked around the sheep wagon. It was all right here, nice and warm and there was plenty of food to eat. Boss was all right too. She had given him her bed and this nightshirt, and she had even covered him up. No one had ever bothered so much about him before, no one but Raidy. He lay back and closed his eyes, suddenly tired again.

When he awakened, a man was standing in the doorway looking at him. The man was young, with dark weather-beaten skin and very light-blue eyes. His clothes were rough and well-worn. He held a pipe in one hand and a bag of flour and tins of food under his arm. Closing the door behind him, he came to the short bench and laid the articles on it.

"Where's Boss?" he asked, and the boy immediately knew he was a Texan. He had the same way of saying words, drawling them slow and easy, like the overseers in the bean fields.

He sat up. "Out with the sheep," he said, feeling comfortable with this man right away.

"When I saw smoke from the chimney, I wondered if she was sick." The man removed his greasy hat and extended a hand. "I'm Tex," he said, "camp tender."

His words meant nothing to the boy, but they shook hands. "I've got kerosene and wood and more groceries in the truck outside. Some mail here." He removed it from his pocket. "If it's all right with you, I'll make some coffee and warm myself up a bit." Without waiting for a reply, he took off his coat, filled the coffee pot from the bucket, and sprinkled a handful of coffee into the water. Setting it on the stove, he lighted his pipe and sat down on the bench.

"You know what a camp tender is?" he asked.

The boy shook his head.

"My job is to come up here every week to see how Boss is makin' out and to bring provisions. Now, there's snow blowin' up in the northwest, so I'm bringin' supplies in early. Tell Boss we're in for some weather, first of the season, and that Bezeleel's dog was rabid. Must have been bit by a coyote before he turned on the old man. And tell her —"

The boy interrupted him. "Who got bit by a coyote?"

"The dog that belonged to the old feller who used to be herder here."

"What's rabid?"

Tex laughed. "You sure got a lot of questions. Say, I thought everyone in Montana knew what rabid meant."

The boy shrugged, "Is that where I am?"

"Sure. Where did you think you were?"

"I didn't know but it didn't seem like what I'd heard about California. Wasn't warm enough. Any crops to pick around here?"

"Whoa, boy. You asked me a question. Rabid means the coyote was sick and he bit the dog and made him sick too, then the dog bit the old man."

"I don't like dogs," the boy said.

Tex looked at him, surprised. "Don't believe I ever knew a boy before who didn't like dogs. I wouldn't let Boss hear you say that. Jup and Juno are the best friends she has. And two of the best sheep dogs in these parts."

"Friends?" the boy said scornfully. "I'd never have a dog for a friend. I been throwing rocks at dogs as long as I can remember. And hitting them, too."

"Why?"

It seemed strange to the boy that Tex didn't know why. "We were both after the same food, that's why." He boasted, "But I usually got it."

Tex stood up and went to the stove. The coffee was boiling and he took a cup from the dish cupboard and filled it with the strong black liquid. When he was sitting down again, he said, "Yes, you're in Montana. But there's no crops to be picked here now. Did you run away?"

The boy considered the question. "No. I just left."

"What about your folks? They'll be worried."

Amazement showed in the boy's eyes. "Worried about me? Nobody's going to be worried about me. I never had any folks."

"Who takes care of you?"

"Takes care of me? I take care of myself, always have."

Tex chuckled. "You sound like a real loner for sure."

"A loner? What's that?"

"Best way I can explain is to tell you how I grew up. I didn't have folks either, nobody to worry about me. I grew up in an orphan's home."

"One of those places?" The boy was horrified.

"Oh, it wasn't so bad. You might say I was a loner too. One of those who didn't believe anyone cared about them or wanted to help. I figured it was up to me to take care of myself, and I didn't need help from anyone."

The boy nodded. This man understood.

"Let me tell you, boy, that's a poor way of livin'. A mighty selfish one too. Somebody will care if you just give 'em a chance."

The boy thought of Raidy.

"There's always people who need you as much as you need them. Don't you forget that. All you got to do is find 'em. When you do, you find you're happier carin' about someone else than just about yourself all the time." Tex took another long swallow of hot coffee. "You thinkin' about stayin' around here? This is mighty pretty country. It's sheep country."

The boy thought it over. "I was planning to get on to California but I might stay a little while — if she'll let me."

Tex leaned back and laughed. "You know what I think? I think Boss has got herself a bum lamb."

"What's that?"

Tex raised his eyebrows into an arch. "Guess you don't know nothin' about sheep raisin'. Let's see how I can explain it. At lambin' time in the spring, the ewe — "

"The what?"

"The mother sheep. Well, sometimes her lamb dies. Or sometimes the ewe dies. Now everybody knows ewes are healthier and happier if they've a lamb to raise, and lambs are better off if they've a mother. So the lambers take an orphan lamb — they call 'em bum lambs — and give it to the ewe that lost hers. Understand?"

"Sure," the boy said. "The mother needs a baby and the baby needs a mother so they put them together. The ewe adopts it the way they say people do sometimes for kids in those orphan homes."

Tex shook his head. "That's where you're wrong. The ewe knows the scent of her own lamb and sometimes she won't take a bum lamb. Sometimes she'll even trample it to death."

"What do they do then?"

"They fool the ewe. They skin her dead lamb and put its wool on the bum. They make slits for the legs and one for the neck and then they slip it over the bum and give him to the ewe. Funniest thing you ever saw. The lamb has two tails and eight legs."

The boy laughed. "Does she take it then?"

"Sure," said Tex. "Just as soon as she sniffs that wool and decides it's her own lamb. And she makes it a real good mother, too. Yes, sir, I think it would be good for Boss to have a bum lamb now."

He drew on his pipe and took a swallow of hot coffee. "You stay here with Boss for a while if she'll let you, hear? But don't tell her I said so. Ever since Ben was killed, she don't take kindly to people figurin' out what she should do."

"Who's Ben?"

Tex didn't answer for a few minutes. He teetered back on the bench, and his eyes looked far off. He seemed to be making up his mind. Finally he decided and he leaned forward.

"I'm goin' to tell you about Boss so you'll understand her a little better. She won't tell you; that is for sure. She doesn't talk much and never about herself. Maybe later on she'll get around to explaining to you about Ben, but I think you should know now. Don't you tell her that I've been talkin' about her." He finished the mug of coffee and rose to refill it. "Ben was her son. He was killed by a grizzly, a bear, two winters back when he was out huntin'. Boss spent a whole year lookin' for that bear and never did find it. There was never anyone in the world like Ben to her. Sometimes I think that's why she took old Bezeleel's place here when he got bit, just so she could be out here and find that bear. Angie said she should try to hire a herder but she wouldn't listen. These ewes in her flock are the best on the ranch, the real money-makers, so it's a special job and Boss decided to do it herself."

The boy was confused. "Who's Angie?"

"Ben's wife, Ben's widow now. She lives on the ranch and teaches school in town. Angie got real upset about Boss comin' way out here alone with the sheep for the winter. That's what I mean by sayin' Boss don't take kindly to people tellin' her what she should do. The more Angie talked, the stubborner Boss got, and I ain't never seen anyone could beat her at bein' stubborn." He slapped his leg. "There I go again. One thing Angie can't stand, bein' a schoolteacher, is someone saying ain't. I been tryin' my best to get over it but it slipped out again."

The boy wanted to hear the rest of the story. "Did you think Boss should have come out here?"

Tex whooped with laughter. "Me? I'm only a hired hand for now. I kept out of it. I'm just here to tend the camps of the herders and to do chores around the ranch. But someday . . ."

His eyes looked far off again. He reminded the boy of how the old man had looked driving down the highways. As though there was something beautiful way past the next hill that no one else could see. "Someday," Tex said, "I'm goin' to have me a sheep ranch, too. Sheep as far as you can see, dottin' the hills all around my ranch."

He slapped his leg again and stood up. "I've talked enough for one day. Got to go now. I'll bring the food and kerosene in and lay the wood under the wagon." He moved toward the door.

"You still a loner?" the boy asked.

A grin spread over Tex's face. "I been gettin' over it lately; that's how come I gave you all that good advice. You better get over it too." He winked. "You put up with Boss as long as she'll have you. When she does talk, you'll hear a lot about Ben and about the bear and about sheep, but I reckon you can stand that. Seems to me you two belong together, a nice old ewe and a bum lamb." He threw up his hands and let out a loud whoop. "Don't tell her I said that, though. She'd skin me alive for callin' her an old ewe." He left, laughing.

When Tex finished his chores, the boy watched him walk down the hill and get into the provision truck. He watched until the truck disappeared down the road between the cottonwoods and the quaking aspens and willows.

The boy thought about Ben and Boss, the bear, and Angie, and Tex for a long time. Tex had advised him to stay here if he could. It made sense. If he kept wandering around the country alone, someday someone would find out he didn't belong anywhere and they'd put him in one of those homes Tex had grown up in. Women who came to visit the pickers' camps were always threatening to put the children in homes somewhere. They said the children ought to be where they could go to school regularly and live like other people. Well, he'd had too much freedom in his life to like the idea of that. Maybe Tex was right. If Boss would have him he'd like to stay here for a while, maybe until next spring.

He began to study how to make Boss want him to stay. He remembered how she'd made him wash last night. That must mean that she liked for people to be clean. All right, if he had to be clean to stay, then he'd get used to it. Finding the pan he had washed in before, he poured water into it from the bucket. The water was warm from standing near the stove so he used it as it was. He stripped off the nightshirt and dropped the soap into the pan. Then, with the end of the towel, he washed himself thoroughly, better than he ever had in his life. Some of the crop-pickers had had portable tubs and he had seen them bathing on Saturday nights, in the middle of their shacks, the whole family waiting in line for their turn. No one he had ever traveled with had carried a tub. The ones he had known had left it up to each person to do what washing he wanted to at the spigot that supplied the whole camp with water. There in the sheep wagon the boy used the towel to dry himself and put his nightshirt back on again. He threw the water out the door as he had seen Boss do.

He ate another biscuit with beans and climbed back into bed. His body cried out for sleep and rest and he curled up under the blankets, grasping the bag of potatoes close to him, although the wagon was warm now. There was no way of knowing what time it was, and even if he had known, it wouldn't have mattered. Boss would be home at sundown. Until then he would sleep.

The boy awoke to sounds outside the wagon. He pulled himself up to the window and looked out. It was late afternoon and the golden haze he remembered from yesterday lay on the dry grass and the slopes near by. The sheep were slowly coming toward the bed-ground, grazing as they moved forward. The reflection of the sky tinted their wool and to the boy they looked like a floating golden cloud lying soft above the ground as far as he could see. Boss wasn't in sight, but he saw a dog working one side of the band. It ran up and down on the outer edge of the flock, guiding, directing the sheep toward the bed-ground. This must be one of the dogs Tex had talked about. He saw it go after one sheep that had strayed a little way off from the others. Taking it gently by the ear, the big black-and-white dog led it back to the others, left it there, and went on with his work.

He heard a low-pitched whistle and then saw another dog, smaller, and all white except for dark-brown ears,

appear from the other side, working the sheep to the right so that they headed toward the bed-ground where the flags marked off the borders.

Boss opened the door a few minutes later, pulling her hat off and running her hands through her short hair as she entered the wagon. "Been all right today?" she asked. Her gaze was so sharp that he felt she knew at once he had bathed but she didn't say anything about it. He nodded, surprised again at her size.

She saw the new supplies and the mail. "Tex been here?"

The boy nodded again. "He said to tell you weather was coming so he brought things out today. And that the old man's dog that bit him was sick. He called it something else but I can't remember what."

Boss nodded. "I figured that." She had pulled her coat off and was getting ready to mix food in two bowls. "Sometimes I wonder if I did wrong, not having all the dogs we own given that vaccine for rabies." She seemed to be talking to herself. "But Ben was so dead set against it after Jup's father died from the shot." She realized the boy was there. "What else did Tex say?"

"Nothing much." He remembered Tex's warning not to let her know they had spent most of the time talking about her.

"He's a good worker but a big talker. If he didn't say more than that he must be off his feed." The boy said nothing and Boss didn't press the matter. She finished mixing the food. "I'm going out and feed the dogs and count the sheep," she said. "Then I'll come in and clean up and get us some supper."

The boy looked at her, round-eyed. "You know enough numbers to count all of them?" he asked. To him the sheep were endless, covering the ground all around the wagon.

She laughed and drew him to the window. "Look out there. You'll see some black sheep among the rest. They're the ones I count. There's one of them for every hundred white and we call them markers. If all nine are there, it's safe to figure we haven't lost any."

She left the wagon with the bowls and the boy stayed at the window and looked out. He counted the number of black sheep he saw. There were only six but he couldn't see all the flock. He couldn't see Boss or the dogs either, but he guessed she was feeding them right outside the wagon. He stayed there, staring at the sheep. Some were slowly grazing their way to the bed-ground on the slant between the flags while others had already kneeled and found a place for the night. He saw with surprise that their fleece was gray and greasy-looking now that the sunlight had gone. Their legs looked too thin for their bodies and they seemed to be standing on the tips of their small split hooves. Tears spilled from their eyes. Now and then they raised their heads and blatted sadly, their cleft upper lips quivering.

After a while Boss came back into the wagon. "No wind tonight," she said, "though it may blow up later if weather's coming. That's the biggest worry I have, along with coyotes."

"Wind don't blow them away, does it?" the boy asked, still thinking of them as they had looked in the golden light — like a cloud, soft and airy.

Boss looked at him quickly to see if he was joking.

"No, though it does seem to blow their wits away. A sheep doesn't like to feel its wool ruffled, so it's just as apt to get up and walk into the wind. And if one goes, they all go."

The boy thought about that. "Guess they're pretty dumb, huh?"

Boss whirled on him. "Dumb? They're not dumb. They're just about the most helpless creatures alive. They've lost all their instinct to take care of themselves because they haven't had to. But it isn't their fault. It's man's. He's bred all the wild animal's independence and cunning out of them for his own gain, to have their meat and their wool with the least possible bother from them. Don't ever use that word about them again in my hearing. I won't have it!"

She stood there, red-faced with anger, and the boy swallowed hard. He wasn't off to a very good start at making her like him and want him to stay. It was a new game to him, and he realized he wasn't very good at it. But if he wanted to stay enough, he could learn how to think of what she'd like before he did or said anything.

Slowly her face relaxed. "I know people call them stupid.

They say they're the only animals alive that are born determined to get themselves killed one way or another as soon as possible. But I happen to love those sheep, every one of them, and Ben did, too. He spent his time caring for them from the time he was just a child. He kept them from straying off and getting lost, kept them out of the coyotes' way, kept them from eating the locoweed that drives them crazy. I know they seem to be bent on doing things that will destroy them, but that's the reason I'm here. To keep them safe, and keep them together."

The boy turned his face to the wall while Boss washed herself and changed her clothes. Evening had come, and the sheep had settled down. The wagon was warm and comfortable, and the deep weariness of his body was almost gone. He thought about what Boss had said. It surprised him to hear her talk like that about sheep. People he'd known spent their time taking care of themselves. Boss took care of sheep.

She pulled the table up and propped it with the folding leg. They ate stewed tomatoes and scrambled eggs and some of the biscuits left over from morning. She opened a glass of blackberry jelly and spread it on the biscuits, and poured a cup of half canned milk and half water for the boy.

"Why didn't you drink some today?" she asked. "Didn't you see the note I left telling you it was on the ledge outside to keep cool?"

He didn't say anything. Raidy had placed such store on reading and writing, maybe Boss did, too. He hadn't even guessed the note was for him. If he said he couldn't read, she might think he ought to go to school and learn. And that would probably mean he would have to live in one of those children's homes. He had to be very careful before he said anything.

Boss watched his face and he was sure she knew what he was thinking. Without saying anything she cleared away the dishes, then brought her boots and a jar of grease to the table. She worked the grease into the leather with her fingers and wiped it off with a cloth. Her large hands were rough, but the nails were evenly trimmed and clean. "Ben cleaned his boots every night of his life," she said. "I never had to tell him to do it."

The boy was glad he had bathed. It had been the right thing to do, something Ben would have done without being told.

When she finished, she put the boots on the floor and went to the long bench. Inside it she found a book and brought it back to the table.

"I've been thinking all day about a name," she said. "Seems to me you ought to pick one out for yourself. There's a lot of fine names in the Bible here."

The boy knew what the Bible was. There had been men who came to the pickers' camps on Sundays, and read out of the Bible to anyone who would listen.

"I decided the best way was to let you hold the Bible and turn to wherever you want. Then put your finger on the page and we'll see what it says."

He took the book and held it between his hands. The cover was of smooth leather, and there were gold letters across the front of it. He hesitated, thinking of Raidy. He wished she could be here now to see him get a name, his own name.

Opening the book, he pressed the pages flat on his knees. Then he placed his finger on a place and held it there. Boss covered his finger with her large one and took the book. For a minute she didn't say anything.

The boy couldn't stand the waiting. "What does it say?" he asked.

Her voice was very low. "You turned to First Samuel, Chapter sixteen. And put your finger on these words, 'Send me David thy son, which is with the sheep!'"

"That mean my name is David?"

She shut the book slowly. "It's a fine name . . ."

He was curious. "Who was he?"

"A shepherd," Boss said. "A very brave and loyal shepherd. When he was only a boy in charge of his father's flock, he risked his life to protect his sheep."

"How?" The boy wanted to know all there was to know about this David whose name he would be taking.

"One day when the sheep were grazing, a hungry lion snatched one out of the flock and ran off with it. David went after him and took the sheep right out of his mouth. The lion turned on him then and David killed it with his bare hands."

"Wow! He sure was brave, wasn't he?"

Boss nodded. "He was. But what I like best about the story is that he didn't stop to think about the danger when

one of his sheep was gone. They were in his care and he knew he had to protect them. That's what a shepherd's for, to look out for his sheep even if it means risking his own life. You could be very proud of a name like that but you'd also have a lot to live up to."

She rose and put the book away. "Get into bed. This one," she was pointing to the one on the bench. "You'll use it after this — David."

He lay in bed thinking about his name, trying it over and over until it began to sound familiar on his tongue. Somewhere, long ago, there had been a David who had taken care of sheep and now he was going to use that name, too.

Author

As wife of a naval officer, Ester Wier has lived in many parts of the world. While her children were in high school, she published magazine stories, articles, poems, and adult books. *The Loner,* her first book for young people, was a Newbery Honor Book and was made into a TV movie. Mrs. Wier says, "My fervent wish is that when children read a book of mine, they find something besides a story to hold their interest, hopefully the opening of a new world of some kind."

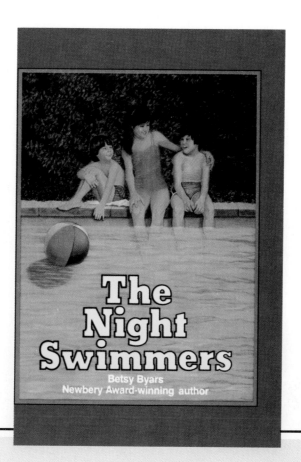

The Night Swimmers
Betsy Byars
Newbery Award-winning author

In the selections you have just read from *Living with Change,* the main characters experienced changes in their lives that were sometimes painful. Even so, such moments of change were also moments of growth and understanding.

Now you will read *The Night Swimmers* by Betsy Byars. Although it concerns the changes in a family shattered by the death of the mother, it also concerns the lessons that come with simply living as a family.

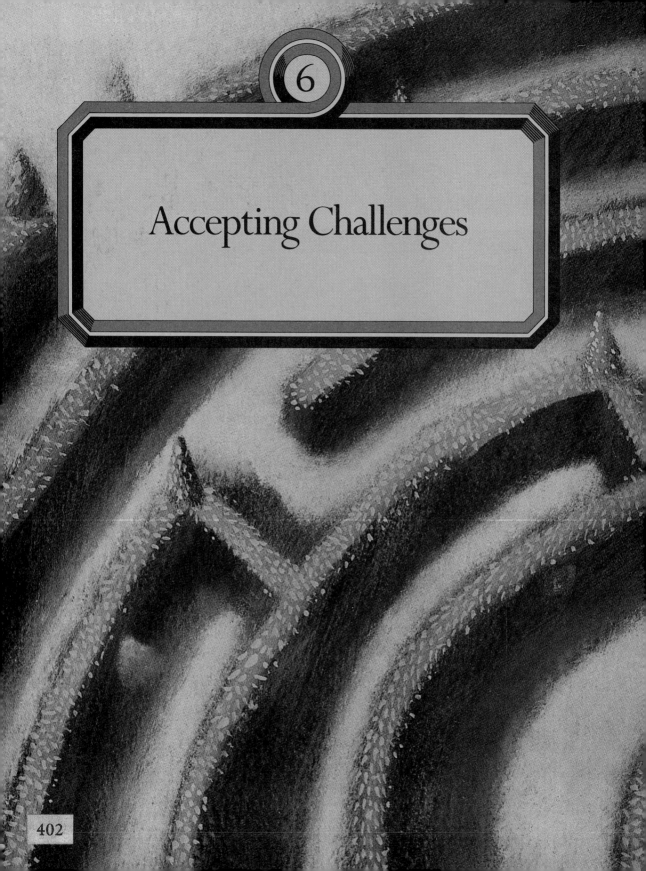

6

Accepting Challenges

Maria Tallchief

The Story of an American Indian

by Marion E. Gridley

As a young adult, Maria Tallchief was a famous ballet dancer — but it seemed she had already spent a lifetime working for that difficult goal. She was born Betty Marie Tall Chief in 1925 in Oklahoma. Her father was Osage and her mother Scottish-Irish and Dutch. When she was eight, the family moved to Los Angeles. There she and her younger sister, Marjorie, worked hard on their dance lessons. At seventeen, Betty Marie joined the Canadian tour of the famed Ballet Russe de Monte Carlo.[1]

It wasn't long before Betty Marie realized that she was a war-time replacement only. She was needed for the tour, but perhaps it would be decided that she was not needed afterwards. She would have to make an impression and convince them that she had ability.

Before the company opened in Ottawa, there were hours and hours of rehearsals. Each day was a round of rehearsals and fittings. Quick meals were snatched on the run. There were only brief rest times. It was exhausting, but the excitement kept her going.

The road company was so much smaller in size that everyone had to learn a number of parts, more than they usually would. And there was less time to learn them. Betty Marie's quick memory made it possible for her to fill in many times where the other dancers could not.

One night, just before curtain time, she was told that she would have a small part in *Gaîté Parisienne*.[2] Danilova[3] was the star. This was a real break for her. She had to do a series of *fouettés*[4] while on her toes. She always did them well, but

---

[1]**Ballet Russe de Monte Carlo** (bă lā′ rōōs′ də mŏn′ tē kär′ lō):
Russian Ballet of Monte Carlo.
[2]**Gaîté Parisienne** (gət ĕ′ pə rē′ zē ĕn′)
[3]**Danilova** (dä nē′ lō vä)
[4]**fouetté** (fwĕ tā′): a ballet step executed with a quick whipping movement of the raised leg, often accompanied by continuous turning.

never so well as she did them that night. The audience clapped loudly and the principal dancers praised her. From then on, she was given other good parts that would not otherwise have been assigned to her. She never knew until almost the last moment what she would dance. Sometimes her part was changed even after she was all dressed and ready.

In Montreal, the company presented a benefit performance for the war effort. The Governor General of Canada and his wife, Princess Alice, would attend. A few days beforehand, Betty Marie was told that she would have a solo role, as Spring in the ballet, *Snow Maiden*. This important role had first been danced by Danilova. For an unknown to follow in the steps of this great ballerina was an honor and challenge. Never in her wildest dreams had Betty Marie hoped for this.

Danilova was her idol of idols. She wanted to become just like the graceful, dynamic star whom people flocked to see. All of her heart and all of her talent went into her performance. She seemed to hear Nijinska[5] saying, "Let the music speak!" She let herself be swept along by it, and with all of her being she reached out to her audience and carried them with her. Her dancing was pure poetry, pure rapture.

That night, praise was heaped on her. Backstage callers complimented her lavishly. One of them was Princess Alice, who spoke with admiration about her lyrical dancing. "You must have worked very hard to do so well," Princess Alice said. She predicted that Betty Marie would become one of the great names in ballet. The newspaper reviews echoed the same thought the next day.

All of this was sweet to hear. Betty Marie's happiness was spoiled by only one harsh note. There was now an air of hostility towards her among the *corps*[6] girls. They made her feel unwelcome, like an outsider.

Betty Marie knew that some of the girls thought her

standoffish. She was naturally reserved and had never had Marjorie's outgoing personality. She had studied and practiced so much by herself that she was not at ease with people. Though she could respond to friendliness and wanted to be friendly, it was hard for her to make friends at once.

The new attitude on the part of the *corps* girls was an active jealousy. They resented the fact that Betty Marie was given so many good parts. They said spitefully that this was because she was a pupil of Madame Nijinska's. There were other cutting remarks, all meant for her to hear. "Her father is a millionaire so she can ride in pullman cars while we have to go by coach," they said. They called her a "wooden Indian" and "Princess Iceberg."

Betty Marie's family had always traveled in pullman cars, so she did so as a matter of course. She had never been with a road company before and did not know it was only the principals who did so. It did not occur to her that this would set her apart from the other girls, or that they would think she thought herself too good to ride with them.

From then on, she went by coach with the rest. But the mean remarks continued. They hurt so much that she withdrew within herself and stayed pretty much alone. She was a member of the *corps* girls, but not "one of the girls."

Now she worked harder than ever. She spent what time she could watching the ballerinas practice and trying to follow their movements. This, too, aroused comment from the girls. "Trying to get in good," they sniffed. "She wants to be noticed."

The Canadian tour was a lonely and depressing experience. If it were not for her good friend Helen Kramer, it would have been nearly unbearable. Betty Marie suffered

---

[5] **Nijinska** (nə jĭn′ skä)
[6] **corps** (kôr)

from the extreme cold weather and from the constant travel. The mean remarks stung like wasps. They added to her tiredness and discouragement. She tried to think only of the pleasant things that took place, although the meanness rankled. She grew pale and sad-looking. She said to Helen that she looked like a picked chicken. She spent much of her time resting and trying to stay well.

At last she learned to steel herself against sullen looks and cold manners. When some of the girls complained to the dance director that she was given parts and they were not, she brushed this aside. She was more concerned over what she heard him reply. "When we get back to New York she won't have those special parts anymore," he said. "She'll be right back in line with the rest of you."

Betty Marie wondered if she would be able to get ahead in New York after all. Or rather, if she could get ahead with Ballet Russe. Again she considered joining Ballet Theatre. Her mother wrote that she was expected to return home after the Canadian tour. This, too, she brushed aside. She did not think at all of return — only of going ahead.

Back in New York, Betty Marie once more prepared to call upon Germain Sevastianov of the Ballet Theatre. Once more she was prevented from doing so. Mr. Denham summoned her to his office. He had been given many good reports about Betty Marie. Everyone said she had a glowing future. So, he would give her a year's contract as a paid member of Ballet Russe. There would be important roles for her, but not at first. She might have to wait a long time for that to happen. Always, she must work very hard. There would be disappointments and frustrations and constant practice.

"If you can't stand up to it all, then you must decide to leave now," Mr. Denham said flatly. "You have got to have what it takes to be a dancer. I think you do."

Betty Marie answered yes at once. Practice she was not afraid of; that she had always done. Hard work she was not afraid of. She had always worked hard. Disappointment she could learn to accept. She would stay with Ballet Russe and hang on, come what may. All that mattered was that she would be dancing. The chance would come to prove herself. She could wait for as long as it took. She would not stay in the *corps* forever.

The New York season began almost at once. On opening night, Betty Marie arrived early. The great stage was ready. Soon the musicians would tune their instruments. The electricians would test their lights. The giant theater would come to life.

In the dressing room, excitement was high. Betty Marie expected to dance the cancan in *Gaîté Parisienne* with a group of *corps* girls. It was a spirited number and she always enjoyed it. She hurried to get ready, pulling on her long hose and slipping her costume with its flouncy skirts over her head. Makeup was put on carefully. A large flower was fastened in the sleek hair. A velvet ribbon was fastened around her throat.

The dressing room was crowded and noisy so she waited in the wings. It was nearly time for the audience to start arriving. Suddenly, a hand was placed on her shoulder and she was given a quick shove.

"Hurry, get out of that costume," she heard the dance director say. "You are going to dance a solo. The soloist who performs the role has not arrived. She cannot be waited for."

Unfastening her costume as she went, Betty Marie ran back to the dressing room. The wardrobe mistress had her new costume ready for her. Her makeup had to be changed. In only a few moments she was ready and about to leave for the wings. She intended to go over her steps.

Just then the soloist dashed in. There was scarcely time for her to get into the costume which Betty Marie quickly slipped off. She smiled as she gave it to the dancer, but she wanted to cry.

There was a titter among the *corps* girls. They were laughing at her. One girl said, "Miss High and Mighty didn't make it this time." Betty Marie remained silent. Only her great dark eyes flashed anger. She would be a good trouper and let no one see how badly she felt. She would not give the girls the satisfaction of letting their jabs upset her.

Quickly she became a cancan dancer again. She danced with a smile on her face, lifting her long tapering legs in perfect *fouettés*. She knew she did them better than anyone else. It gave her a bitter-sweet feeling to see the envious looks of the other dancers. They know it too, she thought. Let them laugh at me if they want to.

As she danced off into the wings, the dance director was waiting. With him was the wardrobe mistress holding out a new costume. The director's face was scarlet. This costume was for another ensemble. Someone had not shown up and Betty Marie had to fill in. Her new dress was barely fastened when she was back on stage.

That night there was a party after the ballet. "You have earned the right to better roles," Mia Slavenska said. "You will have them. But Mr. Denham wants you to have a new name — a Russian one."

Betty Marie refused. She did not want a different name. She wanted to dance as herself. But Mia said that the name Betty Marie was a childish one. It was not the name for someone who will be a great star.

Someone suggested the name of Tallchieva. What could be more Russian than that?

To this, Betty Marie also said no. "I will not change my

last name," she said. "It's a good American name. I'm proud of it. I'm not a Russian."

No amount of argument could persuade her. Even Mr. Denham tried to win her over. "I'll change my first name," she finally gave in. "You can call me Maria. But Tall Chief must stay as it is. You can spell it as one word, if you want to." So it was decided. Maria Tallchief she would be. Maria Tallchief, the Osage dancer. Maria Tallchief, who would go a long way.

When she wrote home to her family, Maria said that it seemed like a miracle. But then, to dance was a miracle. She spoke no word of the mean things that had taken place. She talked only of the promise that lay ahead. When she put aside the name Betty Marie, she also put aside childish feelings. As Maria, she had become a woman.

She had tried out her wings and they had carried her on her first flight. She was eager, now, to fly to new heights.

Six months after Maria first came to New York, she had a small part in *Rodeo*. This was a new, modern ballet choreographed by Agnes de Mille. It met with tremendous success, and it was a small success for Maria. But she was not enjoying herself. She was continually depressed, did not eat well, and grew steadily thinner. It was like a sickness, but she was not sick except in spirit.

Shortly before taking the *Rodeo* part, the Ballet Russe had announced that Madame Nijinska's *Chopin Concerto* would be included in the list of presentations. The names of the cast were posted, but Maria's name was not among them. She tried to tell herself she had been an amateur when she danced the ballet. She was still no more than a small-part dancer. She could hardly expect to be included.

Yet, she longed to dance the *Concerto* with all of her being. Her experience in the Hollywood Bowl came back to haunt her. To dance the ballet well would be to wipe out that early mishap. Surely she could have been given a tiny part! She wanted to dance the *Concerto* so badly that she could think of little else.

Day after day she watched Krassovska rehearse the same role that she had once danced. The movements had been changed somewhat. She studied as she watched so that they became familiar to her. She could have filled in for any of the soloists if an emergency arose, so well did she study all their parts.

When *Chopin Concerto* opened in the Metropolitan Opera House, Maria watched from the wings. She saw herself in every turn, in every graceful position. Her imagining was so vivid it was almost real. But it wasn't real, she was forced to admit. She was only standing on the sidelines.

The program was a great triumph. Danilova, the prima ballerina, received ovation after ovation. Krassovska, too, was applauded enthusiastically. Maria was delighted for her beloved Danilova, for her friend Krassovska, and for Madame Nijinska. But her delight was edged with despair. When was the promised time coming when she would be a great star? Where were the important roles she had been promised? She worked so hard, tried so hard, did everything that was asked of her — and stayed where she was.

In spite of her worries, Maria continued to perfect and polish her dancing. She practiced by herself for hours on end. She paid for extra lessons with her own money. She grew more wan and thin, and she was more than ever driven to succeed.

That fall, the company went on tour. Maria danced in Los Angeles for the first time since she had left home. She did not have a solo part, however, but was still one of the *corps* girls. It was good to see her family again. Marjorie was doing well with her dancing and was certain to find a future in ballet. Mrs. Tall Chief worried about Maria. She was troubled to see her looking so poorly. "You should come home and rest," she urged. "You should stay here and dance. Maybe you should even give up ballet. It is too hard on you."

The ballet returned to New York for a Christmas Day opening. Maria worked for an hour by herself. Then, while she was exercising at the *barre,* the dance director approached her. He said that it was possible she would dance in the *Concerto* the following night. Krassovska was ill and Maria would be allowed to dance that role. She was to stay after the performance and practice the changes.

Maria almost collapsed with joy. It was as though a magic wand had been waved and lifted her up to the clouds. The news spread quickly through the cast and many warm wishes were spoken for good luck. Some of the girls who had been the most unfriendly had left the company and there were better feelings toward Maria. It was admitted that she had been given parts because she deserved them. Maria had something that the rest did not — an inner spark and more than the usual amount of skill.

That night Maria was ready long before curtain time. Then came a message. Danilova wished to see her. Maria hurried to her dressing room and found Mr. Denham there, also. He looked troubled.

As Maria waited with a sinking heart, the two talked in Russian. Somehow, she knew what was being said. She clasped her hands tightly together, afraid for what she would hear.

"Danilova does not think you are ready for the *Concerto,*" Mr. Denham said. "She says you have had no proper rehearsal. She says that you cannot master this difficult role in only a day's time."

Maria pleaded that she could. She knew all of the movements and the music. It was time for the curtain call, so there the matter was left.

The following night, Maria was at the theater early. Her friends clustered around her, eager to help with her hair, her costume, her makeup, or just to be near her in this wonderful hour. When she was ready, she stood in her usual place in the wings.

Then Mr. Denham touched her on the shoulder. She turned, her face shining with happiness. Mr. Denham could not look at her. "You will not be needed," he said shortly, and walked away.

Crushed, Maria went back to the dressing room. The *corps* girls were shocked at her stricken face. No one said a word as she blindly took off her costume and left the room. She stumbled home to sit alone in darkness.

Nothing so terrible had ever happened to her before. "Why? why?" she asked herself over and over. There had to be a reason. But the reason would not come. Only the hurt mounted and mounted.

For the next few days, rumors spread like wildfire. Maria was the talk of the ballet world. There were times when she wanted to run away and hide. But she had an inner toughness, an inner strength, that carried her through. She refused to be defeated by what had taken place. She stayed calm and would not discuss what had happened or what was said.

At last Danilova spoke to her. "Don't hate me," she said. "There just wasn't enough time for you to dance *Concerto*. If you had not done well, your whole career would have been set back. Some day you will dance the *Concerto* and you will be wonderful."

Danilova had a small part for Maria in *Le Beau Danube*[7] and urged her to take it. So Maria swallowed the lump in her

---

[7] **Le Beau Danube** (lĕ bō′ dän yo͞ob′)

throat and began rehearsing. She tried to be grateful for Danilova's attention. She would keep on doing her best.

The winter was a rugged one. One after another, the dancers became ill. Maria, too, caught a cold and was unable to shake it. She was given a solo part in *Schéhérazade*,[8] but her spirits remained low and her health poor. Mrs. Tall Chief again wrote for her to come home. She sensed in Maria's letters that she wasn't well. Marjorie was studying with Madame Nijinska and Maria could study with her.

Maria hung on doggedly. She would not let go. She went on tour with the company in April, even though she was very ill. Her mother wrote again that Marjorie was dancing with the Los Angeles Light Opera Company. Maria must come home. A place would be found for her with the same company.

Again Maria refused. She had a contract with Ballet Russe and would not break it. Once she fainted at a private party. Her friends were alarmed over her health, and she begged them not to let her mother know. She continued to practice and dance, even when she should not have done so.

Then came a never-to-be-forgotten day. May 1, 1943! The day of the big chance, at last!

Krassovska injured her foot and Maria was told that she would take her place in the matinee performance of *Concerto*. She tried to stand quietly while she was being fitted for her costume. But the words "I will show them" kept singing through her head. "I will show them. I will SHOW THEM." She wanted to leap around the room.

When the cue came, she did leap onstage and swirled into the steps as if she were another being. She was part of the music, dancing as if in a dream. She was a new and different Maria, radiant, following her heart in the joy of dancing.

She finished to thunderous applause. Even Danilova

---

[8] **Scheherazade** (shə här′ ə zä′ də)

stood aside as she took her bows. She had proven that she was a dancer — a great dancer. She was the only girl in the company with the promise of becoming a prima ballerina. There was no higher place to go.

All of the principals were elated. They had witnessed the birth of a star. Mr. Denham, in his quiet way, complimented her, too. She would dance the Krassovska role until the foot had recovered. But even when Krassovska returned, Maria continued to dance the role although it was Krassovska's name that appeared in the program. She did not mind. It was not the glory but the doing that mattered.

When Ballet Russe opened its summer season, Krassovska decided to go to Europe. Maria now had the *Concerto* role for good. So far, she had danced it only on tour. Now she would debut in the ballet in New York City. She was only eighteen years old! The world was very good.

Mr. Denham understood the happiness that shone from her eyes. He had been concerned over her sunken cheeks and her pale face. But he knew that happiness was a great healer. Maria's health began to improve almost at once with the *Concerto* assignment.

The New York debut was outstanding. There was no question now of her stature as a dancer. Tears stood in her eyes as she saw the audience rise and heard their shouts and applause. Many bouquets of flowers were brought to the stage. One of them touched her deeply. It was a huge bouquet of roses from the *corps* girls.

Author

Marion E. Gridley was adopted by the Omaha and Winnebago peoples. Her interest in Native Americans led to her more than twenty books on the subject. For many years she edited the magazine *Amerindian*. Ms. Gridley died in 1974.

The Way Things Are

by Myra Cohn Livingston

It's today,
This road,
This knowing the road is there.
A few brambles,
A few tangles,
A few scratches,
A rough stone against your toe,
But still, you've got to go
And take it.
Fast, sometimes,
Or slow,
But go —

         everywhere.
         anywhere
        You need
        to go.

419

AN EXCERPT FROM

Mine for Keeps

by Jean Little

While Sal Copeland had been away at school, her family had moved into a new home. Now she was taking her first close look at the room she was to share with her younger sister Meg.

Home from School

"Hi, Sally," a sweet, small voice was saying, over and over and over.

Sal opened her eyes. Meg stood by her bed, rocking back and forth on her bare feet as she chanted her greeting. She was dressed in an old pair of Kent's pajamas. She had her hands planted on her hips. Her hair was tousled, her big hazel eyes shining. "She's just the same," Sal thought happily.

Meg suddenly came to with a jolt.

"You're awake!" she accused.

Before Sal could answer, her little sister was at the bedroom door shouting the news to everyone living on the block.

"SHE'S AWAKE!! SALLY'S AWAKE!"

At once it sounded as though at least a dozen people were hurrying to the spot. A boy's voice yelled, "Wowie!" Two doors slammed in different parts of the house. Somewhere, water was turned off; and from every direction came footsteps. Startled and excited, Sal watched the door. Mother reached it first. She fixed Meg with a withering look the minute she crossed the threshold.

"Margaret Ann Copeland," she started in sternly, using Meg's whole name to show how serious a matter it was, "I thought I told you quite clearly to leave Sally alone this morning. She was up late last night and she needed to sleep."

Meg defended herself stoutly.

"I never even touched her, did I, Sally? I was just standing looking at her — and she opened her eyes up all by herself, didn't you, Sally?"

Mother was not fooled by this, but she smiled in spite of herself.

Then Melinda and Kent came to the rescue, arriving in the doorway together. Mindy elbowed her way in first. She dived at Sal, giving her a hug and a kiss that left her breathless.

"It's about time you came home," she announced.

Not so ready with words, Kent snapped a salute at Sal from across the room. Then he swung himself up on top of the nearest dresser and perched there to watch whatever happened next.

Last of all, Dad sauntered in, making the family complete.

"Good morning, Miss Copeland," he said solemnly.

"Hi!" Sal got out, grinning at him.

Melinda and Mother were sitting on the two beds. Kent was still aloft on the chest of drawers and Dad leaned up against the doorjamb. Meg, too excited to settle, danced and hopped from one to the other. My whole family, Sal thought, looking around at them all; and then, without any warning, they were all looking at her! Suddenly, the room seemed jammed with people. Ten eyes fixed on her, all in one moment like that, were more than Sally could handle. She gave them back one frantic look. Then she went very red and felt a lump as big as a golfball come into her throat. They were waiting for her to say something — and that lump was so big she could not have gotten one word out, even if she had known what to say.

Mother saved her.

"How do you like your new room, Sarah Jane?" she asked,

gesturing so that everyone's eyes were drawn away from Sal to the bedroom where they were gathered.

Nor did Mother stop there. She went on telling about the troubles she had had in getting just the right material for the drapes. She had asked for yellow drapes, "daffodil" or "buttercup" or even "dandelion," and the store sent "pea-soup green" and "parsnip" and "mustard."

Mindy interrupted to announce eagerly that she had chosen the wallpaper; and, from then on, Sal could relax. Every single one of them had some story to tell. Each corrected the others and, between them, they filled in a dozen funny details that soon had Sal shaking with laughter.

Just as the paperhanger was putting on the wallpaper, Meg had walked under it and had almost been pasted on along with it. "We were nearly rid of her that time, Sally," Dad said, sighing at the way things had turned out. Meg stuck out her tongue at him in reply. When the closets were being painted and the dressers had not arrived, Melinda had almost given all of Sal's and Meg's clothes away to a lady who had come around collecting for the Used Clothing Drive. "Well, how was I to know?" asked Mindy. "There was that big heap of clothes in the hall. I just naturally thought Mother had put them there on purpose." Kent had tried to help the electricians do the wiring and, as Dad put it, he had come "shockingly" close to being electrocuted.

Under cover of their chatter, Sal's blush faded. The lump in her throat melted away. Now, with unabashed delight, she sat and stared around her new room.

It was a big, square room with a southwest window to catch the afternoon sun and a southeast window through which the morning sun now poured. The drapes were yellow and so were the tiny flowers in the wreaths on the wallpaper and the sheepskin rug between the beds. There was a huge bookcase, the top shelves filled with her favorite books, the bottom shelves full of her old favorites which now belonged to Meg. And there was the tall mirror which had always stood in her parents' room in the old house. Sal had never paid much attention to it before, but now she liked it at once. It stood between the two dressers and it had an old frame, curiously carved.

Her family was still talking but Sal had stopped hearing what they said. She smiled, almost shyly, at the small bright flowers in the wallpaper. She turned her head and imagined herself sitting in the captain's chair, over by the window, reading maybe. She picked out which dresser was hers by her brush and comb, which Mother had already unpacked. "This is my room," she said to herself, to see how it sounded. "Mine and Meg's."

"Do you like it, Sarah Jane?" Mother asked, gently.

Sal just looked at her. It took a moment for her to come back from her own thoughts and understand what Mother meant.

"Your room, silly," Mindy prodded, an impatient note in her voice.

"Easy there, Melinda," Mother warned. "I'll do my own asking."

Mindy flushed and was quiet and Sal suddenly came to life.

"It's a beautiful room," she cried. "It's . . . it's beautiful!"

"It's *my* beautiful room too," Meg put in, sounding not quite sure.

"Of course it's yours too, funnyface. Now, I want every one of you to clear out of here and finish dressing. Breakfast will be ready in fifteen minutes. No comics in the bathroom, Kent. Move over, Andrew. Let them through."

Dad grinned at Mother, took Melinda and Kent each by a shoulder and marched them off down the hall singing "Three

Blind Mice" off key. Mother laughed and picked up Sally's braces.

As she began to help Sal into them, Meg put down the sock she had just picked up.

"Why do you have to wear that?" she asked finally.

Sal had known the question was coming. She waited for Mother to explain, but Mother was fitting the braces into the high shoes Sally wore and she paid no attention to Meg.

"Why do you, Sally?"

"Well . . . it's . . . I have to wear them so I can walk," Sal mumbled at last.

"Why?" Meg countered.

Sal hesitated.

"Why?" Meg repeated, a little louder, as though she imagined Sal had not heard the first time.

"Because," Sal snapped.

She knew that would not satisfy Meg, and she looked at her mother again, but Mother was still busy doing up buckles.

"Because why?" came the inevitable small voice.

Sal thought hard. Until today, somebody else had always explained for her.

"Because I have cerebral palsy. It makes you so you can't walk and maybe your hands don't work just right. It makes you kind of stiff."

Then, remembering Bonnie and Alice, Jane Ann and Hilary, she stopped. All of them had cerebral palsy — and yet every single one of them showed it in a different way. Bonnie only limped a bit with her left leg. Alice could not walk but sat in a wheelchair all the time, with her arms and legs bent up and jerking. Jane Ann used crutches, but they were short wrist crutches. They didn't go up under your armpits like Sally's. And Hilary walked without much trouble, but she could not use a fork or a pencil or turn a doorknob or brush her own teeth because her hands were so involved. Then there was Louise, who could walk and use her hands fairly well, but had a terrible time talking. You had to know her for a long time before you could understand what she was trying so hard to tell you. She had cerebral palsy too. Memories of other children crowded into Sally's mind, confusing her still further. They all had cerebral palsy; and yet it suddenly seemed to her that there were dozens of different handicaps among them. She stared helplessly at Meg's waiting face.

Mother caught her expression of dismay and laughed.

"You're right, Sally. Cerebral palsy is pretty complicated. Just the same, I think you and Meg both could understand it better than you do. But, if you don't mind, let's wait till next weekend. You have an appointment then with Dr. Eastman in Toronto, and we'll take Meg along. I could explain, but he told Mindy about it when we first found out you had it and he did such a good job I'd like to see him do it again. Also, right this minute, everybody else in this house is just about ready for breakfast!"

She got up and fetched some clothing from Sal's dresser and the closet.

"Try these on for size, honey." She laid them within Sal's reach and smiled down at her. "You'll find the clothes are brand-new — to match your new room."

Then, without another word, she walked out.

Sal lay very still and stared after her. In one frightened instant, the safe warm feeling which had been growing inside her since Mother first hugged her the night before vanished.

Why, she couldn't dress herself! There were always slippery little blouse buttons impossible to do up and zippers with metal tabs so small your fingers couldn't keep hold of

them! Didn't Mother know that? At school, there was always somebody there to help with the hard parts no matter what Miss Jonas said.

Sal lay very still. She lay and watched the door through which Mother had disappeared. Underneath all the arguments about buttons and zippers and school, she could hear another voice shouting: *She didn't even ask! She just left me! She's not ever going to stay! She doesn't care! She just left! She just left me all alone!*

"Aren't you going to get dressed now, Sally?"

Sal looked away from the door. She had forgotten Meg. How small and sure of herself she looked, sitting cross-legged on the floor, tugging on her socks. Sal almost smiled. Then she knew Meg was no help. She was too small. She couldn't take the place of a whole schoolful of girls with cerebral palsy. She couldn't drive away the fear that now surrounded Sally.

With a jerk, Sal rolled away from her little sister to face the wall, her braces clanking together. A giant sob ached in her throat. As her first tears wet the pillow under her cheek, she took back the wish she had been making so faithfully for such a long time, the wish "come true" just last night. In spite of the feeling she had had when Mother hugged her in the car, in spite of the beautiful room, in spite of Meg, in spite of all the years of waiting and wanting to go home to stay, Sally wanted to go back, back to where she was known and safe and never left alone for a minute. She wanted to go back to school!

"Don't cry!" Meg begged, her voice shrill with alarm. "I'll get Mother. Don't cry, Sally!"

Sal wept on; and Meg scurried off to get help. She always ran to Mother with her own tears. By some special magic, Mother knew every time whether to cure them with a bandage, a cooky or a kiss. Sal, crying into her pillow, was counting on Mother in much the same way.

"Thank you, honey. Now take your clothes to the kitchen and Melinda will help you."

Sal stiffened. There she was now. There. That was Meg leaving. Now Mother would come over and take her in her arms and everything would be all right again. Still lying with her face to the wall, Sal sniffed loudly and sorrowfully. Then she held her breath and waited.

Footsteps crossed the room. There was a creaking sound over by Meg's bed. Far away, Sal heard dishes clinking together and Mindy's voice giving an order. Then a door closed and silence fell. Nothing moved. Nobody spoke. Nothing at all happened.

Sal was stunned. Surely Mother had come in! Yes, of course she had! She had heard her talking to Meg. She had even heard her walking across the room. So why didn't she do something . . . or say something!

Sally gulped. She couldn't look. She was certain that Mother hadn't left the room. But if she were doing anything at all, she would make a noise. And there was no noise.

The answer came to her suddenly. Mother probably thought she was asleep. She must be being extra quiet so as not to waken her. Sal sniffed again; but this time the sniff was very small and uncertain.

At once, the silence swallowed it.

Sal waited. There was nothing else she could think of to do. A minute passed. It seemed an hour. She began to feel sure someone was watching her. Another minute passed, and another. She stuck it out for one more long, long minute. Then, with a gasp, she turned over.

Mother was sitting on Meg's bed.

"That's better," she said quietly, as Sal stared at her. "I'm not in the habit of talking to people's backs. Now suppose you tell me what your trouble is."

Sal was so taken aback she couldn't think of a word to say. Then she found herself in the middle of another silence.

"Don't you know I can't do it all by myself?" she burst out, new tears streaming down her face.

"Do what all by yourself?" Mother asked evenly.

Never had Sarah Jane Copeland felt more muddled and miserable. Once again, silence began to press in on her, but how could she explain to Mother while Mother sat looking so calm and far-off!

"All those buttons, that's what!" she shouted, glaring.

At last, the questions stopped.

"Sally, I have a story to tell you," Mother said.

She tucked her feet up under her as though she had all the time in the world. A little of the fear went out of Sally.

"One summer there was a four-year-old girl who had an older sister and a brother just turned two. Her parents packed up their three children and some clothes and rented a cottage by Lake Huron for one week. The moment they arrived, they all got into their bathing suits, even the baby, and went down to the lake to swim."

Sal said nothing. Her eyes were dark and startled.

"They had been afraid they might have to coax the baby into the water," Mother went on, "but he ran right into it as though it were his bath at home. It was very shallow, so his mother wasn't worried. She just stayed close to him and watched. When the waves hit him, he tried to catch them in his fists and he laughed as though it were a game. The older girl went in more slowly. She put one toe in and squealed 'It's COLD!' But before long she was in up to her neck. Only the little four-year-old girl did not join in and have fun with the others. She began to scream as soon as she saw the water. She buried her head in her father's shoulder and, no matter what anyone said, she wouldn't let even her toes be put into the lake."

Mother paused, but Sal was still silent.

"The little girl's family stayed at the lake for a week. Every day the whole family went in swimming — all but the little girl. Every day, her daddy told her how nice it was, but she wouldn't listen. He waded in to show her how shallow it was, but she wouldn't look. The little girl's name was Sarah, and soon they began to call her 'Scarey Sarey' and tease her

for being so silly, but still, Sarah wouldn't have anything to do with that water.

"On the next to the last day, her father grew tired of coaxing. He knew that, by then, Sarah had herself so scared she'd never go in unless someone made her. So he picked her up and carried her in."

Sal's tears had dried on her cheeks. She remembered that day. It was so long ago it seemed almost a dream, but she could still feel the way she had clutched at Dad and shrieked as he had walked to the lake.

"Her father tried to be gentle" — Mother remembered too — "but Scarey Sarey cried and fought, so at last he had to just pull her hands loose and put her down and leave her. It was so shallow it wasn't dangerous. And since Sarah couldn't walk, she had to stay there whether she wanted to or not. Maybe you remember what happened, Sally, when that little girl stopped crying long enough to notice what the water was really like."

Sal nodded slowly. It did not seem like a dream any longer. The lake had been calm that day. Greenish ripples had broken softly against her. Kent had crowed with excitement and galloped around her, churning up a frothy sparkle. Nearby, Mother had been holding Mindy on her stomach, making her "swim" on top of the bright water. Suddenly giving in completely, she, Sal, had called to Dad, "I want to swim too. Make me swim like Mindy, Daddy."

"Five long days at the beach — wasted!" remarked Mother, as though Sally had spoken her memories aloud. "Five days wasted because Scarey Sarey didn't wait to find out whether there was anything to cry about before she started crying. . . . But, of course, she was only four. You can forgive a little girl like that for not taking time to think."

Sal blushed, a slow, deep, burning blush right up to her ears. She looked at the rug.

"Have you really looked at the clothes I put out for you to wear this morning, Sal?"

Unable to speak, Sal only shook her head. Mother rose and reached for the clothes. One piece at a time, she spread them out across Sal's knees.

"Now show me those buttons you're so worried about!"

With her head bent and her heart thumping uncomfortably, Sal inspected the clothing. The expression on her face grew more and more sheepish as she looked.

There were no buttons. Not a single button anywhere! In fact, the clothes on her lap were the simplest clothes to put on that Sal had ever seen. The skirt was full with an elasticized top. No zipper! No tricky fastening at all! And the soft yellow blouse had a wide boat neck with a rolled-over collar. No hooks and eyes! No skimpy little puffed sleeves! Even the underwear was specially made with generous openings for arms and legs. All the things that made dressing difficult were missing — and yet the clothes themselves looked lovely.

"I — I'm sorry. They're wonderful clothes," Sal gulped.

Mother dropped down on the bed beside her and circled Sal lightly with her arms.

"Sally, Sally, don't be so afraid," she said softly. "If not being able to do up buttons were all that was troubling you, you wouldn't be wanting to cry again this minute. You're scared to death that I'm going to walk out and leave you with nobody to look after you. Don't you know that I would never do that if I didn't know, for certain sure, that you didn't need me?"

Astonishment held back Sal's tears. How could Mother see inside a person's thoughts like that?

"Now guess who suggested those new clothes for you."

"You must have," Sal faltered.

"Wrong. Miss Jonas did."

"Miss Jonas!"

"Miss Jonas. When you left Allendale, she wrote us a long letter about you. You'd be surprised at some of the things she knows about you, Sarah Jane. Most important, she told us that if we all, including you, started working on it right away, there will come a day when you, Sal Copeland, will be an independent adult. An independent adult is a person who decides things for herself and does things for herself and for others. It would mean having your own job, your own friends, your own money, your own freedom."

To Sal it sounded frightening and far off, but fun too. Her own friends! She had wanted a special friend badly for a long time now.

"But to be independent someday means beginning practicing independence *today;* and the first step is dressing yourself. Only, before you begin, I'm going to cut your hair."

Sal had thought she was past feeling surprised, but Mother's announcement knocked the breath clean out of her. *Cut her hair!* Why, she'd had long pigtails ever since she could remember. Miss Jonas had braided them every morning and neither she nor Carla, who also had them, had dared so much as squeak when she raked the snarls out with a strong hand. Surely her mother didn't really mean to . . .

Twenty minutes later, Mother stood back, looked over her handiwork one last time, and declared it was perfect. The floor was littered with long strands of wheat-colored familiar-looking hair. Gingerly, Sal put up a hand to feel what was left, but Mother batted her exploring fingers down.

"None of that," she ordered. "No looking in the mirror, either. Here are your clothes. Get yourself dressed. Then you can see your whole new self at once. Now get busy."

She hoisted Sal back to the bed, from the captain's chair where she had sat to have her hair cut, put her crutches within reach, and left.

For one long moment, Sal sat and stared down at the clothes beside her. Then she began to move. She hitched the short nightgown out from under her and hauled it over her head. For the first time, she noticed that it was new and different too, like the other clothes. Only the gay up and down stripes saved it from looking like a plain sack with holes in it for her head and arms.

But it was too cold in the room to sit in her bare skin and admire it. If she didn't get into something quickly, she'd freeze.

Just the same, frozen or thawed, it took a long time. Wriggling into and tugging at each garment in turn soon had her puffing and red in the face. Her fingers, always a little awkward, seemed to stiffen on purpose to make things harder. She put her arm through the hole in her blouse which was meant for her head and it took ages to pull it free again. The skirt twisted itself around her legs and, however hard she yanked at it, it refused to straighten out. More than once, she came close to giving up, but something about that "Scarey Sarey" story kept her going doggedly until she was done.

She looked down at herself and drew a sharp little breath of excitement. She had managed it! She was dressed. She wriggled forward until her feet were firmly on the floor and reached for her crutches. Leaning down, she got her braces locked and then put her weight solidly on the handgrips. After trying a couple of times, she was up. Holding her breath, she turned and started for the mirror.

Without warning, the door swung wide and the other Copelands crowded in. Forever afterwards, Sal was to wonder whether they had been watching her through the keyhole.

"Is that Sally?" Meg asked, her eyes round.

Kent gave a wolf whistle, and Mindy breathed "Gee!"

"Hush," Mother said. "Let her see for herself."

Shyly, shakily, Sally approached the glass. As she caught sight of herself, she stopped in her tracks. Even though she had known she would be different, she was totally unprepared for this girl in the mirror.

Sal was not used to seeing herself in a looking glass. At

school she had practiced walking in front of one, but the therapist had always been telling her to watch her knees or keep her elbows in. Over the years, Sally had grown to look at herself a piece at a time. She had come to have a vague picture of herself, a girl all elbows and knees and crutches, with a face and clothes too ordinary to notice much.

This was a new Sally.

She was dressed in bright, soft colors. In place of the long braids she wore a smooth shining cap of hair with no part at all. It was almost as short as a boy's, but it had bangs straight across the front and it curved in just a little on the ends. From all her hard work, and excitement, her cheeks glowed like roses. In spite of herself, her mouth tipped up in a delighted smile and her blue eyes shone bluer than ever with wonder.

Sal glanced away from the glass at her family. At the admiration on their faces, her cheeks grew rosier.

"I look like somebody else," she half-whispered at last. "Not me."

"Somebody beautiful," smiled Dad, and bowed to her with a flourish.

Author

Jean Little was born in Taiwan and grew up in Guelph, Ontario. Blind at birth, she later gained some sight in one eye and graduated from the University of Toronto. *Mine for Keeps,* from which this excerpt was taken, was her award-winning first book.

An excerpt from

Mrs. Frisby and the Rats of NIMH

by Robert C. O'Brien

One evening a young rat, Nicodemus, and his friend, Jenner, were feasting with dozens of other rats in the market square at the edge of the city. As they began to eat, Nicodemus noticed a white truck parked nearby. Printed on both its sides were the letters NIMH. Suddenly, several people jumped out of the truck, surrounded the rats, caught them in nets, and dumped them into a wire cage at the back of the truck. The doors shut, and they drove away.

After several hours, the truck came to a stop beside a large building. The rats were taken into a large, white room with a lot of bottles, boxes, and mysterious-looking equipment. One whole end of the room was filled with small cages. A man whom the others called "Dr. Schultz" locked each rat into a cage and left. Nicodemus and his companions wondered where they had been brought, and for what purpose.

Escape from NIMH

That cage was my home for a long time. It was not uncomfortable; it had a floor of some kind of plastic, medium soft and warm to the touch; with wire walls and ceiling, it was airy enough. Yet just the fact that it was a cage made it horrible. I, who had always run where I wanted, could go three hops forward, three hops back again, and that was all. But worse was the dreadful feeling — I know we all had it — that we were completely at the mercy of someone we knew not at all, for some purpose we could not guess. What were their plans for us?

As it turned out, the uncertainty itself was the worst suffering we had to undergo. We were treated well enough, except for some very small, very quick flashes of pain, which were part of our training. And we were always well fed, though the food, scientifically compiled pellets, was not what you'd call delicious.

But of course we didn't know that when we arrived, and I doubt that any of us got much sleep that first night. I know I didn't. So, in a way, it was a relief when early the next morning the lights snapped on and Dr. Schultz entered. There were two other people with him, a young man and a young woman. Like him, they were dressed in white laboratory coats. He was talking to them as they entered the room and walked toward our cages.

". . . three groups. Twenty for training on injection series A, twenty on series B. That will leave twenty-three for the control group. They get no injections at all — except, to keep the test exactly even, we will prick them with a plain needle. Let's call the groups A, B, and C for control; tag them and number them A-1 through A-20, B-1 through B-20, and so on. Number the cages the same way, and keep each rat in the same cage throughout. Diet will be the same for all."

"When do we start the injections?"

"As soon as we're through with the tagging. We'll do that now. George, you number the tags and the cages. Julie, you tie them on. I'll hold."

So the young woman's name was Julie; the young man was George. They all put gloves on, long, tough plastic ones that came to their elbows. One by one we were taken from our cages, held gently but firmly by Dr. Schultz while Julie fastened around each of our necks a narrow ribbon of yellow plastic bearing a number. I learned eventually that mine was number A-10.

They were kind, especially Julie. I remember that when one rat was being tagged, she looked at it and said, "Poor little thing, he's frightened. Look how he's trembling."

"What kind of biologist are you?" said Dr. Schultz. "The 'poor little thing' is a she, not a he."

When my turn came, the door of my cage slid open just enough for Dr. Schultz to put his gloved hand through. I cowered to the back of the cage, which was just what he expected me to do; one hand pressed me flat against the wire wall; then his fingers gripped my shoulders. The other hand held my head just behind the ears, and I was powerless. I was lifted from the cage and felt the plastic collar clipped around my neck. I was back inside with the door closed in less than a minute. The collar was not tight, but by no amount of tugging, twisting or shaking was I ever able to get it off.

I watched through the wire front of my cage as the others were caught and tagged. About six cages down from me, on the same shelf, I saw them put a collar on Jenner; but once he was back in his cage, I could see him no longer.

A little later in the morning they came around again, this time pushing a table on wheels. It was loaded with a bottle of some clear liquid, a long rack of sharp needles, and a plunger. Once more I was lifted from the cage. This time George did the holding while Dr. Schultz fastened one of the needles to the plunger. I felt a sharp pain in my hip; then it was over. We all got used to that, for from then on we got injections at least twice a week. What they were injecting and why, I did not know. Yet for twenty of us those injections were to change our whole lives.

During the days that followed, our lives fell into a pattern, and the reason for our captivity gradually became clear. Dr. Schultz was a neurologist — that is, an expert on brains, nerves, intelligence, and how people learn things. He hoped, by experimenting on us, to find out whether certain injections could help us to learn more and faster. The two younger people working with him, George and Julie, were graduate students in biology.

"Watch always," he told them, "for signs of improvement, faster learning, quicker reaction in group A as compared to group B, and both as compared to the control group."

My own training began on the day after the first injections. It was George who did it; I suppose Julie and Dr. Schultz were doing the same test on other rats. He took my cage from the shelf and carried it to another room, similar to the first one but with more equipment in it, and no shelves of cages. He placed the cage in a slot against a wall, slid open the end, opened a matching door in the wall — and I was free.

Or so I thought. The small doorway in the wall led into a short corridor, which opened, or seemed to, directly onto a green lawn. I could see it clearly, and behind it some bushes, and behind them a street — all outdoors, and nothing but air between me and them. Furthermore, I could smell the fresh outdoor breeze blowing in. Were they letting me go?

I made a dash toward the open end of the corridor — and then jumped back. I could not go on. About two feet from my cage (still open behind me) there was something dreadfully wrong with the floor. When I touched my feet to it, a terrible, prickling feeling came over my skin, my muscles cramped, my eyes blurred and I got instantly dizzy. I never got used to that feeling — no one ever does — but I did experience it many times, and eventually learned what it was: electric shock. It is not exactly a pain, but it is unbearable.

442

Yet I was in a frenzy to reach that open lawn, to run for the bushes, to get away from the cage. I tried again — and jumped back again. No use. Then I saw, leading off to the left, another corridor. I had not noticed it at first because I had been looking so eagerly at the open end of the one I was in. The second one seemed to stop about five feet away in a blank wall. Yet there was light there: it must turn a corner. I ran down it, cautiously, not trusting the floor. At the end it turned right — and there was the lawn again, another opening. I got closer that time; then, just as I thought I was going to make it — another shock. I pulled back and saw that there was still another corridor, leading off to the right. Again I ran, again I saw the open escape hole, and again I was stopped by shock. This was repeated over and over; yet each time I seemed to get a little closer to freedom.

But when finally I reached it and the grass was only a step away, a wire wall snapped down in front of me, another behind me; the ceiling opened above me and a gloved hand reached in and picked me up.

A voice said: "Four minutes, thirty-seven seconds."

It was George.

I had, after all my running through the corridors, emerged into a trap only a few feet from where I had started, and through a concealed opening up above, George had been watching everything I did.

I had been in what is called a maze, a device to test intelligence and memory. I was put in it many times again, and so were the others. The second time I got through it a little faster, because I remembered — to some extent — which corridors had electric floors and which did not. The third time I was still faster; and after each trial George (or sometimes Julie, sometimes Dr. Schultz) would write down how long it took. You might ask: Why would I bother to run through it at all, if I knew it was only a trick? The answer is

I couldn't help it. When you've lived in a cage, you can't bear *not* to run, even if what you're running toward is an illusion.

There were more injections, and other kinds of tests, and some of these were more important than the maze, because the maze was designed only to find out how quickly we could learn, while some of the others actually taught us things — or at least led up to actual teaching.

One was what Dr. Schultz called "shape recognition." We would be put into a small room with three doors leading out — one round, one square, and one triangular. These doors were on hinges, with springs that held them shut, but they were easy to push open, and each door led into another room with three more doors like the first one. But the trick was this: If you went through the wrong door, the room you entered had an electric floor, and you got a shock. So you had to learn: In the first room, you used the round door; second room, triangle, and so on.

All of these activities helped to pass the time, and the weeks went by quickly, but they did not lessen our longing to get away. I wished for my old home in the storm sewer; I wished I could see my mother and father, and run with my brother to the marketplace. I know all the others felt the same way; yet it seemed a hopeless thing. Still there was one rat who decided to try it anyway.

He was a young rat, probably the youngest of all that had been caught, and by chance he was in the cage next to mine; I might mention that like Jenner and me, he was in the group Dr. Schultz called A. His name was Justin.

It was late one night that I heard him calling to me, speaking softly, around the wooden partition between our cages. Those partitions generally kept all of us from getting to know each other as well as we might have done, and discouraged us from talking much to one another; it was quite hard to hear around them, and of course you could never see the one you were talking to. I think Dr. Schultz had purposely had them made of some soundproof material. But you *could* hear, if you and your neighbor got in the corners of the cages nearest each other and spoke out through the wire front.

"Nicodemus?"

"Yes?" I went over to the corner.

"How long have we been here?"

"You mean since the beginning? Since we were caught?"

"Yes."

"I don't know. Several months — I think, but I have no way to keep track."

"I know. I don't either. Do you suppose it's winter outside now?"

"Probably. Or late fall."

"It will be cold."

"But not in here."

"No. But I'm going to try to get out."

"Get out? But how? Your cage is shut."

"Tomorrow we get injections, so they'll open it. When they do, I'm going to run."

"Run where?"

"I don't know. At least I'll get a look around. There might be some way out. What can I lose?"

"You might get hurt."

"I don't think so. Anyway *they* won't hurt me."

By they he meant Dr. Schultz and the other two. He added confidently:

"All those shots, all the time they've spent — we're too valuable to them now. They'll be careful."

That idea had not occurred to me before, but when I thought about it, I decided he was right. Dr. Schultz, Julie and George had spent most of their working hours with us for months; they could not afford to let any harm come to us. On the other hand, neither could they afford to allow any of us to escape.

Justin made his attempt the next morning. And it did cause a certain amount of excitement, but not at all what we expected. It was Julie who opened Justin's cage with a hypodermic in her hand. Justin was out with a mighty leap, hit the floor (about four feet down) with a thump, shook himself and ran, disappearing from my view heading toward the other end of the room.

Julie seemed not at all alarmed. She calmly placed the needle on a shelf, then walked to the door of the laboratory and pushed a button on the wall near it. A red light came on over the door. She picked up a notebook and pencil from a desk near the door and followed Justin out of my sight.

A few minutes later Dr. Schultz and George entered. They opened the door cautiously and closed it behind them. "The outer door is shut, too," said Dr. Schultz. "Where is it?"

"Down here," said Julie, "inspecting the air ducts."

"Really? Which one is it?"

"It's one of the A group, just as you expected. Number nine. I'm keeping notes on it."

Obviously the red light was some kind of a warning signal, both outside the door and in — "laboratory animal at large." And not only had Dr. Schultz known one of us was out, but he had expected it to happen.

". . . a few days sooner than I thought," he was saying, "but so much the better. Do you realize . . ."

"Look," said Julie. "He's doing the whole baseboard — but he's studying the windows, too. See how he steps back to look up?"

"Of course," said Dr. Schultz. "And at the same time he's watching us, too. Can't you see?"

"He's pretty cool about it," said George.

"Can you imagine one of the lab rats doing that? Or even one of the controls? We've got to try to grasp what we have on our hands. The A group is now three hundred per cent ahead of the control group in learning, and getting smarter all the time. B group is only twenty per cent ahead. It's the new DNA that's doing it. We have a real breakthrough, and since it is DNA, we may very well have a true mutation, a brand new species of rat. But we've got to be careful with it. I think we should go ahead now with the next injection series."

"The steroids?"

(Whatever that meant.)

"Yes. It may slow them up a little — though I doubt it. But even if it does, it will be worth it, because I'm betting it will increase their life span by double at least. Maybe more. Maybe *much* more."

"Look," said Julie, "A-9 has made a discovery. He's found the mice."

George said: "See how he's studying them."

"Probably," said Dr. Schultz wryly, "he's wondering if they're ready for their steroid injections, too. As a matter of fact, I think the G group is. They're doing almost as well as A group."

"Should I get the net and put him back?" George asked.

"I doubt that you'll need it," Dr. Schultz said, "now that he's learned he can't get out."

But they were underestimating Justin. He had learned no such thing.

Of course, Justin did not escape that day, nor even that year. When they — Julie — put on a glove and went to pick him up, he submitted meekly enough, and in a short time he was back in his cage.

Yet he had learned some things. He had, as Julie noticed, examined the air ducts — the openings along the wall through which warm air flowed in winter, cool air in summer — and he had studied the windows. Mainly he had learned that he could, occasionally at least, jump from his cage and wander around without incurring any anger or injury. All of this, eventually, was important. For it was Justin, along with Jenner, who finally figured out how to get away. I had a part in it, too. But all that came later.

I won't go into details about the rest of our training except for one part of it that was the most useful of all. But in general, during the months that followed, two things were happening:

First, we were learning more than any rats ever had before, and were becoming more intelligent than any rats had ever been.

The second thing could be considered, from some points of view, even more important — and certainly more astonishing — than the first. Dr. Schultz (you will recall) had said that the new series of injections might increase our life span by double or more. Yet even he was not prepared for what happened. Perhaps it was the odd combination of both types of injections working together — I don't know, and neither did he. But the result was that as far as he could detect, in the A group the aging process seemed to stop almost completely.

For example — during the years we were in the laboratory, most of the rats in the control group grew old and sickly, and finally died; so did those in B group, for though they were getting injections, too, the formula was not the same as ours. But among the twenty of us in A group, no one could see any signs that we were growing older at all. Apparently (though we seldom saw them) the same thing was happening with the G group, the mice who were getting the same injections we were.

Dr. Schultz was greatly excited about this. "The short life span has always been a prime limiting factor in education," he told George and Julie. "If we can double it, and speed up the learning process at the same time, the possibilities are enormous." Double it! Even now, years later, years after the injections were stopped, we seem scarcely any older than we were then.

We could not detect either of these things ourselves. That is, we didn't *feel* any different, and since we had no contact with the other groups, we had no basis for comparison. All we had to go by was what Dr. Schultz said. He and the others were preparing a research paper about us — to be published in some scientific journal — so each morning he dictated the results of the previous day's tests into a tape recorder. We heard all of it, though there was a lot of technical stuff we couldn't understand, especially at first. Until the paper was published (he kept reminding George and Julie of this) the whole experiment was to be kept secret.

The one important phase of training began one day after weeks of really hard work at the "shape recognition" that I mentioned before. But this was different. For the first time they used sounds along with the shapes, and pictures, real pictures we could recognize. For example, one of the first and simplest of these exercises was a picture, a clear photograph, of a rat. I suppose they felt sure we would know what that was. This picture was shown on a screen, with a light behind it. Then, after I had looked at the picture and recognized it, a shape flashed on the screen under it — a sort of half circle and two straight lines, not like anything I had seen before. Then the voice began:

"Are."

"Are."

"Are."

It was Julie's voice, speaking very clearly, but it had a tinny sound — it was a record. After repeating "are" a dozen times or so, that particular shape disappeared and another one came on the screen, still under the picture of the rat. It was a triangle, with legs on it. And Julie's voice began again:

"Aiee."

"Aiee."

"Aiee."

When that shape disappeared a third one came on the screen. This one was a cross. Julie's voice said:

"Tea."

"Tea."

"Tea."

Then all three shapes appeared at once, and the record said:

"Are."

"Aiee."

"Tea."

"Rat."

(You will already have recognized what was going on: they were teaching us to read. The symbols under the picture were the letters R-A-T.) But the idea did not become clear to me, nor to any of us, for quite a long time. Because, of course, we didn't know what reading *was*.

Oh, we learned to recognize the shapes easily enough, and when I saw the rat picture I knew straight away what symbols would appear beneath it. In the same way, when the picture showed a cat, I knew the same shapes would appear, except the first one would be a half-circle, and Julie's voice would repeat: "See — see — see." I even learned that when the photograph showed not one but several rats, a fourth shape would appear under it — a snaky line — and the sound with that one was "ess — ess — ess." But as to what all this was *for,* none of us had any inkling.

It was Jenner who finally figured it out. By this time we had developed a sort of system of communication, a simple enough thing, just passing spoken messages from one cage to the next, like passing notes in school. Justin, who was still next to me, called to me one day:

"Message for Nicodemus from Jenner. He says important."

"All right," I said, "what's the message?"

"Look at the shapes on the wall next to the door. He says to look carefully."

My cage, like Jenner's and those of the rest of A group, was close enough to the door so I could see what he meant: Near the doorway there was a large, square piece of white cardboard fastened to the wall — a sign. It was covered with an assortment of black markings to which I had never paid any attention (though they had been there ever since we arrived).

Now, for the first time, I looked at them carefully, and I grasped what Jenner had discovered.

The top line of black marks on the wall were instantly familiar: R-A-T-S; as soon as I saw them I thought of the picture that went with them; and as soon as I did that I was, for the first time, reading. Because, of course, that's what reading is: using symbols to suggest a picture or an idea. From that time on it gradually became clear to me what all these lessons were for, and once I understood the idea, I was eager to learn more. I could scarcely wait for the next lesson, and the next. The whole concept of reading was, to me at least, fascinating. I remember how proud I was when, months later, I was able to read and understand that whole sign. I read it hundreds of times, and I'll never forget it:

RATS MAY NOT BE REMOVED FROM THE LABO-RATORY WITHOUT WRITTEN PERMISSION. And at the bottom, in smaller letters, the word NIMH.

But then a puzzling thing came up, a thing we're still not sure about even now. Apparently Dr. Schultz, who was running the lessons, did not realize how well they were succeeding. He continued the training, with new words and new pictures every day; but the fact is, once we had grasped the idea and learned the different sounds each letter stood for, we leaped way ahead of him. I remember well, during one of the lessons, looking at a picture of a tree. Under it the letters flashed on: T-R-E-E. But in the photograph, though the tree was in the foreground, there was a building in the background, and a sign near it. I scarcely glanced at T-R-E-E, but concentrated instead on reading the sign. It said:

NIMH. PRIVATE PARKING BY PERMIT ONLY. RE-SERVED FOR DOCTORS AND STAFF. NO VISITOR PARKING. The building behind it, tall and white, looked very much like the building we were in.

I'm sure Dr. Schultz had plans for testing our reading ability. I could even guess, from the words he was teaching us, what the tests were going to be like. For example, he taught us "left," "right," "door," "food," "open," and so on. It was not hard to imagine the test: I would be placed in one chamber, my food in another. There would be two doors, and a sign saying: "For food, open door at right." Or something like that. Then if I — if all of us — moved unerringly toward the proper door, he would know we understood the sign.

As I said, I'm sure he planned to do this, but apparently he did not think we were ready for it yet. I think maybe he was even a little afraid to try it; because if he did it too soon, or if for any other reason it did not work, his experiment would be a failure. He wanted to be sure, and his caution was his undoing.

Justin announced one evening around the partition:

"I'm going to get out of my cage tonight and wander around a bit."

"How can you? It's locked."

"Yes. But did you notice, along the bottom edge there's a printed strip?"

I had not noticed it. I should perhaps explain that when Dr. Schultz and the others opened our cages we could never quite see how they did it; they manipulated something under the plastic floor, something we couldn't see.

"What does it say?"

"I've been trying to read it the last three times they brought me back from training. It's very small print. But I think I've finally made it out. It says: To release door, pull knob forward and slide right."

"Knob?"

"Under the floor, about an inch back, there's a metal thing just in front of the shelf. I think that's the knob, and I think I can reach it through the wire. Anyway, I'm going to try."

"Now?"

"Not until they close up."

"Closing up" was a ritual Dr. Schultz, George and Julie went through each night. For about an hour they sat at their desks, wrote notes in books, filed papers in cabinets, and finally locked the cabinets. Then they checked all the cages, dimmed the lights, locked the doors and went home, leaving us alone in the still laboratory.

About half an hour after they left that night, Justin said: "I'm going to try now." I heard a scuffling noise, a click and scrape of metal, and in a matter of seconds I saw his door swing open. It was as simple as that — when you could read.

"Wait," I said.

"What's the matter?"

"If you jump down, you won't be able to get back in. Then they'll know."

"I thought of that. I'm not going to jump down. I'm going to climb up the outside of the cage. It's easy. I've climbed up the inside a thousand times. Above these cages there's another shelf, and it's empty. I'm going to walk along there and see what I can see. I think there's a way to climb to the floor and up again."

"Why don't I go with you?" My door would open the same way as his.

"Better not this time, don't you think? If something goes wrong and I can't get back, they'll say: It's just A-9 again. But if two of us are found outside, they'll take it seriously. They might put new locks on the cages."

He was right, and you can see that already we both had the same idea in mind: that this might be the first step toward escape for all of us.

And so it was.

By teaching us how to read, they had taught us how to get away.

Justin climbed easily up the open door of his cage and vanished over the top with a flick of his tail. He came back an hour later, greatly excited and full of information. Yet it was typical of Justin that even excited as he was, he stayed calm, he thought clearly. He climbed down the front of my cage rather than his own, and spoke softly; we both assumed that by now the other rats were asleep.

"Nicodemus? Come on out. I'll show you how." He directed me as I reached through the wire bars of the door and felt beneath it. I found the small metal knob, slid it forward and sideward, and felt the door swing loose against my shoulder. I followed him up the side of the cage to the shelf above. There we stopped. It was the first time I had met Justin face to face.

He said: "It's better talking here than around that partition."

"Yes. Did you get down?"

"Yes."

"How did you get back up?"

"At the end of this shelf there's a big cabinet — they keep the mouse cages in it. It has wire mesh doors. You can climb up and down them like a ladder."

"Of course," I said. "I remember now." I had seen that cabinet many times when my cage was carried past it. For some reason — perhaps because they were smaller — the mice were kept in cages-within-a-cage.

Justin said: "Nicodemus, I think I've found the way to get out."

"You have! How?"

"At each end of the room there's an opening in the baseboard at the bottom of the wall. Air blows in through one of them and out the other. Each one has a metal grid covering it, and on the grid there's a sign that says: Lift to adjust air flow. I lifted one of them; it hangs on hinges, like a trapdoor. Behind it there is a thing like a metal window — when you slide it wide open, more air blows in.

"But the main thing is, it's easily big enough to walk through and get out."

"But what's on the other side? Where does it lead?"

"On the other side there's a duct, a thing like a square metal pipe built right into the wall. I walked along it, not very far, but I can figure out where it must go. There's bound to be a duct like it leading to every room in the building, and they must all branch off one main central pipe — and that one has to lead, somewhere, to the outside. Because that's where our air comes from. That's why they never open the windows. I don't think those windows *can* open."

He was right, of course. The building had central air conditioning; what we had to do was find the main air shaft and explore it. There would have to be an intake at one end and an outlet at the other. But that was easier said than done, and before it was done there were questions to be answered. What about the rest of the rats? There were twenty of us in the laboratory, and we had to let the others know.

So, one by one, we woke them and showed them how to open their cages. It was an odd assembly that gathered that night, under the dimmed lights in the echoing laboratory, on the shelf where Justin and I had talked. We all knew each other in a way, from the passing of messages over the preceding months; yet except for Jenner and me, none of us had ever really met. We were strangers — though, as you can imagine, it did not take long for us to develop a feeling of comradeship, for we twenty were alone in a strange world. Just how alone and how strange none of us really understood at first; yet in a way we sensed it from the beginning. The group looked to me as leader, probably because it was Justin and I who first set them free, and because Justin was obviously younger than I.

We did not attempt to leave that night, but went together and looked at the metal grid Justin had discovered, and made plans for exploring the air ducts. Jenner was astute at that sort of thing; he could foresee problems.

"With a vent like this leading to every room," he said, "it will be easy to get lost. When we explore, we're going to need some way of finding our way back here."

"Why should we come back?" someone asked.

"Because it may take more than one night to find the way out. If it does, whoever is doing the exploring must be back in his cage by morning. Otherwise Dr. Schultz will find out."

Jenner was right. It took us about a week. What we did, after some more discussion, was to find some equipment: first, a large spool of thread in one of the cabinets where some of us had seen Julie place it one day. Second, a screwdriver that was kept on a shelf near the electric equipment — because, as Jenner pointed out, there would probably be a screen over the end of the airshaft to keep out debris, and we might have to pry it loose. What we really needed was a light, for the ducts, at night, were completely dark. But there was none to be had, not even a box of matches. The thread and the screwdriver we hid in the duct, a few feet from the entrance. We could only hope they would not be missed, or that if they were, we wouldn't be suspected.

Justin and two others were chosen as the exploration party (one of the others was Arthur). They had a terrible time at first: Here was a maze to end all mazes; and in the dark they quickly lost their sense of direction. Still they kept at it, night after night, exploring the network of shafts that laced like a cubical spiderweb through the walls and ceilings of the building. They would tie the end of their thread to the grid in our laboratory and unroll it from the spool as they went. Time and time again they reached the end of the thread and had to come back.

"It just isn't long enough," Justin would complain. "Every time I come to the end, I think: if I could just go ten feet farther . . ."

And finally, that's what he did. On the seventh night, just as the thread ran out, he and the other two reached a shaft that was wider than any they had found before, and it seemed, as they walked along it, to be slanting gently upward. But the spool was empty.

"You wait here," Justin said to the others. "I'm going just a little way farther. Hang on to the spool, and if I call, call back." (They had tied the end of the thread around the spool so they would not lose it in the dark.)

Justin had a hunch. The air coming through the shaft had a fresher smell where they were, and seemed to be blowing harder than in the other shafts. Up ahead he thought he could hear the whir of a machine running quietly, and there was a faint vibration in the metal under his feet. He went on. The shaft turned upward at a sharp angle — and then, straight ahead, he saw it: a patch of lighter-colored darkness than the pitch black around him, and in the middle of it, three stars twinkling. It was the open sky. Across the opening there was, as Jenner had predicted, a coarse screen of heavy wire.

He ran toward it for a few seconds longer, and then stopped. The sound of the machine had grown suddenly louder, changing from a whir to a roar. It had, obviously, shifted speed; an automatic switch somewhere in the building had turned it from low to high, and the air blowing past Justin came on so hard it made him gasp. He braced his feet against the metal and held on. In a minute, as suddenly as it had roared, the machine returned to a whisper. He looked around and realized he was lucky to have stopped; by the dim light from the sky he could see that he had reached a point where perhaps two dozen air shafts came together like branches into the trunk of a tree. If he had gone a few steps farther he would never have been able to distinguish which shaft was his. He turned in his tracks, and in a few minutes he rejoined his friends.

We had a meeting that night, and Justin told all of us what he had found. He had left the thread, anchored by the screwdriver, to guide us out. Some were for leaving immediately, but it was late, and Jenner and I argued against it. We did not know how long it would take us to break through the screen at the end. If it should take more than an hour or two, daylight would be upon us. We would then be unable to risk returning to the laboratory, and would have to spend the day in the shaft — or try to get away by broad daylight. Dr. Schultz might even figure out how we had gone and trap us in the air shaft.

Finally, reluctantly, everyone agreed to spend one more day in the laboratory and leave early the next night. But it was a hard decision, with freedom so near and everyone thinking as I did: "Suppose . . ." Suppose Dr. Schultz grew suspicious and put locks on our cages? Suppose someone found our thread and pulled it out? (This was unlikely — the near end, tied to the spool, was six feet up the shaft, well hidden.) Just the same, we were uneasy.

Then, just as we were ending our meeting, a new complication arose. We had been standing in a rough circle on the floor of the laboratory, just outside the two screen doors that enclosed the mice cages. Now, from inside the cabinet, came a voice:

"Nicodemus." It was a clear but plaintive call, the voice of a mouse. We had almost forgotten the mice were there, and I was startled to hear that one of them knew my name. We all grew quiet.

"Who's calling me?" I asked.

"My name is Jonathan," said the voice. "We have been listening to your talk about going out. We would like to go, too, but we cannot open our cages."

As you can imagine, this caused a certain consternation, coming at the last minute. None of us knew much about the mice, except what we had heard Dr. Schultz dictate into his tape recorder. From that, we had learned only that they had been getting the same injections we were getting, and that the treatment had worked about as well on them as on us. They were a sort of side experiment, without a control group.

Justin was studying the cabinet.

"Why not?" he said. "If we can get the doors open."

Someone muttered: "They'll slow us down."

"No," said the mouse Jonathan. "We will not. Only open our cages when you go, and we will make our own way. We won't even stay with you, if you prefer."

"How many are you?" I asked.

"Only eight. And the cabinet doors are easy to open. There's just a simple hook, half way up."

But Justin and Arthur had already figured that out. They climbed up the screen, unhooked the hook, and the doors swung open.

"The cages open the same way as yours," said another mouse, "but we can't reach far enough to unlatch them."

"All right," I said. "Tomorrow night, as soon as Dr. Schultz and the others leave, we'll open your cages, and you can follow the thread with us to get out. After that you're on your own."

"Agreed," said Jonathan, "and thank you."

"And now," I said, "we should all get back to the cages. Justin, please hook the doors again."

I had latched myself into my cage and was getting ready for sleep when I heard a scratching noise on the door, and there was Jenner, climbing down from above.

"Nicodemus," he said, "can I come in?"

"Of course. But it's getting on toward morning."

"I won't stay long." He unlatched the door and entered. "There's something we've got to decide."

"I know," I said. "I've been thinking about it, too."

"When we do get out, where are we going to go?"

I could not see Jenner's face in the dark of the cage, but I knew from his voice that he was worrying. I said:

"At first I thought, home, of course. But then, when I began remembering, I realized that won't work. We could find the way, I suppose, now that we can read. But if we did — what then? We wouldn't find anyone we know."

"And yet," Jenner said, "you know that's not the real point."

"No."

"The real point is this: We don't know where to go because we don't know what we are. Do you want to go back to living in a sewer-pipe? And eating other people's garbage? Because that's what rats do. But the fact is, we aren't rats any more. We're something Dr. Schultz has made. Something new. Dr. Schultz says our intelligence has increased more than one thousand per cent. I suspect he's underestimated; I think we're probably as intelligent as he is — maybe more. We can read, and with a little practice, we'll be able to write, too. I mean to do both. I think we can learn to do anything we want. But where do we do it? Where does a group of civilized rats fit in?"

"I don't know," I said. "We're going to have to find out. It won't be easy. But even so, the first step must be to get out of here. We're lucky to have a chance, but it won't last. We're a jump ahead of Dr. Schultz; if he knew what we know, he wouldn't leave us alone in here another night. And he's sure to find out soon."

"Another thing to worry about," Jenner said. "If we do get away, when he finds we're gone — won't he figure out how we did it? And won't he realize that we must have learned to read?"

"Probably."

"And then what? What will happen when he announces that there's a group of civilized rats roaming loose — rats that can read, and think, and figure things out?"

I said: "Let's wait until we're free before we worry about that."

But Jenner was right. It was a thing to worry about, and maybe it still is.

The next day was terrible. I kept expecting to hear Dr. Schultz say: "Who took my screwdriver?" And then to hear Julie add: "My thread is missing, too." That could have happened and set them to thinking — but it didn't, and that night, an hour after Julie, George, and Dr. Schultz left the laboratory, we were out of our cages and gathered, the whole group of us, before the mouse cabinet. Justin opened its doors, unlatched their cages, and the mice came out. They looked very small and frightened, but one strode bravely forward.

"You are Nicodemus?" he said to me. "I'm Jonathan. Thank you for taking us out with you."

"We're not out yet," I said, "but you're welcome."

We had no time for chatting. The light coming in the windows was turning gray; in less than an hour it would be dark, and we would need light to figure out how to open the screen at the end of the shaft.

We went to the opening in the baseboard.

"Justin," I said, "take the lead. Roll up the thread as you go. I'll bring up in the rear. No noise. There's sure to be somebody awake somewhere in the building. We don't want them to hear us." I did not want to leave the thread where it might be found: the more I thought about it, the more I felt sure Dr. Schultz would try to track us down, for quite a few reasons.

Justin lifted the grid, pushed open the sliding panel, and one by one we went through. As I watched the others go ahead of me, I noticed for the first time that one of the mice was white. Then I went in myself, closing the grid behind me and pushing the panel half shut again, its normal position.

With Justin leading the way, we moved through the dark passage quickly and easily. In only fifteen or twenty minutes we had reached the end of the thread; then, as Justin had told us it would, the shaft widened; we could hear the whir of the machine ahead, and almost immediately we saw a square of gray daylight. We had reached the end of the shaft, and there a terrible thing happened.

Justin — you will recall — had told us that the machine, the pump that pulled air through the shaft, had switched from low speed to high when he had first explored through there. So we were forewarned. The trouble was, the forewarning was no use at all, not so far as the mice were concerned.

We were approaching the lighted square of the opening when the roar began. The blast of air came like a sudden whistling gale; it took my breath and flattened my ears against my head, and I closed my eyes instinctively. I was still in the rear, and when I opened my eyes again I saw one of the mice sliding past me, clawing uselessly with his small nails at the smooth metal beneath him. Another followed him, and still another, as one by one they were blown backward into the dark maze of tunnels we had just left. I braced myself in the corner of the shaft and grabbed at one as he slid by. It was the white mouse. I caught him by one leg, pulled him around behind me and held on. Another blew face-on into the rat ahead of me and stopped there — it was Jonathan, who had been near the lead. But the rest were lost, six in all. They were simply too light; they blew away like dead leaves, and we never saw them again.

In another minute the roar stopped, the rush of air slowed from a gale to a breeze, and we were able to go forward again.

I said to the white mouse: "You'd better hold on to me. That might happen again."

He looked at me in dismay. "But what about the others? Six are lost! I've got to go back and look for them."

Jonathan quickly joined him: "I'll go with you."

"No," I said. "That would be useless and foolish. You have no idea which shaft they were blown into, nor even if they all went the same way. And if you should find them — how would you find your way out again? And suppose the wind comes again? Then there would be eight lost instead of six."

The wind did come again, half a dozen times more, while we worked with the screwdriver to pry open the screen. Each time we had to stop work and hang on. The two mice clung to the screen itself; some of us braced ourselves behind them, in case they should slip. And Justin, taking the thread

466

with him as a guideline, went back to search for the other six. He explored shaft after shaft to the end of the spool, calling softly as he went — but it was futile. To this day we don't know what became of those six mice. They may have found their way out eventually, or they may have died in there. We left an opening in the screen for them, just in case.

The screen. It was heavy wire, with holes about the size of an acorn, and it was set in a steel frame. We pried and hammered at it with the screwdriver, but we could not move it. It was fastened on the outside — we couldn't see how. Finally the white mouse had an idea.

"Push the screwdriver through the wire near the bottom," he said, "and pry up," We did, and the wire bent a fraction of an inch. We did it again, prying down, then left, then right. The hole in the wire grew slowly bigger, until the white mouse said: "I think that's enough." He climbed to the small opening and by squirming and twisting, he got

through. Jonathan followed him; they both fell out of sight, but in a minute Jonathan's head came back in view on the outside.

"It's a sliding bolt," he said. "We're working on it." Inside we could hear the faint rasping as the two mice tugged on the bolt handle, working it back. Then the crack at the base of the screen widened; we pushed it open, and we were standing on the roof of NIMH, free.

Author

Robert O'Brien was the pen name of Robert L. Conly, a writer and editor for newspapers and magazines. His several books for young people include *The Silver Crown* and *Mrs. Frisby and the Rats of NIMH,* winner of the Newbery Medal and other awards.

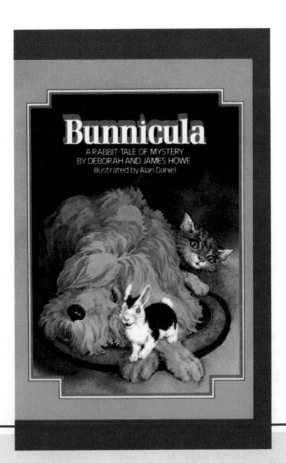

In each of the selections you have just read from *Accepting Challenges,* the main characters overcame hardships as they accepted the challenges that came their way.

The idea of accepting challenges is given a comic twist in *Bunnicula: A Rabbit Tale of Mystery* by James and Deborah Howe. In this story, a seemingly ordinary household pet presents many challenges to its owners. To tell you any more would be to give away Bunnicula's secret!

Glossary

Some of the words in this book may have pronunciations or meanings you do not know. This glossary can help you by telling you how to pronounce those words and by telling you their meanings.

You can find out the correct pronunciation of any glossary word by using the special spelling after the word and the pronunciation key at the bottom of each left-hand page.

The full pronunciation key below shows how to pronounce each consonant and vowel in a special spelling. The pronunciation key at the bottom of each left-hand page is a shortened form of the full key.

Full Pronunciation Key

Consonant Sounds

b	**bib**		p	**pop**
ch	**church**		r	**roar**
d	**deed**		s	**miss, sauce, see**
f	**fast, fife, off, ph**ase, rou**gh**		sh	**dish, ship**
g	**gag**		t	**tight**
h	**hat**		th	pa**th, thin**
hw	**wh**ich		*th*	ba**the, this**
j	**judge**		v	ca**ve, valve, vine**
k	**c**at, **k**ick, pi**que**		w	**with**
l	**l**id, need**l**e		y	**yes**
m	a**m, m**an, **mum**		z	ro**se**, si**ze**, **x**ylophone, **z**ebra
n	**no**, sudde**n**		zh	gara**ge**, plea**s**ure, vi**s**ion
ng	thi**ng**			

Vowel Sounds

ă	pat	ô	alter, caught, for, paw
ā	aid, they, pay	oi	boy, noise, oil
â	air, care, wear	ŏŏ	book
ä	father	o͞o	boot, fruit
ĕ	pet, pleasure	ou	cow, out
ē	be, bee, easy, seize	ŭ	cut, rough
ĭ	pit	û	firm, heard, term, turn, word
ī	by, guy, pie	yo͞o	abuse, use
î	dear, deer, fierce, mere	ə	about, silent, pencil, lemon, circus
ŏ	pot, horrible		
ō	go, row, toe	ər	butter

Stress Marks

Primary Stress′
bi·ol′o·gy   (bī ŏl′ə jē)

Secondary Stress ′
bi′o·log′i·cal   (bī′ə lŏj′ĭ kəl)

ab·sence (ăb′səns) *n.* **1.** Being away from someone or from a place. **2.** The time during which someone or something is away. **3.** The fact of not existing or not being present.

ab·sent·mind·ed (ăb′sənt mīn′dĭd) *adj.* Not paying attention; forgetful: *I am so absent-minded that I am always losing my glasses.*

a·cre·age (ā′kər ĭj) *n.* Land area measured in units, each equal to 4,840 square yards, called acres.

ad·a·mant (ăd′ə mənt) *or* (-mănt′) *adj.* Firm and unyielding. — **ad·a·mant·ly** *adv.*

ad·van·tage (ăd văn′tĭj) *n.* A benefit or favorable position: *My early start gave me an advantage.*

a·gue (ā′gyōō) *n.* **1.** A fever, like that of malaria, in which there are periods of chills, fever, and sweating. **2.** A chill.

aisle (īl) *n.* **1.** A passageway between rows of seats, as in a theater. **2.** Any passageway, as between counters in a department store.

aisle

al·lot·ment (ə lŏt′mənt) *n.* Something given out or distributed: *Each sailor received an allotment of meat and beans before the voyage.*

am·a·teur (ăm′ə chŏŏr′) *or* (-chər) *or* (-tyŏŏr′) *n.* A person who engages in an art, science, or sport for enjoyment rather than for money.

a·mi·a·bly (ā′mē ə blē) *adv.* To do or say something in a friendly, good-natured manner.

a·muse (ə myōōz′) *v.* **1.** To give enjoyment to; entertain pleasantly: *Playing checkers amuses me.* **2.** To cause to laugh or smile: *The clown's tricks amused us.*

an·ti·sep·tic (ăn′tĭ sĕp′tĭk) *adj.* Thoroughly clean. *n.* A substance capable of destroying germs.

an·vil (ăn′vĭl) *n.* A heavy block, usually of iron or steel, with a smooth, flat top on which objects are shaped by hammering.

anvil

ap·a·thet·ic (ăp′ə thĕt′ĭk) *adj.* Lacking or not showing strong feeling: uninterested; indifferent.

ă pat / ā pay / â care / ä father / ĕ pet / ē be / ĭ pit / ī pie / î fierce / ŏ pot / ō go / ô paw, for / oi oil / ōō book / ōō boot / ou out / ŭ cut / û fur / *th* the / th thin / hw which / zh vision / ə ago, item, pencil, atom, circus

ap·er·ture (ăp′ər chər) *n.* The opening in a camera lens that allows the amount of light passing through it to be controlled.

ap·pre·hen·sive (ăp′rĭ hĕn′sĭv) *adj.* Anxious or fearful; uneasy.

ar·bor (är′bər) *n.* A shaded place closed in by shrubs or trees or a frame on which climbing plants such as vines grow.

ar·id (ăr′ĭd) *adj.* Having little or no rainfall; dry: *The settlers irrigated the arid land.*

a·ris·to·crat·ic (ə rĭs′tə krăt′ĭk) *adj.* Of, relating to, or like the social class whose members enjoy greater wealth and status than the rest of society; noble.

a·stern (ə stûrn′) *adj.* Behind a ship or toward the rear of one.

au·to·graph (ô′tə grăf′) *n.* A person's signature in his or her own writing. — *v.* To write one's signature in or on: *I asked the author to autograph my book.*

az·ure (ăzh′ər) *n.* A light to medium blue, like that of the sky on a clear day.

bar·bar·i·an (bär bâr′ē ən) *adj.* Rough and uncivilized; savage.

bar·ren (băr′ən) *adj.* Lacking or unable to produce growing plants or crops: *barren soil.*

beau (bō) *n., pl.* **beaus** *or* **beaux.** The sweetheart of a woman or girl.

bel·lig·er·ent (bə lĭj′ər ənt) *adj.* Inclined to fight; hostile.

bel·lows (bĕl′ōz) *or* (-əz) *n.* *(used with a singular or plural verb)* A device for pumping air, consisting of a chamber with openings controlled by valves so that air can enter only at one end and leave only at another as the chamber is forced to expand and contract.

bi·ol·o·gy (bī ŏl′ə jē) *n.* The scientific study of living things and life processes, including growth, structure, and reproduction.

bole (bōl) *n.* The trunk of a tree.

bole

boon (bōōn) *n.* A help or benefit, often unexpected.

borscht (bôrsht) *n.* A Russian beet soup served hot or cold, often with sour cream.

brack·en (brăk′ən) *n.* **1.** A large fern with branching leaves. **2.** A place overgrown with such ferns.

bu·reau (byōōr′ō) *n., pl.* **bu·reaus** (byōōr′ōz) A chest of drawers.

bureau

cap·tiv·i·ty (kăp tĭv′ĭ tē) *n., pl.* **cap·tiv·i·ties.** A period or the condition of being held prisoner.

car·cass (kär′kəs) *n.* The dead body of an animal.

cas·ing (kā′sĭng) *n.* A metal pipe or tubing used as a lining in wells.

ca·ter (kā′tər) *v.* **ca·ter·ing** **1.** To provide food, supplies, and sometimes service and entertainment, as for a banquet. **2.** To show preference in business to a particular group of people.

cau·tion (kô′shən) *n.* **1.** Care so as to avoid possible danger or trouble: *He climbed the icy steps with caution.* **2.** A warning: *a word of caution.* —*v.* To warn against possible trouble or danger: *She cautioned them not to go near that dog.*

ce·les·tial (sə lĕs′chəl) *adj.* **1.** Of or related to the sky: *Stars and planets are celestial bodies.* **2.** Of heaven; divine: *Angels are celestial beings.*

ces·sa·tion (sĕ sā′shən) *n.* The act of stopping; a halt: *a cessation of activity.*

chan·nel (chăn′əl) *n.* **1.** The part of a river or harbor deep enough for ships to pass through. **2.** A body of water that connects two larger bodies of water.

cha·os (kā′ŏs′) *n.* Great disorder or confusion.

chis·el (chĭz′əl) *n.* A metal tool with a sharp, beveled edge, used in cutting and shaping stone, wood, or metal.

chisel

cho·re·o·graph (kôr′ē ə grăf′) *or* (-gräf′) *or* (kōr′-) *v.* To create the arrangement of a ballet or other stage work.

coax (kōks) *v.* **1.** To persuade or try to persuade by gentle urging: *He coaxed the monkey into the cage.* **2.** To obtain by such persuasion: *coax a smile from the baby.*

com·rade·ship (kŏm′răd shĭp′) *n.* Companionship; a sharing of one's activities.

con·cept (kŏn′sĕpt′) *n.* A general idea or understanding, especially one based on known facts or observation: *the concept that all matter is made up of elements.*

con·sec·u·tive (kən sĕk′yə tĭv) *adj.* Following in order, without a break or interruption; successive: *It rained for five consecutive days.*

ă pat / ā pay / â care / ä father / ĕ pet / ē be / ĭ pit / ī pie / î fierce / ŏ pot / ō go / ô paw, for / oi oil / o͞o book / o͞o boot / ou out / ŭ cut / û fur / th the / th thin / hw which / zh vision / ə ago, item, pencil, atom, circus

con·ster·na·tion (kŏn′stər nā′ shən) *n.* Great alarm, shock, or amazement; dismay.

con·verse (kən **vûrs′**) *v.* **con· versed, con·vers·ing.** To talk informally with others: *converse about family matters.* **con·verse** *n.* Association.

con·vul·sive (kən **vŭl′**sĭv) *adj.* Of or like a seizure or fit.

cop·pice (kŏp′ĭs) *n.* A thicket or grove of small trees.

copse (kŏps) *n.* A group of small trees or bushes.

copse

cra·dle (krād′l) *v.* **cra·dled, cra· dling.** To hold closely; support.

cres·cen·do (krə **shĕn′**dō) *or* (-**seň′**-) *n., pl.* **cres·cen·dos.** A gradual increase.

crest·fall·en (krĕst′fô lən) *adj.* Dejected; sad.

cue (kyōō) *n.* A word or signal given to remind a performer to begin a speech or movement.

cun·ning (kŭn′ĭng) *n.* Slyness; craftiness: *The fox is an animal of great cunning.*

cur·rent (kûr′ənt) *n.* **1.** A steady and smooth onward movement, as of water. **2.** A mass of liquid or gas that is in motion. **3.** A flow of electricity.

de·but *or* **dé·but** (dā **byōō′**) *or* (**dā′**byōō′) *n.* A first public appearance, as of a performer.

de·ci·sive (dĕ **sī′**sĭv) *adj.* Firm. —**de·ci·sive·ly** *adv.*

deign (dān) *v.* To be kind or gracious to: *He wouldn't deign to answer the reporter's questions.*

de·lir·i·ous (dĭ **lîr′**ē əs) *adj.* **1.** Out of one's senses: *The child was delirious from the high fever.* **2.** Wildly excited.

del·uge (dĕl′yōōj) *n.* A great flood; heavy downpour.

des·ig·nat·ed (dĕz′ĭg nāt′ĭd) *adj.* Selected for a particular duty, office, or purpose; appointed.

des·o·late (dĕs′ə lĭt) *adj.* **1.** Having little or no vegetation; barren. **2.** Having few or no inhabitants; deserted: *a desolate wilderness.*

de·tain (dĭ **tān′**) *v.* To delay.

de·tour (dē′tōōr′) *or* (dĭ **tōōr′**) *n.* **1.** A road used temporarily instead of a main route. **2.** A change from a direct route or course. —*v.* To take or cause someone to take a detour.

dev·as·tate (dĕv′ə stāt′) *v.* **dev·as· tat·ed, dev·as·tat·ing.** To lay waste; ravage; spoil.

di·lap·i·dat·ed (dĭ lap′ĭ dā′tĭd) *adj.* Shabby from great neglect: *the dilapidated old house.*

dis·cour·age (dĭ skûr′ĭj) *v.* **dis· cour·aged, dis·cour·ag·ing. 1.** To make less hopeful or enthusiastic. **2.** To try to prevent or hinder; deter: *They lit a fire to discourage mosquitoes.*

dis·rep·u·ta·ble (dĭs rĕp′yə tə bəl) *adj.* Not respectable, as in appearance: *His old, worn-out clothes made him look more disreputable than he really was.*

dog·ged (dô′gĭd) *or* (dŏg′ĭd) *adj.* Not giving up easily; stubborn. **—dog′ged·ly** *adv: She doggedly refused to join us.*

down·y (dou′nē) *adj.* **down·i·er, down·i·est.** Of or like soft, fluffy feathers.

driz·zle (drĭz′əl) *v.* To rain lightly, as in very fine drops.

dron·ing (drōn′ing) *adj.* Making a continuous low, dull humming sound.

drought (drout) *n.* A period of little or no rain.

drowse (drouz) *v.* **drowsed, drows·ing.** To be half asleep; doze: *A dog drowsed in the sun.*

duct (dŭkt) *n.* A tube or pipe through which liquid or gas flows.

dug·out (dŭg′out′) *n.* A long, low shelter at the side of a baseball field in which team members stay when they are not playing.

dugout

dy·nam·ic (dī năm′ĭk) *or* **dy·nam·i·cal** (dī năm′ĭ kəl) *adj.* Energetic; vigorous.

ed·dy (ĕd′ē) *n., pl.* **ed·dies.** A current, as of a liquid or gas, that moves against the direction of a main current, especially in a circular motion.

e·ject (ĭ jĕkt′) *v.* To throw out forcefully; expel.

e·late (ĭ lāt′) *v.* To raise the spirits of; make very happy or joyful: *We're elated by our surprise victory.*

e·lu·sive (ĭ lōō′sĭv) *adj.* **1.** Tending to avoid or escape. **2.** Difficult to describe.

e·ma·ci·at·ed (ĭ mā′shē āt′ĭd) *adj.* Thin, as from starvation or illness.

em·bat·tle·ment (ĕm băt′l mənt) *or* (ĭm-) *n.* A low protective wall containing positions that soldiers have prepared to defend.

en·dur·ance (ĕn dŏor′əns) *or* (ĕn dyŏor′əns) *n.* The ability to withstand strain, pain, hardship, or use.

en·ter·prise (ĕn′tər prīz′) *n.* **1.** An undertaking or venture: *a new business enterprise.* **2.** Economic activity: *free enterprise.* **3.** Initiative in undertaking new projects; adventurous spirit.

ă pat / ā pay / â care / ä father / ĕ pet / ē be / ĭ pit / ī pie / î fierce / ŏ pot / ō go / ô paw, for / oi oil / ōō book / ōō boot / ou out / ŭ cut / û fur / *th* the / th thin / hw which / zh vision / ə ago, item, pencil, atom, circus

etch (ĕch) *v.* **1.** To make (a shape or pattern) on a metal plate by dissolving parts of it with acid. **2.** To show clearly as in a print.

ewe (yōō) *n.* A female sheep.

ex·as·per·a·tion (ĭg zăs′ pə rā′ shən) *n.* The condition of extreme irritation.

ex·pel (ĭk spĕl′) *v.* **ex·pelled, ex·pel·ling.** To force or drive out; to eject forcefully: *expel air from the lungs.*

fal·low (făl′ō) *adj.* Plowed and tilled but left unseeded during a growing season: *a fallow field.*

fath·om (făth′əm) *n.* A unit of length equal to six feet, used mainly to measure the depth of water. — *v.* To measure the depth of water, especially with a line that has a weight at one end.

faun (fôn) *n.* In Roman mythology, a rural god represented as having the body of a man and the horns, ears, tail, and sometimes legs of a goat.

faun

feign (fān) *v.* To give a false appearance of; pretend: *feign illness.*

flat·i·ron (flăt′ī′ərn) *n.* A heated device, usually having a flat base, used for pressing clothes.

for·age (fôr′ĭj) *or* (fŏr′-) *v.* **for·aged, for·ag·ing.** To search for food or provisions.

fren·zy (frĕn′zē) *n., pl.* **fren·zies.** Wild excitement or a display of emotion suggesting madness, often accompanied by violent activity.

froth·y (frô′thē) *or* (frôth′ē) *adj.* **froth·i·er, froth·i·est. 1.** Of, like, or covered with foam: *a wave's frothy spray.* **2.** Light, frivolous, and playful: *a frothy comedy.*

frus·tra·tion (frŭs trā′shən) *n.* The condition of being prevented from accomplishing a goal; a feeling of discouragement.

fun·nel (fŭn′əl) *n.* **1.** A utensil with a narrow open tube at one end, used in pouring something into a container with a small opening. **2.** Something shaped like a funnel, as a tornado.

funnel

fur·tive (fûr′tĭv) *adv.* Stealthily; shiftily.

fu·tile (fyōōt′l) *or* (fyōō′tīl′) *adj.* Having no useful result; useless; vain: *futile efforts.*

gam·bol (găm′bəl) *v.* **gam·boled**
or **gam·bolled, gam·bol·ing** or
gam·bol·ling. To play or frolic
about.

gin·ger·ly (jĭn′jər lē) *adv.* In a
very cautious or careful way: *He
gingerly patted the large dog.*

gloom (gloom) *n.* **1.** Partial or to-
tal darkness: *He peered into the
gloom.* **2.** Lowness of spirit; sad-
ness; depression: *the gloom that de-
feat always brings.*

gloom·y (gloo′mē) *adj.* **gloom·i·
er, gloom·i·est. 1.** Partly or
completely dark. **2.** Sad: *gloomy
about his future.*

gorge (gôrj) *n.* A deep, narrow
passage with steep, rocky sides, as
between mountains.

grim·ace (grĭm′ĭs) *or* (grĭ mās′)
n. A tightening and twisting of
the face to express pain, contempt,
or disgust.

grimace

gro·tesque (grō těsk′) *adj.* **1.**
Distorted and odd: *a grotesque
monster.* **2.** Outlandish; very
strange.

ham·let (hăm′lĭt) *n.* A small village.

hand·i·cap (hăn′dē kăp′) *n.* Any
defect in the structure or func-
tioning of the body or mind that
prevents someone from living nor-
mally; a disability.

har·poon (här poon′) *n.* A spear
with a rope attached, used for
catching sea animals.

harpoon

hawk (hôk) *v.* To offer for sale by
shouting.

herb (ûrb) *or* (hûrb) *n.* A plant
with leaves, roots, or other parts
used to flavor food or as medicine.

horde (hôrd) *or* (hōrd) *n.* A large
group or crowd; swarm.

hos·til·i·ty (hŏ stĭl′ĭ tē) *n., pl.*
hos·til·i·ties. 1. The condition
of feeling ill will; hatred. **2. hos-
tilities.** Open warfare.

hy·dro·phob·ic (hī′drə fō′bĭk) *adj.*
1. Having a fear of water. **2.**
Having rabies, a serious disease
that attacks the central nervous
system.

hy·po·der·mic (hī′pə dûr′mĭk)
n. A hollow needle that pierces
the skin and through which a dose
of medicine can be injected.

ă pat / ā pay / â care / ä father / ĕ pet / ē be / ĭ pit / ī pie / î fierce / ŏ pot / ō go / ô paw, for / oi oil /
oo book / oo boot / ou out / ŭ cut / û fur / th the / th thin / hw which / zh vision / ə ago, item, pencil, atom, circus

i·dol (īd′l) *n.* **1.** An image that is worshiped as a god. **2.** A person or thing adored or greatly admired.

il·lu·mi·na·tion (ĭ lōō′mə nā′ shən) *n.* The act of providing or brightening with light.

il·lu·sion (ĭ lōō′zhən) *n.* **1.** An appearance or impression that has no real basis. **2.** A mistaken notion or belief.

im·per·son·ate (ĭm pûr′sə nāt′) *v.* To act the character or part of; to pretend to be.

im·pulse (ĭm′pŭls′) *n.* **1.** A short, sudden burst of energy: *an electrical impulse.* **2.** A sudden urge; whim.

in·ces·sant (ĭn sĕs′ənt) *adj.* Continuing without interruption; constant.

in·cred·u·lous (ĭn krĕj′ə ləs) *adj.* 1. Disbelieving; skeptical. **2.** Expressing disbelief: *an incredulous stare.* — **in·cred·u·lous·ly** *adv.*

in·ex·pli·ca·bly (ĭn ĕk′splĭ kə blē) *or* (ĭn′ĭk splĭk′ə blē) *adv.* In an unexplainable manner.

in·fal·li·ble (ĭn făl′ə bəl) *adj.* Not capable of making a mistake.

in·jec·tion (ĭn jĕk′shən) *n.* The process of forcing a liquid medicine into the body by the use of a hypodermic needle.

in·quis·i·tive (ĭn kwĭz′ĭ tĭv) *adj.* **1.** Eager to learn: *an inquisitive mind.* **2.** Unduly curious; prying.

in·stinct (ĭn′stĭngkt′) *n.* **1.** An inner feeling or way of behaving that is automatic rather than learned. **2.** A natural talent or ability.

in·su·late (ĭn′sə lāt′) *or* (ĭns′yə- lāt′) *v.* **in·su·lat·ed, in·su·lat·ing.** To cover, surround, or line something with material that slows or stops the passage of heat, sound, or electricity.

in·trude (ĭn trōōd′) *v.* To come in rudely or inappropriately. — **in·trud·er** *n.*

in·va·lid (ĭn′və lĭd) *n.* A sick, weak, injured, or disabled person, especially someone in poor health for a long time.

i·so·la·tion (ī′sə lā′shən) *n.* The condition of being kept apart from others: *living in isolation from the world.*

jade (jād) *n.* Either of two minerals that are used as gemstones and as materials from which objects are carved.

la·goon (lə gōōn′) *n.* A shallow body of water along a coast or shore.

lagoon

la·ment (lə **mĕnt′**) *v.* **1.** To express grief for or about; mourn. **2.** To regret deeply; deplore. *n.* **1.** A feeling or expression of grief; elegy. **2.** A song or poem expressing grief; elegy.

league[1] (lēg) *n.* **1.** A group of nations, people, or organizations working together for a common goal. **2.** An association of sports teams that compete mainly among themselves.

league[2] (lēg) *n.* A unit of length equal to about three miles.

lit·er·al·ly (**lĭt′**ər ə lē) *adv.* **1.** Word for word. **2.** Really or actually.

lon·gev·i·ty (lŏn **jĕv′**ĭ tē) *n.* Long life.

loom (lo͞om) *v.* **1.** To come into view, often with a threatening appearance: *Storm clouds loomed on the horizon.* **2.** To seem close.

ma·chet·e (mə **shĕt′**ē) *or* (**-chĕt′**ē) *n.* A large, heavy knife with a broad blade, used for cutting vegetation and as a weapon.

mag·a·zine (**măg′**ə **zēn′**) *or* (**măg′** ə zēn′) *n.* **1.** A periodical containing written matter, such as articles or stories, and usually also illustrations and advertising. **2.** A place where ammunition is stored.

ma·lig·nant (mə **lĭg′**nənt) *adj.* **1.** Having or showing ill will; malicious: *malignant thoughts.* **2.** Threatening to life or health.

mal·lard (**măl′**ərd) *n.* A wild duck of which the male has a glossy green head and neck.

mallard

mam·moth (**măm′**əth) *adj.* Huge; gigantic.

man·da·rin (**măn′**də rĭn) *n.* In imperial China, a high public official.

ma·raud·ing (mə **rôd′**ing) *adj.* Roving in search of or raiding to seize booty.

mat·i·nee *or* **mat·i·née** (**măt′**n **ā′**) *n.* A theatrical performance given in the afternoon.

me·an·der (mē **ăn′**dər) *v.* **1.** To follow a winding and turning course: *The river meanders through the town.* **2.** To wander aimlessly and idly. — **me·an′der·ing** *adj.*

men·ace (**mĕn′**əs) *v.* To threaten with harm; endanger: *an oil slick menacing the shoreline of California.* — **men′ac·ing** *adj.*: *a menacing look.*

me·te·or·ol·o·gist (mē′tē ə **rŏl′**ə jĭst) *n.* A scientist who studies weather and weather conditions.

ă pat / ā pay / â care / ä father / ĕ pet / ē be / ĭ pit / ī pie / î fierce / ŏ pot / ō go / ô paw, for / oi oil / o͞o book / o͞o boot / ou out / ŭ cut / û fur / *th* the / th thin / hw which / zh vision / ə ago, item, pencil, atom, circus

miffed (mĭft) *adj.* Offended or annoyed.

mo·bile (**mō′**bəl) *adj.* Capable of moving or being moved: *Mobile cameras filmed the parade.* — *n.* (mō bēl′) A type of sculpture consisting of parts that sway in a breeze.

mol·ten (**mōl′**tən) *adj.* Made liquid by heat; melted.

mon·i·tor (**mŏn′**ĭ tər) *n.* A device used to record or control a process or activity. — *v.* To keep watch over, record, or control.

moon·stone (**mōōn′**stōn′) *n.* A pearly stone that lets light pass through, valued as a gem.

mor·sel (**môr′**səl) *n.* A small piece, especially of food; a bit.

muse (myōōz) *v.* **mused, mus·ing.** To consider at length; ponder; meditate.

ob·sta·cle (**ŏb′**stə kəl) *n.* Something that stands in the way of reaching a goal.

of·fal (**ô′**fəl) *or* (**ôf′**əl) *n.* Waste parts, especially of a butchered animal.

ok·ra (**ō′**krə) *n.* **1.** A tall tropical or semitropical plant. **2.** The edible pods of the okra plant, used in soups or as a vegetable.

o·men (**ō′**mən) *n.* A thing or event regarded as a sign of future good or bad luck.

op·pres·sive (ə **prĕs′**ĭv) *adj.* **1.** Difficult to bear; tyrannical. **2.** Causing physical or mental distress: *an oppressive silence.*

op·ti·mis·tic (ŏp′tə **mĭs′**tĭk) *adj.* Taking a hopeful view of a situation, expecting the best possible outcome.

o·va·tion (ō **vā′**shən) *n.* A loud and enthusiastic display of approval, usually in the form of shouting or hearty applause.

pact (păkt) *n.* A formal agreement, as one between nations; a treaty.

par·cel (**pär′** səl) *n.* A bundle; package.

parcel

par·ti·tion (pär **tĭsh′**ən) *n.* Something, as a partial wall, that di vides a room or space.

pa·tron (**pā′**trən) *n.* A person who supports a certain activity or institution: *a patron of the arts.*

per·ish·a·bles (**pĕr′**ĭ shə bəlz) *pl. n.* Things, such as food, that spoil or decay easily.

per·plexed (pər **plĕkst′**) *adj.* Confused or puzzled; bewildered.

per·sist·ent (pər **sĭs′**tənt) *adj.* Refusing to give up or let go.

plague (plāg) *v.* To annoy or bother; pester.

plain·tive (**plān′**tĭv) *adj.* Sad; mournful: *a plaintive song.*

pli·a·ble (**plī′**ə bəl) *adj.* **1.** Easily bent or shaped without breaking; flexible: *pliable strips of wood.* **2.** Tending to be easily influenced or dominated: *a pliable mind.*

plun·der (**plŭn′**dər) *v.* To take booty or valuables from; rob: *Pirates plundered the coastal city.*

pro·ceeds (**prō′**sēdz′) *n.* All the money that comes from a business or fund-raising activity.

pro·jec·tile (prə **jĕk′**təl) *or* (-tīl′) *n.* An object, such as a bullet or an arrow, that is fired, thrown, or otherwise launched through space.

pros·per·ous (**prŏs′** pər əs) *adj.* Enjoying or marked by wealth or success: *My parents have built a prosperous business.*

Pull·man (**pŏŏl′**mən) *n.* Often **Pullman car.** A railroad car having private sleeping compartments.

pun·gent (**pŭn′**jənt) *adj.* Sharp to the taste or smell: *a pungent sauce.*

rap·ture (**răp′**chər) *n.* Overwhelming delight; great joy.

rasp (răsp) *or* (räsp) *v.* To make a harsh, grating sound.

ra·vine (rə **vēn′**) *n.* A deep, narrow cut, similar to a canyon or gorge, in the earth's surface.

ray (rā) *n.* **1.** Any of several ocean fishes having a flattened body, often with the fins forming winglike extensions, and a long narrow tail. **2.** A narrow beam of light.

re·as·sure (rē′ə **shŏŏr′**) *v.* **re·as·sured, re·as·sur·ing.** To make less fearful or worried; to restore confidence to.

reef (rēf) *n.* A strip or ridge of rock, sand, or coral that rises to or close to the surface of a body of water.

re·mote (rĭ **mōt′**) *adj.* **re·mot·er, re·mot·est.** Far away; not near.

ren·dez·vous (**rän′**dā vōō) *or* (-də-) *n.* A prearranged meeting: *a rendezvous of the explorers in the wilderness.*

re·signed (rĭ **zīnd′**) *adj.* Accepting what is happening without complaining.

rig (rĭg) *n.* **1.** A vehicle. **2.** Any special equipment or gear.

rig

scal·a·wag (**skăl′**ə wăg) *also* **scal·ly·wag** (**skăl′**ē-) *n.* A dishonest, unprincipled person.

ă pat / ā pay / â care / ä father / ĕ pet / ē be / ĭ pit / ī pie / î fierce / ŏ pot / ō go / ô paw, for / oi **oil** /
o͞o **book** / o͞o **boot** / ou **out** / ŭ **cut** / û **fur** / *th* **the** / th **thin** / hw **which** / zh **vision** / ə **ago, item, pencil, atom, circus**

scraw·ny (**skrô′**nē) *adj.* **scraw·ni·er, scraw·ni·est.** Thin and bony; skinny.

scur·ry (**skûr′**ē) *v.* **scur·ried, scur·ry·ing, scur·ries. 1.** To move with or as if with light, rapid steps; scamper. **2.** To race about in a hurried or confused manner; rush.

self-suf·fi·cient (sĕlf′sə **fĭsh′**ənt) *adj.* Able to provide for oneself without help; independent.

se·rene (sə **rēn′**) *adj.* **1.** Peaceful and calm. **2.** Perfectly clear and bright.

se·ver·i·ty (sə **vĕr′**ĭ tē) *n.* The state or quality of being unsparing and harsh in treating others.

shaft (shăft) *n.* **1.** A spear or arrow or the long, slender stem of a spear or arrow. **2.** A long, narrow passage or opening, such as one leading into a mine.

sheep·ish (**shē′**pĭsh) *adj.* **1.** Embarrassed and apologetic. **2.** Meek; timid.

shud·der (**shŭd′**ər) *v.* To tremble or shiver suddenly, especially from fear or cold.

si·lo (**sī′** lō) *n.* A tall, round building in which food for farm animals is stored.

smug (smŭg) *adj.* **smug·ger, smug·gest.** Too pleased or satisfied with oneself. — **smug′ly** *adv.*

sol·i·tar·y (**sŏl′**ĭ tĕr′ē) *adj.* Being or living alone: *I saw a solitary runner at the side of the road.*

spare (spâr) *adj.* **1.** Ready when needed: *There's a spare tire in the car trunk.* **2.** Beyond what is needed; extra.

spas·mod·ic (spăz **mŏd′**ĭk) *adj.* Happening occasionally; in sudden bursts.

spec·i·men (**spĕs′**ə mən) *n.* A sample of something that one studies.

spi·ral (**spī′**rəl) *n.* **1.** A curve that gradually widens as it coils around. **2.** Something, such as the thread of a screw, that resembles a spiral. — *v.* To move or cause to move in the form of a spiral: *Smoke spiraled from the chimney.* — *adj.* Of, relating to, or being a spiral: *The tower had a spiral staircase.*

spiral

splay·foot·ed (**splā′**fo͝ot′ĭd) *adj.* Walking with feet turned outward.

spunk·y (**spŭng′**kē) *adj.* Spirited; plucky.

stat·ure (**stăch′**ər) *n.* Reputation gained by achievement.

stol·id (**stŏl′**ĭd) *adj.* Having or showing little emotion. — **stol′id·ly** *adv.*

stub·ble (**stŭb′**əl) *n.* **1.** Short, stiff stalks, as of grain, left after a crop has been harvested. **2.** Something resembling this, such as a short, stiff growth of beard.

sub·mis·sive (səb **mĭs′**ĭv) *adj.* Yielding; obedient.

sub·mit (səb **mĭt′**) *v.* **sub·mit·ted, sub·mit·ting.** To yield or surrender (oneself) to the will or authority of another.

sul·len (**sŭl′**ən) *adj.* Showing ill humor or resentment; sulky.

su·per·sti·tious (sōō′pər **stish′**əs) *adj.* Believing in or resulting from a superstition.

sym·pa·thet·ic (sĭm′pə **thĕt′**ĭk) *adj.* **1.** Of, feeling, expressing, or resulting from understanding or affection between persons. **2.** In agreement.

tak·en a·back (tā′kən ə **băk′**) *adv.* Surprised: *I was taken aback by your decision to leave your job.*

tech·nique (tĕk **nēk′**) *n.* A procedure or method by which a task, especially a difficult or complicated one, is accomplished.

ter·rain (tə **rān′**) *or* (tĕ-) *n.* A tract of land: *hilly terrain.*

Tex·as lea·guer (tĕk′səs lē′gər) *n. Baseball.* A fly ball that drops between the infielder and the outfielder for a hit.

the·o·ry (thē′ə rē) *or* (thîr′ē) *n., pl.* **theories. 1.** An idea or set of ideas made up to explain why something happened or continues to happen. **2.** An assumption or guess based on limited information or knowledge.

ther·a·pist (**thĕr′**ə pĭst) *n.* Someone who specializes in treating a physical or mental illness.

this·tle (**thĭs′**əl) *n.* Any of several prickly plants with usually purplish flowers and seeds tufted with silky fluff.

thistle

thong (thông) *or* (thŏng) *n.* A narrow strip of leather used to fasten something.

trans·con·ti·nen·tal (trăns′kŏn tə **nĕnt′**tl) *adj.* Crossing one of the main masses of the earth: Africa, Antarctica, Asia, Australia, Europe, North America, or South America.

tri·um·phant (trī **ŭm′**fənt) *adj.* **—tri·um·phant·ly** *adv.* Victorious, successful.

trough (trôf) *n.* **1.** A long, narrow hollow, as between ocean waves. **2.** A long, narrow container for holding food or water for animals.

tyke (tīk) *n.* A mongrel, or dog of mixed breeding.

ă pat / ā pay / â care / ä father / ĕ pet / ē be / ĭ pit / ī pie / î fierce / ŏ pot / ō go / ô paw, for / oi oil /
ōō book / ōō boot / ou out / ŭ cut / û fur / *th* the / th thin / hw which / zh vision / ə ago, item, pencil, atom, circus

un·a·bashed (ŭn′ ə băsht′) *adj.*
Not embarrassed or ashamed.

un·ceas·ing·ly (ŭn sē′sĭng lē) *adv.*
In a continuous manner.

un·der·es·ti·mate (ŭn′dər ĕs′tə-māt′) *v.* **-es·ti·mat·ed, -es·ti·mat·ing.** To judge or guess too low the value, amount, quality, or capacity of.

un·fal·ter·ing (ŭn fôlt′ər ĭng) *adj.* Not wavering in confidence; not hesitating. — *adv.* **un·fal·ter·ing·ly**

un·in·hab·it·ed (ŭn′ĭn hăb′ĭ tĭd) *adj.* Without people; not lived in.

un·sea·son·a·bly (ŭn sē′zə nəb lē) *adv.* In a manner that is not suitable for the season.

ush·er (ŭsh′ər) *n.* A person who shows people to their seats, as in a theater.

vague (vāg) *adj.* **vagu·er, vagu·est. 1.** Not clearly expressed; lacking clarity: *a vague statement; a vague promise.* **2.** Lacking definite shape, form, or character.

var·nish (vär′nĭsh) *n.* An oil-based paint that dries to leave a surface coated with a thin, hard, glossy film that is relatively transparent and almost colorless.

vast (văst) *adj.* Very great in area, size, or amount: *The ship sailed the vast ocean.*

ver·vain (vûr′vān′) *n.* Any of several varieties of plants having slender spikes of small blue, purplish, or white flowers.

vin·dic·tive (vĭn dĭk′tĭv) *adj.* Having or showing a desire for revenge; vengeful.

wan (wŏn) *adj.* **wan·ner, wan·nest. 1.** Unnaturally pale, as from illness: *a wan face.* **2.** Weak or faint: *a wan smile.*

ward·robe (wôr′drōb′) *n.* **1.** A person's clothes. **2.** A closet or tall piece of furniture in which clothes are kept.

wardrobe

war·y (wâr′ē) *adj.* **war·i·er, war·i·est. 1.** Alert to danger; watchful: *The possibility of discovery kept him wary.* **2.** Distrustful: *wary of the weather.*

wor·ry (wûr′ē) *or* (wŭr′ē) *v.* **wor·ried, wor·ry·ing. 1.** To feel or cause to feel uneasy or anxious: *worried about his health.* **2.** To grasp and tug at repeatedly: *a kitten worrying a ball of yarn.*

wretch·ed (rĕch′ĭd) *adj.* **1.** Full of or attended by misery or woe. **2.** Shabby. **3.** Inferior in quality: *a wretched performance.*

zo·o·log·i·cal (zō′ə **lŏj′ĭ** kəl) *or* **zo·o·log·ic** (zō ə **lŏj′ĭk**) *adj.* Of animals or the scientific study of animals: *a zoological collection.* — **zo′o·log′i·cal·ly** *adv.*

zwie·back (**zwī′**băk′) *or* (-băk′) *or* (**zwē′**-) *or* (**swī′**-) *n.* A type of biscuit first baked in the form of a slightly sweetened loaf of bread often sliced and oven-toasted.

ă pat / ā pay / â care / ä father / ĕ pet / ē be / ĭ pit / ī pie / î fierce / ŏ pot / ō go / ô paw, for / oi oil / o͞o book / o͞o boot / ou out / ŭ cut / û fur / *th* the / th thin / hw which / zh vision / ə ago, item, pencil, atom, circus

Credits

Cover Design: James Stockton & Associates

Illustrators: 10−19 Mou-Sien Tseng
20−49 Richard Loehle **50−65** Floyd Cooper
66−67 Mary Azarian **68−92** Paul O. Zelinski
93−118 Cheri Wyman **119** Nanette Biers
120−121 Robert Stein III **122−139** Charles
Shaw **140−157** Tony Smith **158−168** Robert
Lawson **169** Jan Wills **179−188** Julie Downing
189 Jaclyne Scardova **217−230** Tony Smith
232−254 Graham Humphreys **255** Shelley
Austin, Ernest Shepard **258−265** Edward Gorey
266−267 Laura Cornell **268−285** Robert
Giuliani **302−316** Pauline Baynes **317** Symeon
Shimin **320−331** Chris Calle **332−345** Tony
Smith **346−368** Margot Thomes **370−400** Ben
F. Stahl **401** Troy Howell **402−403** Kevin
Hawkes **419** Cecilia von Rabenau
420−437 Francien van Westering **438−468** Jan
Pyk **469** Alan Daniel

Photographers: 8−9 Gerard Vandystadt/Photo
Researchers **170** Shostal Association
171−172 Susanah Brown **174, 175, 177** Nebraska
Historical Society **178** Four by Five **190−191** E.
Bordis/Leo DeWys, Inc. **192−203** © Randall
Davis **204−209** © Howard B. Bluestein/Univer-
sity of Oklahoma **214** Dan McCoy/Rainbow
231 SUNLIGHT ON THE COAST by Winslow
Homer/Toledo Museum of Art **256−257** Joseph
Nettis/Photo Researchers **286−287** © James A.
Sugar/Black Star **288** © Margaret Bourke-
White/Life Magazine **292−297** © Margaret
Bourke-White/Life Magazine/George Arents
Research Library (Syracuse University) **299** Oscar
Graubner/Life Magazine/George Arents Research
Library (Syracuse University) **300−301** © Margaret
Bourke-White/Life Magazine **318−319** John
Marshall **365−368** © Jean Fritz **369** RESTING
IN THE WOODS by John George Brown/Collection
of JoAnn and Julian Ganz, Jr. **404, 411** Courtesy
Maria Tallchief Paschen **415** Martha Swope